ACHIEVING PROBLEM FREE PROJECT MANAGEMENT

ACHIEVING PROBLEM FREE PROJECT MANAGEMENT

Sydney F. Love

JOHN WILEY & SONS
New York • Chichester • Brisbane • Toronto • Singapore

Copyright © 1989 by Sydney F. Love
Published by John Wiley & Sons, Inc.

All rights reserved. Published simultaneously in Canada.

Reproduction or translation of any part of this work
beyond that permitted by Section 107 or 108 of the
1976 United States Copyright Act without the permission
of the copyright owner is unlawful. Requests for
permission or further information should be addressed to
the Permissions Department, John Wiley & Sons, Inc.

This publication is designed to provide accurate and
authoritative information in regard to the subject
matter covered. It is sold with the understanding that
the publisher is not engaged in rendering legal, accounting,
or other professional service. If legal advice or other
expert assistance is required, the services of a competent
professional person should be sought. *From a Declaration of
Principles jointly adopted by a Committee of the
American Bar Association and a Committee of Publishers.*

Library of Congress Cataloging in Publication Data:

Love, Sydney F.
  Achieving problem free project management / by Sydney F. Love.
      p.   cm.
  Bibliography: p.
  ISBN 0-471-63522-7
  1. Industrial project management: I. Title.
HD69.P75L68   1989
658.4'04—dc20   89-8914
                                                         CIP

Printed in the United States of America

10 9 8 7 6 5 4 3 2 1

PREFACE

This book is for the nontechnical person. There has been an aura of mystery about managing projects for too long. One does not need to be an engineer or a computer expert. Anyone who can add, subtract, and multiply can master the subject of project management. For that matter, two-thirds of project management is dealing with people and organizations. The number crunching and drawing can be done by an easy-to-use-computer program. It follows that most people in a business or government situation can become proficient at managing projects. This includes project leaders, project officers, project managers, and project team members—in fact, anyone who is required to get people to work together to achieve new goals. In our society, where the rate of change is increasing, intelligent project management is the way to achieve change without wrecking the productivity of the ongoing operations.

I have a technical background as an engineer, and that's how I got into project management soon after it started in the early 1960s. For over ten years I have conducted public and in-house seminars on that subject—hundreds of seminars. Thousands of people have taken my course and applied it. I have trained many engineers, scientists, and technical personnel. However, over the past decade I have increasingly trained nontechnical people for nontechnical projects. I have conducted special in-house courses in Project Management for insurance companies, drug firms, and publishers. The attendees ranged from loan officers and social workers to system analysts and executive assistants. For them, I prepared special course materials. I was able to test, revise, validate, and fine-tune these materials. Now I am using them in this book.

Along the way, I learned about Neurolinguistic Programming. It is a new paradigm for learning, and I use it in this book. Through anecdotal cases, I build a visual picture in the reader's mind to stimulate the imaginative portion of the brain. Then I implicitly state the principle for use by the judgmental part of the brain. This is right and left brain learning combined. After this induction to principles, I use deduction to show the reader a range of practical examples with which they can identify. Finally, I get to the kinesic part. The reader is drawn vicariously into the action by the dialogue, and then at the end of each chapter, and sometimes within a chapter, the reader is invited to do some practical pencil pushing. All of this is the new way of learning by Neurolinguistic Programming.

This book has some chapters about getting computer assistance in the easy way. In the years to follow, computers will provide even more assistance to project managers on all kinds of projects. I have used a few current software programs to show what computers can do. This subject is treated in a timeless fashion, so that it will still be useful a decade from now.

Most people doing nontechnical projects are also involved with multiple projects. There is no theory to guide us on multiple projects. Most books ignore it, but not this one. I have included practical ways to cope with the problems of multiple projects—which is what the reader needs anyway.

Whether you are new at project management or are a seasoned practitioner, this book shows you the who, what, and when of problem free project management.

SYDNEY F. LOVE

North Hollywood, California
June 1989

ACKNOWL-
EDGMENTS

An objective of this book was that it be understandable by a nontechnical person. I tested every chapter with my wife, May, who is an elementary school teacher, without any inclination to be proficient in math or science. How fortunate for me! As you know, engineers are more able to write for engineers than for the nontechnical reader. As it turned out, I had to rewrite the whole chapter on scheduling so it would pass May's scrutiny. She also did much to improve the grammar and spelling.

Another great help was Paul Sparrow, a project manager with an uncanny ability to pick out errors within a sentence. Besides this, he is a graduate of my course and was able to help in the continuity of project management items.

It's not the custom to give acknowledgments to computers, but I will, if not to the computer, then to the authors of the software I used. Every chapter was analyzed by "RIGHTWRITER," and it reminded me frequently to shorten sentences, close parentheses, and use the active voice. Another help was a spelling check program, which not only advised on spelling, but also picked up typos within a word.

Patricia Ward was the secretary who saw me through two years of transcriptions and revisions. She inserted useful little notes in the text where it didn't seem quite right.

The editor who chose to publish this book is John Mahaney, of

John Wiley & Sons. He arranged for developmental editing early in the book, and this gave me a chance to respond to the comments of a professional reader who was not involved directly in the subject matter.

To the thousands of people who have attended my seminars, I owe a special debt. By presenting their real problems for open discussion at the seminar, we have learned together what it takes to make project management work.

S.F.L.

FOREWORD

I am very pleased to provide a foreword to Syd Love's new book on project management. We have been witnessing a rapidly growing acknowledgment of project management by industry over the past few years. This has been accompanied by the emergence of a group of highly esteemed theoreticians and practitioners who see the tremendous operational leverages that are possible by applying the fundamentals of project management. Syd Love is a member of this group.

You might ask: Why is project management important when prominent business issues involve downsizing, corporate mergers, new business ventures, balance of trade deficits, needs for productivity improvements, a rise in entrepreneurial activity, increased competition, and related phenomena? Many people are realizing that being an "organization man" is not the answer to these issues. Roseabeth Moss Kanter, a best-selling author, Harvard professor, and management consultant, relates to this observation in her book *When Giants Learn to Dance*. She advises today's managers to focus their allegiance on their projects, rather than their employees. Viewing work as a series of projects will enable departures from the bureaucratic conformities and rigidities of hierarchy that characterize the organization man approach, and will unleash higher levels of creativity and results. By associating rewards with project performance, in the form of formal pay and recognition, unlocked productivity is expected to flourish. This assumes, of course, that project management tools and techniques are well known and effectively applied. Unfortunately, such is often not the case. In a typical situation, one is given the assignment of a project and expected to perform admirably on the basis of intuition alone. This approach can backfire and result in project cost overruns, time overruns, labor inefficiencies, poor quality, low morale, high turnover, and any number of other undesirable consequences. How, then, does one convert from being an organization man to a project person? People who wish to succeed as project managers have a number of learning opportunities.

To gain knowledge about project management, one can attend short seminars, perhaps take college courses, join a professional society like the Project Management Institute, read articles, and study books written on the subject. Since project management is a contemporary management style, the subject matter is both fascinating and wide ranging. A very sound foundation in project management is contained in *Achieving Problem Free Project Management*.

In authoring this book Syd Love has capitalized on his many years of experience in consulting, leading seminars, writing, and practicing the profession of project management. The entire spectrum of project managers, from novice to accomplished, will benefit from his practical advice on the "keys to the kingdom" as recorded in these chapters. By following the steps outlined for project planning, scheduling, and control, from both the behavioral and the quantitative viewpoints, one's success at project work will be enhanced. The chapter on computer assistance presents important considerations for the acquisition and application of project management computer software, particularly for the personal computer. And, for those who own such software and who tried to learn project management from it, this book should clarify many unanswered questions. Moreover, *Achieving Problem Free Project Management* will be most useful to those concerned with the management of small to medium-sized projects, especially in multiproject, multiresource situations. Very little is available at present in the project management literature on this subject, but applications of it abound in industries such as banking, real estate, marketing and advertising, printing, computer software, theatrical productions, business startup, research and development, architecture, and home improvement.

It is also my hope that this book will help academics to further realize the full and rich breadth of the project management discipline, and to go beyond the few short lectures often devoted to the topic. It is time that the subject of project management be incorporated into the curricula of collegiate schools of business, to help our country's productivity and thereby address some of the critical needs of our economy. *Achieving Problem Free Project Management* is an important contribution to these goals.

> Roger B. Glaser, Ph.D.
> President Emeritus, San Diego Chapter
> of Project Management Institute
> and
> Information Systems Division
> San Diego Gas & Electric Company

CONTENTS

List of Figures   xxi

CHAPTER 1.   MANAGEMENT BY PROJECTS (MBP):
Why It Is Different from the Usual Form of
Management   1

Case 1: It Looked Easy, So Joe Did It Himself   2
Case 2: Fun and Games with Computerization   4
When Should Work Be a Project   5
Small Project Example   7
An Example of a Medium Project   10
Multiple Projects   12
Case 3: She Almost Took On More Than She Could Handle   12
The Project Management Planning Phase   16
The Project Management Controlling Phase   21
The Role of the Project Leader/Project Manager   23
Summary   25
Questions for Discussion or Assignment   26

CHAPTER 2.   THE DYNAMIC PROJECT PLAN:
Its Approval Precedes the Real Start   29

Case 1: The Banker Gets Bucked   30
Case 2: The Software That Never Got Finished   31
The Dynamic Project Plan   33

Purposes of the Dynamic Project Plan 37
Details of the Dynamic Project Plan 38
The Projectics Dynamic Project Plan Form 44
Summary 44
Questions for Assignment or Discussion 50

CHAPTER 3. DEFINING THE PROJECT OBJECTIVES AND TASKS: Pinning Them Down 55

Case 1: The Banker Creates New Problems 56
Case 2: The Software Project for Personnel Records 57
Setting Objectives 57
Application to a Small Project 58
The Delphi Study Project 59
Application to a Medium Project 60
Objectives for the Multiple-Project Insurance Firm 62
Comprehensive and Balanced Objectives 63
Time and Cost Considerations 64
Pinning Down the Objectives 64
Questions for Discussion or Assignment 69

CHAPTER 4. SCHEDULES FOR BEING ON TIME: You Need Them for Control 71

Case 1: They Ran Out of Letterhead 72
Case 2: Due Process Is Not Fast Enough 73
The Projectics Method of Scheduling 74
Production of a Schedule with the Projectics Methods 82
Application to a Small Project: The Bank's Goodwill Project 87
Application to a Medium Project: The Personnel Records Project 88
Uses of Float Information 89
The Work Breakdown Structure 94
Adjustment of Schedules for Resource Availability 95
Putting It All Together 96
Questions for Discussion or Assignment 97

CHAPTER 5. BUDGETING AND CONTROLLING THE COST: How to Avoid Overruns 99

Case 1: The Banker Loses Money 100
Case 2: The Purchasing Department Did Their Own Thing 101

Application to a Small Project   103
Application to a Medium Project   104
Application to Annual Budget Control of Multiple Projects   106
Application to Multiple Projects   107
The Activity Budget   108
Accuracy of Estimates   110
Milestone Reporting Versus Periodic Reporting   111
Committed Cost at a Milestone   112
Choosing Milestones   113
Cost Is a Tradeoff   114
Delays Are Sometimes Very Expensive   115
Ways to Keep the Cost Under Control   115
Questions for Discussion or Assignment   116

CHAPTER 6. ENHANCEMENTS TO THE DYNAMIC PROJECT PLAN:
Items That Need Attention   119

Case 1: The Meticulous Banker   120
Case 2: The Personnel Manager Blows the Whistle   121
Case 3: You Got It, Boss   123
Other Planning Considerations   124
Small to Large Projects   128
Summary   129
Questions for Assignment or Discussion   130

CHAPTER 7. RESOURCES AND MOTIVATION:
Assignments Become Commitments   131

Case 1: Differences in Motivation   132
Case 2: Off to a Bad Start   133
Application to a Small Project   134
Application to a Medium Project   134
Assessing the New Situation   136
More People, Less Time?   137
Allocation of Account Numbers   138
Whose Estimate Is Best?   138
Commitment and Motivation   139
Summary   140
Questions for Assignment or Discussion   140

CONTENTS

CHAPTER 8. REPORTS, ACTIONS, AND SOLUTIONS:
You Seize Control Again   143

Case 1: The Banker Learns from Experience   144
Case 2: The CEO Gets What He Asks For   145
Application to a Small Project   146
Application to a Medium Project   147
The Concept of a Baseline Plan   149
Schedule Progress   151
Budget Progress   152
Results Progress   154
Balanced Reporting   154
Major and Minor Tradeoffs   155
Milestone Decision Reviews   156
Coping with Uncertainty   157
Reserves of Money and Time   158
Additional Control Points   159
Earned Value Reporting   160
Summary   160
Questions for Assignment or Discussion   161

CHAPTER 9. MOTIVATION:
Keeping the Team Enthusiastic throughout the
Project   163

Case 1: A Critical Attitude Did Not Recharge the
Batteries   164
Case 2: Marvin Screws Up the Project   165
Application to a Small Project   167
Application to a Medium Project   168
Praise as a Motivator   168
Peer Praise as a Motivator   172
The Project as a Motivator   173
The Participative Approach   175
Power and Influence   178
Questions for Discussion or Assignment   180

CHAPTER 10. THE PROJECT MANAGER'S SPECIAL AUTHORITY:
With It, You Can Win   181

Case 1: The Banker Who Couldn't Wait   182
Case 2: He Didn't Attend the Meeting   183
Application to a Small Project   185

CONTENTS

Application to a Medium Project   186
The Rights of Project Managers   187
Task Reporting in Different Forms of
    Organization   191
The Project Charter   194
The Task Form   194
Questions for Discussion or Assignment   198

CHAPTER 11. COMPUTER ASSISTANCE:
Do It Right and Save Time   201

Case 1: The Neat Drawings Impressed the
    Management   202
Case 2: High Gear Was Really Low Gear   205
Application to Small Projects   206
Application to a Medium Project   209
Common Mistakes in Adopting Computer
    Assistance   213
Export or Import of Project Data to and from Other
    Software   213
Cost Data with Software Assistance   215
Which Computer to Use   216
Selection of PM Software for a PC   217
An Example of a Medium Project   221
Multiuser Programs   222
Questions for Assignment or Discussion   226

CHAPTER 12. MULTIPLE PROJECTS:
Look at the Load on the Resources   229

Case 1: The Merger Creates a Bottleneck   230
Case 2: The Past Projects Wouldn't Settle Down   233
Discussion   235
Application to a Multiple-Project Load   235
Resource Availability Affects the Schedule   236
Competition between Project Leaders   237
Analyzing Your Own Workload   238
Priorities within a Project   238
Priorities among Projects   239
An Application of Project Priorities   240
Rapidly Changing Priorities   241
A Computer Will Help   244
Which Method to Use   245

Systematic Changing of Priorities   246
All Departments Need to Get Organized   247
Software with Multiproject Capability   247
Summary   251
Questions for Assignment or Discussion   253

CHAPTER 13. MANAGING TIME:
For the Busy Project Manager   255

Case 1: Harry Did the Project but Neglected Operations   256
Case 2: Jack in the Pressure Cooker   258
Application to a Part-Time Project Manager   260
Application to a Full-Time Project Manager with Multiple Projects   262
Priority on Your Time Has Two Dimensions   265
What Is Long-Term Payoff?   266
Interruptions Waste Your Time   268
Coping with Interruptions   269
Quiet Time and Available Time   270
Meetings That Waste Time   271
Workload Analysis   272
A 3 × 5 Card Organizer for Tracking Projects   274
A Memo Book and Software Combination for Managing Your Time   277
Questions for Assignment or Discussion   280

APPENDIX A. LOGIC DIAGRAMS   283

A Comparison of the Two Kinds of Logic Diagrams   284
Answers to Exercises in Chapter 4   287

APPENDIX B. SOURCES FOR PROJECT MANAGEMENT MATERIALS   291

Project Management Software Summaries   292
Project Management Software Used as Examples in This Book   293
Time Management Organizers and Software Mentioned in Chapter 13   294

Index   295

LIST OF FIGURES

1-1	Mary-Helen's expected workload.	15
1-2	Project management is like basic management, but the detail increases with the size of the project.	17
2-1	Harry's dynamic project plan for the bank's Goodwill Project.	34
2-2	Jack's dynamic project plan for the Personnel Records Project.	36
2-3	A parameter range forecast.	43
2-4	Dynamic project plan for the Goodwill Project.	45
2-5	Dynamic project plan for the Personnel Records Project.	47
3-1	Objectivity scales and opinions.	65
3-2	Using scales to go from objective to specification.	67
4-1	A precedence logic diagram.	76
4-2	A precedence diagram with a milestone added.	76
4-3	A precedence diagram with parallel activities.	77

LIST OF FIGURES

4-4	A precedence diagram with parallel and series activities.	78
4-5	A precedence diagram with different relationships between activities.	78
4-6	A logic diagram exercise.	79
4-7	Another logic diagram exercise.	80
4-8	A more extensive logic diagram exercise.	80
4-9	Examples of diagram labeling.	82
4-10	Scheduling symbols for the Projectics method.	83
4-11	A scheduling exercise.	84
4-12	The Projectics method of scheduling.	85
4-13	The two kinds of float.	86
4-14	A logic diagram for the Goodwill Project.	88
4-15	Goodwill Project activity list.	89
4-16	Projectics method schedule for the Goodwill Project.	90
4-17	Level 2 phases and level 3 activity list for the Personnel Records Project.	91
4-18	A logic diagram for the Personnel Records Project.	92
4-19	Projectics method schedule for the Personnel Records Project.	93
4-20	Work breakdown structure for constructing a hi-fi set.	95
5-1	The Goodwill Project budget.	103
5-2	Level 2 and level 3 budget for the Personnel Records Project.	105
7-1	Jack's attempt to save time by fast-tracking the tasks.	135
8-1	A summary milestone report for managers using MBO.	148
8-2	A project status report.	150
8-3	A periodic report on schedule progress.	152
8-4	A budget and actuals report.	153
9-1	Praise as a motivator.	171

LIST OF FIGURES

9-2	Peer praise as a motivator.	173
9-3	Sample risk chart.	179
10-1	The eight basic rights of project managers.	190
10-2	Task reporting in a line organization.	191
10-3	Task reporting in a matrix organization.	192
10-4	The full-time project team.	194
10-5	Activity/task form for the Goodwill Project.	195
10-6	Activity/task form for the Personnel Records Project.	196
10-7	Activity/task form (owners of this book may copy this form for their own use).	197
11-1	A neat schedule produced by a microcomputer program.	204
11-2	The graphics capability of software is a consideration.	208
11-3	A schedule and a resource management histogram from PMS-II.®	212
11-4	Good software will prevent or detect this loop.	218
11-5	Good software will report on this open end.	219
11-6	PC software criteria in order of importance.	222
11-7a	Harvard Project Manager, version 2.01, levels 2 and 3 logic diagrams.	223
11-7b	Harvard Project Manager, version 2.01, level 3 schedule for part of a project.	224
11-7c	Harvard Project Manager, version 2.01, PERT and Gantt charts for a subproject.	225
11-8a	Time Line ® version 3.0, levels 2 and 3 logic diagram.	226
11-8b	Time Line ® version 3.0, levels 2 and 3 schedule.	227
12-1	Forecasted resource load.	236
12-2	Mary-Helen's projects and their priorities.	241
12-3	True multiproject capability of software.	248
12-4	The multiproject capability of Harvard Total Project Manager II, version 2.01.	249

12-5	The multiproject capability of Time Line ®, version 3.0.	250
12-6	Load leveling for Personnel Records Projects.	252
13-1	Harry's daily timetable.	260
13-2	Harry's task list.	261
13-3	One of Jack's daily schedules.	263
13-4	One of Jack's priorities cards (task list).	263
13-5	Time Mastery Form for Agenda and Instant Minutes.	273
13-6	The Scan/Plan Creative Organizers.	275
13-7	A Scan/Plan organizer for a small project.	276
13-8	Time/Design™ project worksheet.	278
13-9	Control Center, for the project manager with a portable computer.	279
A-1	An arrow-node diagram.	284
A-2	A precedence diagram.	285
A-3	Nodes become edges joined by a line.	286
A-4	Adding milestones.	286
A-5	Answers to exercise in Figure 4-6.	288
A-6	Answers to exercise in Figure 4-7.	288
A-7	Answers to exercise in Figure 4-8.	289
A-8	Answers to exercise in Figure 4-12.	290

CHAPTER one

MANAGEMENT BY PROJECTS (MBP)

why it is different from the usual form of management

> **Key Idea**
>
> Project management requires much more detail in planning and control than general management does.

One-time-only jobs require special management. They should be treated as *projects*—that is, as unique jobs with definable end points. Project management, as we shall see, entails its own set of planning and control procedures. First, however, to establish the need for project management, we will examine some cases in which its principles should have been—but were not—applied.

CASE 1:
IT LOOKED EASY, SO JOE DID IT HIMSELF

Joe Manfred of Los Angeles was successful as the owner and manager of a specialty shop on Hollywood Boulevard. Because his revenues covered his mortgage payments and because he always paid his bills on time, he had a good line of credit with his suppliers and his bank.

Although business was good, it bothered Joe that he didn't have a more secure layout that would compel shoplifters to pass by the cash register when leaving the store with merchandise. Also, he had a winner in a new line and he wanted space to sell it. First, he would open up the wall to the storeroom and introduce the new line in that area. The need for storage would be diminished by going to an immediate delivery format that he had negotiated with his principal supplier. Because he was a good customer, the supplier had agreed to give him the large-order discount on small orders.

Joe hired a carpenter, who obtained the building permit, opened up the wall, and reinforced the ceiling. As the job progressed, Joe decided to have the carpenter also make a new counter for the cash register and credit card sales. He also had the carpenter install a railing to guide people past this point at the door. Before the front counter could be finished, however, the carpenter mysteriously disappeared, as contractors are apt to do when they have work elsewhere. Things were makeshift for two weeks. The carpenter didn't show up or even answer telephone calls. Finally, on a busy Friday night, he appeared and offered to finish the job. Joe didn't have the heart to say no. Finally, when Joe was satisfied that Phase One was done, he started looking for a cabinetmaker. At about this time, he noticed that his sales were down for the month, but he was not worried.

Halfway through the installation of new counters and cabinets in the rear, Joe got the idea of having one unit on display and the remainder of the stock visible but secure. This was too good an idea to dismiss, so the cabinetmaker had to rip everything out and start over again. Naturally, being somewhat proud of his work, he was a little nonplussed and disappeared for a week. When he finally reappeared, he was drunk, and another day was lost. Good cabinetmakers were hard to find, however, so Joe went ahead with his renovation plans. At the end of the second month, the back room was ready for display of the new specialty line.

Joe now called up the supplier of the new specialty and ordered his stock. Much to his dismay, he found that there was no stock available because the sales were so good. (He truly was onto a good idea.) It would take another six weeks to get his stock for display. As if that wasn't enough, there were problems at the checkout. The railing was too close to the counter and wobbly enough to make an insurance inspector threaten to cancel Joe's liability insurance. Furthermore, Joe's most experienced clerk simply refused to adapt to the new electronic cash register, which did inventory control as well. Worst of all, while making out his sales tax report for the month, Joe noticed that his sales were down for the second month in a row. He was neglecting sales. Not only that, his wife was making snide remarks about neglected spouses.

What are the lessons from this sad story? Joe was good at selling, but he was not good at renovating and expanding his store. It took him away from his selling activity. If he had hired an architect or an interior designer, he would have been astounded by their consulting fees. On the other hand, an experienced person could have put everything in place with minimum disturbance to the business. His lost sales for the past two months would have more than paid for the extra cost. Also, he probably wouldn't have so much fence mending to do at home.

CASE 2:
FUN AND GAMES WITH COMPUTERIZATION

A small manufacturer of biofeedback devices, working out of Denver, was ready for the benefits of computerization. The company had an engineering department, a manufacturing department, a sales department, and a finance department. In addition, it was soon to have a personnel department. Wilf Baker, the owner/manager, had seen a business computer system at a medical equipment show and was enthusiastic about the possibilities. A customer's order could be entered into the computer, which would then print a copy of the existing inventory or the materials to be ordered to build a custom unit. Wilf's people could charge their time and materials to a job number, and the information would be entered into the computer. Wilf would then know what the true cost was. Finally, the computer would issue a shipping advice and an invoice and keep track of collections.

Currently, Wilf's company did all this manually on different pieces of paper: Some were letters of authorization; some were forms Wilf had picked up; and one was a work order sheet that he had to authorize personally. As the paperwork went from department to department, it sometimes got lost in the shuffle. If a customer wanted a status report, it took a tremendous effort to find out what was going on. As the sales manager had pointed out, and as Wilf had agreed, a computer could tidy up the situation. It would also free people to do other work. After a demonstration at their offices, the department managers agreed to go ahead. Only his old-fashioned production manager protested, but the sales manager handled this with aplomb. First, he got the production manager interested in playing a game of Ding-Bat on the computer. Then he led him to try out a subprogram for inventory control. Things popped up on the screen and danced from right to left and top to bottom. The production manager was intrigued. Before long, the unit was sitting in the front office. Wilf assigned Larry, his chief accountant, to make the system operational. After three weeks of instruction and practice with the computer, Larry told Wilf he couldn't do anything until he changed over all the account numbers so that they would fit the computer program. "Okay," said Wilf. "Go ahead. Let's go for it."

Two months later, when Wilf was scanning his profit statement, he found that they were paying ten times as much for electronic sensors as they had paid in the past. This turned out to be a small problem of account number jumbling, and Larry promised to correct it. Meanwhile, Wilf decided to process sales through the computer, although that required close cooperation between his accountant and the sales manager, who did not like each other. Indeed, in the fourth month, Wilf questioned Larry more closely and was told that the sales manager had refused to do as Larry had requested. The sales manager retorted that he was busy selling and didn't have time to organize all the new paperwork. Besides, what was wrong with what they were doing already? Weren't they selling plenty?

Consequently, Wilf found himself getting more and more involved in the implementation of computerization. He had to redesign the existing forms and also convince the sales manager that this was a good thing to do. Next, he tackled Engineering. They were a little bit angry because the new computer would not work with their kind of software. However, with a little coercion, they entered their bill of materials into the computer. On their own, they decided it would be good to put the specifications on the computer as well. This led to a need for a word-processing package.

Wilf's saga is common. Like many others, he did not immediately get the benefits of computerization. After one year, he was ready to throw the whole thing out, but by this time his emotional and financial investment was too large for him to quit. Being the entrepreneur that he was, Wilf was determined to triumph over the computer. And he did—after about two years. In the meantime, some of the things that were important to the firm had been neglected. For example, he didn't have a new personnel manager; in fact, he had nobody for Personnel at all. Several key testers in the production area had left for other jobs, partly because of the lack of a good benefit package.

Computerization does not have to be a bad experience. There is a better way to run a project.

WHEN SHOULD WORK BE A PROJECT?

It is clear from the foregoing cases that something new and different can have a bad impact on the operations of an organization. A one-time job that affects operations and people should be managed as a *project*. A project, then, is something with an *end point,* and each project is *unique*. The more things there are to be done and the more people to be coordinated, the more need there is for the detailed planning and control of *project management*.

Small Projects

Joe Manfred's expansion of his store was a small project—as are such activities as opening a second store, opening another restaurant, putting a small addition on a factory, computerizing a payroll, purchasing and installing a computer printer, or introducing a product variation. Such a project, when complete, may be good for the business, but its impact if it is not well done may be costly because of its interference with regular operations.

Medium Projects

A medium project is one that requires the coordination of several departments. Examples are the expansion of a department store into other locations, the development of a restaurant chain, the installation of a management information system, or the acquisition of new equipment. Such medium projects require definition of all the tasks to be done and coordination of the involved people. If these are not done, the project will be costly in lost production or sales, and there will be discontent in the ranks—sometimes total confusion. It is best to have a single person to coordinate the whole thing. This person can be called a Project Manager, Project Leader, Project Coordinator, or some similar title—perhaps in addition to another title if the project is not a full-time job.

The Principle of Project Planning

For a project to succeed, you must plan the details and coordinate the actions of the people involved. As you go from small to medium projects, the degree of planning must increase. One person should be put in charge of the project.

SMALL PROJECT EXAMPLE

Let's do Joe Manfred's store expansion over again, and do it as a project. This is not like setting up a new sales record keeping scheme or arranging for a daily cleaning service. This is a one-time event. Even if Joe does expand his store again, it will never be the same experience as this one.

First, we will appoint Joe as the project manager. He can do this project and run the store as well. Besides, he's the only person available. The first thing Joe should do is to clarify what he wants to accomplish. He has some hazy ideas for getting more space and for having better security. Joe should ask himself, "Is this really what I want to accomplish? Let's define the project now in terms of what is to be achieved:

1. To provide space for exhibiting a new specialty line (about 100 square feet of floor space should suffice)
2. To provide control of people leaving the store with merchandise

These are the main objectives. Overriding them, however, is the need to make money. So let's add a few more:

3. To accomplish the first two objectives with not more than a five percent loss in sales volume over a two-month period
4. To complete the job in a two-month period
5. An objective to be named or discovered later (we frequently think of extras once a project is under way)

Because this is a small project, it's not difficult to set out the objectives. In fact, they're probably not much different from what Joe had in mind originally. However, the objective to minimize disruption to the business might well have occurred later in the planning exercise. You will notice that I also added a *time objective*, (item 4). What about a cost objective?

6. To complete the job at an expenditure of between $5,000 and $10,000 (Joe is not an estimator, so the cost objective is very approximate)

Next, Joe should make a list, in any order, of things that have to be done, including:

Tear down the partition

Put shelves in the new area

Install the new merchandise

Move the counter closer to the doorway and install a railing

When Joe has written this basic list, it may prompt him to think of other things, such as:

Cut down the counter height in the center aisle to improve visibility

Install mirrors to watch customers who are hidden behind counters

Leave room at the front counter for installation of a computerized cash register and inventory control

Put security alarm on the back door and window

In many projects, extras have a way of creeping in, just as Joe's second list shows. You should list them up front, so that you can assess their cost and their impact on the completion time.

Now Joe is ready for a *rough schedule*. Approximate times are satisfactory for a job of this sort. For example: Tear down partition on Sunday, June 25, and Monday, June 26 (store closing days). Install cabinets on the following weekend—say, July 3. Install new merchandise on weekend of July 10.

Now we have a schedule stretching out over three weeks. Is this possible? We haven't allowed for waiting periods. How long will it take to get a carpenter? How long will it take to get the cabinets made off-site? How long will it take to get the merchandise? At this point, Joe should elaborate his checklist of things to do and finalize his schedule. Suppose that after a couple of days, Joe has done some checking and the schedule works out to be six weeks. This is fine, because his target was eight weeks. It allows a comfortable two-week time cushion in case something goes wrong and he needs an extra weekend to do some work that would otherwise upset store operations.

Joe could use a parallel schedule for the alterations at the front of the store. They are more or less independent of the others and could be deferred if necessary. On the other hand, there are some savings in time and money if he gets a carpenter to do both jobs at once. Suppose that Joe decided to use a carpenter recommended by a fellow storekeeper down the street. It would save him the time of getting different quotes. Besides, this is not such a big job that it requires three separate quotes.

Somewhere along the line, Joe will discover that he needs a building permit. With luck, the carpenter or cabinetmaker will tell him about the permit and take care of it.

Joe would be wise to go over his plans with the carpenter and cabinetmaker in order to make use of their experience. Undoubtedly, they could make some worthwhile suggestions to cut his cost, cut the time, or do the job better. If Joe is to be a project manager, he should draw the project team into the work planning as much as possible. This is called *participative planning*.

All in all, Joe doesn't need to do much work in this planning phase. Objectives and schedules should be written down and reviewed by Joe and by others at this time. Even if all the bases aren't covered, it is probably better to plan than to dash in and start tearing things down. There will be problems, but someone with Joe's enterprising skills should be able to handle them.

Suppose that Joe is too busy to do this planning, but he still wants to go ahead. He could then find an architect or an interior designer who specializes in store interiors. He might be a little shocked when he hears their daily consulting charges, but when he considers the overall job, he should realize that they are reasonable. For example, if a store designer is also the project manager, he or she will make a plan without major flaws. Materials will be chosen that won't have to be ripped out and replaced later or kept with a lot of regret. Moreover, this specialist may have contact with carpenters and cabinetmakers who are willing to work for a better price. In other words, project management costs something, but there are some hidden payoffs. Not the least of these is that Joe himself would be free to mastermind the new sales strategy and would be able to explore other avenues of merchandising.

AN EXAMPLE OF A MEDIUM PROJECT

Let's do Wilf's computerization as a planned project. First, he needs to designate a project manager. That person should be free to devote at least 50 percent of his or her time to the project for as long as necessary. Wilf can then sit back and be the idea man. He can do the other things that the president of a growing company should be doing. Also, because the company is growing, Wilf can hire another person to assist in the accounting function. He would thus free up his chief accountant, Larry, to look after the computerization. He should enroll Larry in a seminar on project management, because accountant training does not usually include these skills. Such a seminar can give a person 20 years of experience in a matter of a few days.

As in the small project, the project manager should clarify the objectives. Larry should talk to Wilf and the department managers and find out the areas that can be improved through the use of a computer. He could arrange for briefings by several software suppliers. The executive staff could contribute worthwhile ideas and make informed decisions. This could take a month. Wilf might get impatient with a project manager who does all this preparation work. Actually, Wilf should worry only if the preparation is *not* done.

By now, the project manager will have come up with a *list of requirements* for the computer and the software they are going to purchase. (For example, it should provide the 17 reports requested by the department managers.) The project manager will also have a rough idea of the cost and will be able to make a *cost–benefit comparison*. (For example: "The new computer reports should save labor and fine-tune the operation.") Suppose that the benefits are worth $100,000 per year; then it makes sense to spend up to $100,000 for the project. However, subtracting the salary of the project manager and the cost of the time spent by other people leaves very little money for the computer and software.

In the meantime, the project manager, if properly trained, will be roughing out a schedule. It will contain time for defining the requirements, installing the equipment, pilot-testing the new system, and implementing the system. Even though the project manager has no expertise in these areas, he can get estimates from suppliers based on the time required for similar installations.

AN EXAMPLE OF A MEDIUM PROJECT

Now, at last, the project manager should be ready to present his plan. Wilf is likely wondering why the computer isn't already installed in the front office; after all, he saw one operating at a show several months ago. This reaction is not unusual. When they first introduce project management, executives are often surprised to find how slowly a project moves at the startup. They are used to having things happen shortly after the idea occurs to them. The executives need to understand that although careful project work starts slowly, it has a fast finish. The overall saving in time and money is well worth the effort. Of course, one can dash into a project and get something operating, but the results seldom justify the rush. The history of business computerization is well laced with stories of horrible massacres to organizations that did it without careful planning.

The plan that Wilf will approve should say what money and people *resources* will be required, how much *time* will be required, and what *results* are to be achieved. We can well imagine that someone who spends several months preparing such a project plan will probably come across several software and computer combinations. All the software vendors will claim to do the job superbly, accurately, cheaply, and without the problems of their competitors. A knowledge of potential problems will be valuable to the project manager during the implementation process, so that he will know what to look for.

It might be six months before the computer is sitting in the main office, with figures dancing on the screen and the printer drumming out reports. It will likely be a year before the system is operational for Sales and Production. It could be a year and a half before Engineering and Personnel get into the act. There will be some trying times. Not all the reports will be as expected. Some departments will be required to generate information in a form that the computer requires, something that they may not have expected to do. The system will require some debugging, some hand-holding, and occasionally the passing around of the crying towels.

With this kind of project, it is hard to know when the end has been reached. In fact, if the end points are not defined early, the project can go on and on. Computerization can be extended to other aspects of the business, ad infinitum. However, these extensions should be handled as separate projects. The project manager, Larry, should be able to cover himself with glory by having the first project completed on a specified date. (Begin the project by issuing a statement like: "When 95 percent of all the original requirements are met, the project shall be considered complete.") Wilf will have the secret satisfaction of having done a better job than some other small companies that are still floundering about. He should arrange for a dinner party, with a ceremonial ribbon cutting, at which he can pass out accolades to the whole team. Then someone can program the computer to print out a statement that says, "I am happy to be one of your family. Thanks for everything."

MULTIPLE PROJECTS

If you are assigned a number of small projects, there is some additional planning to do in order to cover the interaction of one project with another. Although the projects may be relatively independent of each other in terms of results, they become related because *you* are the shared resource. If you don't plan your workload, you may end up jumping from project to project in order to meet deadlines. This is a very inefficient way of working. The result is that you will be late with some of the key projects. Next, we will examine a case of multiple small projects.

CASE 3:
SHE ALMOST TOOK ON MORE THAN SHE COULD HANDLE

Imagine that you are able to tune in on a day with Mary-Helen, an insurance officer with the ABC Insurance Company in Boston. She is seated at her desk working on a project when the telephone rings. It is the boss's secretary, who says that Bill would like to see Mary-Helen if she has a few moments. Translated, this means: "Get over here on the double." Mary-Helen grabs a note pad and proceeds immediately to the boss's office. Soon she is hearing, "This new insurance policy is a great challenge, Mary-Helen. I am only giving

CASE 3: MORE THAN SHE COULD HANDLE

it to you because of your superior experience. We have found a niche in the insurance market that involves retiring teachers who qualify for the State Pension Fund. A recent court case has ruled that the State must use the same actuarial rate for men and for women. If a female teacher retires and her husband is older and she chooses a survivor's option, she doesn't get as good a deal as we can arrange for her. Our rate for males is less than for females because, as you know, females live longer."

Mary-Helen's eyes brighten, because she has heard about this idea before, and she thinks there are possibilities. Bill drones on: "There are about 100,000 teachers in this state, of whom 30,000 are close to retirement. I estimate that if we can get to them, we could sell at least 5,000 policies. We can show a retiring female teacher with an older male spouse that she can save money by taking the full pension instead of the reduced one with a survivor's benefit. She can cover her husband with a life insurance policy on herself. Normally, we would take one year to develop, test, and deploy such a policy, but the court action I mentioned took place about six months ago. I suspect that some of our competition may be working on the same scheme. Therefore, I think our new policy should be ready within six months. I would need a preliminary report in order to make a decision within six weeks. Now, here are preliminary notes and a letter from one of our field managers. Get back to me after you have had a look at this project."

On her way back to her office, Mary-Helen is euphoric. She knows the boss is beginning to recognize her abilities, because he's giving her the whole job without a lot of boring details. She gets back to her desk and looks for a place to put down the new bundle of notes. To her dismay, she realizes that she already has a lot of work ahead of her. What about that budget she is preparing for the Miller project? Then there is this joint project with another insurance company, which has a deadline of only five weeks.

She gets out her project list and tidies it up a bit. Then she adds a new one at the bottom: Teachers' Pension Alternative. Thinks Mary-Helen: "If I drop everything and work on the teachers' pension project, Bill will be pleased. But sooner or later, he's going to want results on these others. Not only that, but there are a couple of projects here that have a high executive profile because of agreements with other companies. I can't let them slide very long. I'm already working two evenings a week. Something's not right here.

This is an interesting job, but Bill doesn't realize that I can't do everything at once. There is no use in my telling him I am overloaded. He always says 'So what; I'm overloaded, too. So is everybody. We've just got to do the best we can!' I think that this time I'll take a look at my load in hours per week before discussing the situation with Bill. I'll do it the way it was mentioned in that newsletter about project management—the one that was circulated around here by Bill."

So Mary-Helen takes a piece of graph paper and lists her projects down one side (see Figure 1-1). Across the top, she marks off the months and makes a column for each week. Then, for each project, she puts an X at its promised date of delivery. She puts in the hours per week that she thinks the project will require of her, continuing across the row for each project. Finally, she gets down to the last project—the Teachers' Pension Alternative. She estimates 10 hours per week for the first four weeks, 25 for the next two, 5 for two more weeks, and then 15, except for the last seven weeks, where she bumps it up to 30. Then she adds a row for her miscellaneous workload, which includes answering the telephone, taking odd assignments from the boss and from other departments, going to unplanned meetings, and so forth. She allows 10 hours per week for the miscellaneous workload. Finally, across the bottom, she sums up her load in hours per week.

Mary-Helen looks at the totals (Figure 1-1) and finds that she is currently booked at 50 hours per week. This includes the two evenings per week that she is working. However, there is a sustained workload coming up that averages about 80 hours per week. She knows that she can't do it. It boils down to this: If the new project is really that important, then something will have to be either delayed or given to someone else. She really should have more help, but she knows that Bill will be unable to give it to her in the current fiscal year.

After rechecking the figures and tidying them up a bit, she takes the chart to her manager. "Bill," she says, "I want you to take a look at my workload. I'm not complaining about the things that you have given me to do. I would like to do them all, but I can't."

Bill takes a look at the chart and says, "I'm impressed, Mary-Helen. I wish more people would do this for me. I certainly didn't realize that the load had built up to this point. When I give you an assignment, and you take it on, I naturally assume that you are able

EXPECTED WORKLOAD

of ___Mary-Helen___

PROJECT	Month					
	JAN	FEB	MARCH	APRIL	MAY	JUNE
MILLER	10 10 10 10	15 5 5 15	25*			
JOINT	15 15 15 15	15*				
HIGH PROFILE #1	5 5 5 5	15 25 25 25	10 10 30 30*			
HIGH PROFILE #2		20 20 20 20	15 15 15 15	30 30 30 30		
TEACHERS PENSION ALT.	10 10 10 10	25 25* 5 5	15 15 15 15	15 15 15 15	15 30 30 30	30 30 30 30*
MISC.	10 10 10 10	10 10 10 10	10 10 10 10	10 10 10 10	10 10 10 10	10 10 10 10
TOTAL HRS/WK	50 50 50 50	100 85 65 75	75 50 50 70	55		

Figure 1-1. Mary-Helen's expected workload.

to do it, unless you say otherwise. Too many people don't tell me the consequences until it's already too late. Then they're failing to deliver the projects that I have promised to other people. Here's what we'll do. I want you to keep the Teachers' Pension Alternative. This High Profile 1 on your list can be put on hold for another six months because of new developments. I think I'll take High Profile 2 and give it to John, because the Sales Department just canceled a big one that he was doing. Okay, now take another look at your workload, and let me know what the delivery dates will be for the remaining projects."

On her way back to her office, Mary-Helen feels pleased with herself. Finally, she has found a way to communicate with her manager. She is glad that she has done some project planning, and she resolves to do more. That little piece of paper seemed to aid in communications with her boss much better than anything else she had previously tried.

Mary-Helen's situation was very much like those of project leaders, project engineers, project architects, or project officers who have specialties. In large organizations, they are assigned more than one project at a time. Also, it is typical for people who handle small projects to have a number of them at once. It is this overload on themselves that seems to be the prime cause of failure. Yet, as is evident from the example, the extra bit of planning is not difficult to do.

THE PROJECT MANAGEMENT PLANNING PHASE

As you can see from Figure 1-2, project management, like general management, is broken down into *planning* and *controlling*. However, there is a great deal of detail in the planning and controlling phases of project management. I will describe this detail in the sequential steps shown in the figure. In many cases, you may do the steps out of this order. However, it is important that you do all of them, or at least check them out within each phase.

Step 1: Preliminary Plan

Once a project is assigned to you, it is time to do some preliminary planning. Most small projects can be put on one sheet of paper.

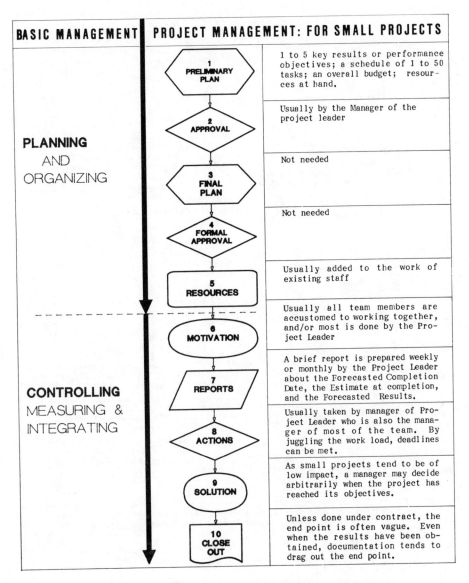

Figure 1-2. Project management is like basic management—but the detail increases with the size of the project.

FOR MEDIUM SIZE PROJECTS

5 to 25 results, performance objectives, specifications; a schedule of 10 to 100 tasks; a Work Breakdown Structure; approximate overall budget; resources to be negotiated.

Most likely by Senior Management or a Project Office

5 to 50 results, performance objectives, specifications; a schedule of 50 to 500 tasks; a Work Breakdown Structure and a code of accounts; subschedules; accurate overall budget; sub-budgets; benefit-to-cost analysis; availability of key resources; requests for additional authority; a priority rating.

Most likely by Senior Management, client, customer, or all; Funds held until the approval is given.

Requires commitments from other key resource managers; may use written task agreements; contracts let; overloads identified.

Project Manager must establish new cooperative relationship with other departments and sustain them; may need to build teamwork.

Schedules and sub-schedules are updated by Forecasted Completion Dates; Budgets and sub-budgets are updated by Estimates at Completion;; Overall and subsystem results are forecasted; Period of reporting according to the approved plan; Summary reports prepared for Management, client, or customer.

The project manager renegotiates the best new schedule and budget that can be obtained from the resource managers; reasonable tradeoffs are made; if project is seriously off track, the Dynamic Project Plan is revised and resubmitted for approval.

The end point is clearly defined in the approved Project Plan; tests may be performed to prove out the results before payments are completed.

The close-down step is usually detailed in the Dynamic Project Plan; the project account number can be closed off; additions require the raising of new projects.

(Figure 1-2 continued)

THE PROJECT MANAGEMENT PLANNING PHASE 19

Medium-size projects may require additional pages for each of the subplans for the involved subdepartments.

You first need to clarify the objectives. The objectives state the performance or results that will be achieved by the project. If you are developing a race car, then *performance* is the appropriate word. If you are developing a new insurance policy, then *results* is a more suitable word. In our project planning, *performance* or *results* will pertain to anything other than the budget or schedule.

Once you have made up a list of activities or tasks to accomplish the results (or performance), you should prepare a preliminary schedule. A preliminary schedule need not be very precise. You may lose time on some tasks and gain it on others. Also, you don't yet know which activities are going to be critical to the overall completion date.

Associated with the list of activities is a budget for each item; when these are totaled, you will have the budget for the project. You should include any out-of-pocket expenses, the costs for contracted work, and the required person-hours for completion of the project. A common mistake in preparing the budget is not to include the person-hours of the department that is in charge of the project. All resources used in the project should be included in the budget so they can be controlled.

Step 2: Approval

A project plan is a description of what is to be achieved, the necessary time, and the required resources and authority. These resources are usually under the control of someone else, so you will need your manager's approval of the plan. Your manager can take it to a higher level if it requires resources from other departments. Thus, a project plan is like a contract between you and your management, customer, or client. You are promising to get a specific result within a stated time frame in return for a stated allocation of resources. That is why you should get approval. On the other hand, if you are the boss, and you have assigned a project to a subordinate, you should require that he or she draft a preliminary plan. It should be brought to you for your approval. In that way, you will know whether he or she is working toward the same targets that you have in mind. You can also bring up the matter of the other work that has been assigned, keeping in mind that those who handle small projects often have multiple projects to deal with.

Step 3: Final Plan

For medium to large projects, you should do additional planning. Sometimes the targets need alteration after you have discussed them with your management, customer, or client. The final plan is more detailed and precise than the preliminary plan. You now have specific dates when you will require end items. Suppose that for your preliminary plan, another department manager said they would normally require about two weeks to do a task. When you actually specify a date—say, January 30—you may find that they are loaded with other work. They may actually take six weeks to deliver an item that requires only two weeks of work. Your final plan is like a final contract. It needs to be fine-tuned for the commitments of other parties; for other work that you have; and for the priority given to the project if it is to be done in a multiple-project work environment. This is the plan that you and your manager, customer, or client will go by. Therefore, it needs approval once again by whatever authority is involved.

Step 4: Formal Approval

As depicted in Figure 1-2, a final plan and formal approval are usually not required for small projects. The adjustments to schedule that will be necessary once the project is launched are usually done by the manager of the project leader on an "as needed" basis. Moreover, on small projects commitments are frequently not required from other departments, as the preliminary plan can be realized within one working unit.

Step 5: Resources

The plan is now approved and the project goes ahead. There may have been some delays in getting approval. This means that many of the prior commitments to the plan must be renegotiated. For small projects, you assign the tasks and it gets under way. For medium to large projects, the tasks are grouped into packages—for your own department and for other departments. You must now get a commitment to a definite schedule. Note that this is a two-way commitment. For example, if Department B works on the output of Department A, it will be up to you to see that A is ready on time. Then B can keep its commitment to you. For medium to large projects, the resources to be committed to projects can be quite substantial. Additional approvals might be needed. For example, outside expenditures beyond a certain dollar value may need approval at the executive level.

At the end of this step, the project has been planned, the people are organized, and the work should be under way. Now we will go on to the controlling phase of project management.

THE PROJECT MANAGEMENT CONTROLLING PHASE

Step 6: Motivation

For small projects involving the same team members, motivation is usually not the direct concern of the project leader. Although motivation can affect the results obtained in the project, the project leader is usually not able to give tangible rewards or punishments that can affect the motivation. As you will see, however, there are things that project leaders can do to enhance the cooperation they will get. A later chapter will show you how to get enthusiastic cooperation from other departments when dealing with medium and large projects. For these, some overt acts may be necessary to increase motivation. The project manager may do some team-building. He or she may talk to people about the benefits of the project so that they can see the big picture. The project manager should develop whatever enthusiasm is needed to do the work. If the motivation is inadequate for the project, you will soon know it. You would then go back to this step because of failure to meet targets.

Step 7: Reports

How is the project going? Fortunately, when you have a plan, you have a baseline against which you can measure your current progress. It boils down to this: You look at the progress to date, compare it with the scheduled progress, and then make judgments about the future. You then report the forecasted completion date (FCD) of the project and the estimate at completion (EAC).

For a small project, the reports are prepared by the project leader. He or she is in frequent communication with other team members and can scan the results in order to make a subjective estimate of the future of the project. This estimate probably will fit into the weekly or monthly reporting that is customarily the project leader's responsibility.

Medium to large projects require more formal reporting. First, you must decide in advance whether the reports will be monthly or weekly. The overall reporting on the project may depend on the submission of subreports by other departments, contractors, or even distant government agencies. On medium to large projects, a computer will probably be used to summarize the results and prepare reports.

Step 8: Actions

From Step 7, you now have reports. You have projected these out into the future to the best of your ability. This may not be the future you want, however, so you may decide to take *corrective action*. For example, you may schedule overtime to catch up on some tasks that are running behind. You may give one project priority over other projects for a short time. You may have some problem-solving meetings with other departments in order to get better commitments to the schedule. You may even decide to forgo some features that are expendable in order to be sure that the project adheres to a tight schedule.

A more profound action would be to go back to the planning phase and replan the rest of the project. You get approval for new completion dates, new budgets, and possibly modified results. Once you have replanned the project, it is then under control again. By the very act of getting new commitments from team members, you seize control of the project once again. If, at this point, you are unable or unwilling to act, and your project is running out of control, it will most certainly get worse. Going back to a previous step, which can improve the result, is known as *iteration*. Iteration is necessary and desirable if an organization is going to learn from experience. Fortunately, the effort required to update an existing plan is not nearly as great as the effort required to do the original plan. The main thing is to do it and do it promptly.

Step 9: Solution

One day, the last task will be done and the project will be completed. If you haven't defined the results too well, then completion may be vague, and the project can go on indefinitely. You build the termination of the project into the original plan by defining the end points. When the end points or results are achieved, the project is over. Any requirements that are added at this point should go into a modified and reapproved plan or be considered additional projects.

Step 10: Close Out

There are frequently things to do to close out a project. These should be included in the original plan. Such project tasks as final correction of file drawings, documentation, or preparation of manuals are often deferrable. Unless you put deadlines on them, they may be deferred to the point where they never get done. Sometimes the knowledgeable people are long gone and these items can't be done properly. It is best that the closing of the project be part of the project. There should be assigned tasks and commitments, which you monitor. One day, the project will finally be completed, and you can get on with other work.

THE ROLE OF THE PROJECT LEADER/PROJECT MANAGER

In order to manage a project properly, one person is assigned authority and responsibility for the coordination and completion of the project. This is one of the reasons why project management works. Even in this age of consensus-seeking, we still need a designated person to keep a project moving forward and to make key decisions in a timely fashion.

Regardless of the actual title given, we will use the term *project manager* for the role that this key individual performs. For instance, the person's job title might be insurance officer, such as Mary-Helen in the foregoing example. For the part of her time that she is doing project work, she is a project manager, even if she is not given that title. Project leader, project coordinator, project sponsor, and project officer are some of the other possible titles. Having a project management title is a good idea in an organization, even when the project management is part of another job. For example, the manager of operations may have several key projects under his wing. For those projects, he is the project manager, even though he has another permanent title. When a document about the project needs to be signed by the project manager, he will sign it, regardless of his other titles.

What does a project manager do? He or she plans and coordinates the project from beginning to end, or at least from point A to point B. Many organizations have difficulty in evaluating this position properly and operate without proper job descriptions. People are often doing project management work in addition to their regular job descriptions. Sometimes they are not getting credit for it, and frequently they do not have the appropriate authority, either.

The authority of project managers is sufficiently important to rate a full chapter later in this book. At this point, you should learn about two modes of operation: the team approach and task reporting (matrix form).

The Team Approach

In this mode, all of the people necessary for the completion of the project should report to the project manager. For the duration of the project, the project manager is the boss; he or she is in charge of such important matters as pay, promotions, and assignment of parking spaces. At the conclusion of the project, the team is disbanded. Team members may go back to their previous jobs, may be assigned other work, or may be given pink slips. In the team approach, the project manager is not really lacking in authority. He or she has all the authority that any manager needs with his or her subordinates. As we shall see later, the team approach is generally used only for very large projects. It is rather inefficient for medium projects. The team approach is seldom applied to a small project unless that project has a high profile in the organization.

Task Reporting and Matrix Form

In the task reporting mode, the project manager has no direct subordinates. He or she gets the work done through subordinates of other managers. For small projects, the project leader, project engineer, or project manger usually is at the working level and reports to one of the line managers. This person is very dependent on his or her manager in order to get cooperation from other people within the department and from other departments.

In the matrix form of an organization, the position of project manager is recognized as a full-time job. It is usually on a level equal to that of line manager (frequently called *functional manager* or *resource manager*). On the other hand, project managers have no direct subordinates to do the work; they depend on other departments to get the work done. Their authority, however, is formally recognized, and there are procedures to define the mode of cooperation that is to take place. This is not to say that it is always done this way. In some matrix organizations, the project managers do not have the commensurate authority to get the work done. In such cases, the organization is either ineffective or falls apart, or no one cares if all the projects are late and over the budget.

SUMMARY

When unique projects are added to routine operations, chaos can result. The planning and controlling that is suitable for repeated operations is simply not intensive enough or deep enough or sophisticated enough for managing projects that are different from each other. Thus, although project management is similar to general management, it is also different because it requires more management effort.

Managing a project requires the development of a project plan, its subsequent approval, and assignment of resources. Not only do project managers assign the work, they follow it up in an organized fashion at checkpoints. At these checkpoints, they measure their progress against the plan and take corrective action. They then forecast a new outcome for the project. If the new outcome is substantially different from the original one, they may seek reapproval for a revised plan.

It is customary to assign the responsibility for managing a project to one person. This person may have all other resources under his or her control, as subordinates. In other cases, the resources are under the control of other managers. Naturally, the latter case is a little more difficult for the project manager. Medium projects often operate under these conditions.

Managing a project requires the acquisition of a body of knowledge about scheduling, budgeting, defining results, and the planning and controlling of these factors toward a successful project outcome. That is what the rest of this book is all about.

QUESTIONS FOR DISCUSSION OR ASSIGNMENT

1. The dividing line between small and medium projects is not very precise. Make a list of ten projects that you know about and classify them as small, medium, or large. Give your reasons. Try to have a range from small to large.
2. What is the basic reason that a project plan requires approval?
3. Name two situations in which a project plan might be resubmitted for approval after you have reached the action step.
4. What are the three basic components of any project plan?
5. Take a project that you have been assigned and prepare a preliminary project plan for it. Discuss the plan with other members of your work group, or your manager, or your instructor.

QUESTIONS FOR DISCUSSION OR ASSIGNMENT

6. If a project plan were submitted to you for approval, what would you look for?
7. Why is one person usually designated to be in charge of a project?
8. List three advantages and three disadvantages of preparing a project plan.

CHAPTER
two

THE DYNAMIC PROJECT PLAN
its approval precedes the real start

THE DYNAMIC PROJECT PLAN

> ### Key Idea
>
> Use a dynamic project plan to define the targets for results, time, and cost and the means of controlling them. The plan is dynamic in that it may be revised during the project.

The temptation to get started immediately on a project is strong, particularly when the task is challenging and the improvements are obviously needed. However, the project manager must first establish a *dynamic project plan* (dynamic because it evolves with the project) that defines when the project will be completed, how much it will cost, and what it will accomplish. Such a plan is essential for securing management's guidance and commitment so that the project manager will be headed in the direction approved by senior management and will have the resources and authority to see the job through.

CASE 1:
THE BANKER GETS BUCKED

Cal was the new manager of a bank in a small midwestern town. He had brought Harry with him from his previous bank. Cal was determined to make a good show at his new location. In poring through the files, he found quite a few letters from disgruntled customers. A few discreet inquiries about his predecessor's reign showed that customers had been leaving the bank and going to another down the street. This unhappy migration was certainly not due to differences in interest rates or charges. Cal showed the letters to Harry and said, "Look, Harry, there's a problem here, and I want you to do something about it. Let's call it the Goodwill Project. I want you to institute some kind of program that will get our customers back. Make them so happy that they'll bring others."

"Right," said Harry. He needed no more direction. From experience, Harry knew that Cal expected him to find his own way.

Two weeks later, Cal asked Harry how the Goodwill Project was doing. "Oh that," said Harry. "I'm thinking about giving up on it. There is nothing I can really do without more authority and some money. Would you like to talk about it?"

Back in Cal's office, Harry explained. First, he had wanted to do a mail survey of the bank's customers. However, someone at headquarters told him that a mail survey was their responsibility, not his. Besides, they didn't think it was necessary. Then he thought that he would do an informal survey by taking some corporate clients out to lunch, but he didn't have an entertainment account. Moreover, he knew that the accountants at headquarters wouldn't go for that. Harry did have one definite clue to the customer loss, though: "Cranky Mary," one of the old-time tellers. Something had happened in her life that had made her crotchety toward most of the customers. He had heard her with his own ears. He had talked to the Personnel Department at headquarters about her. They said that since she was a long-time employee, and Cal was new to the bank, they didn't think they could do anything to help.

"Look," said Harry, "I would like to do something about the problem, but I get resistance whichever way I turn. If you could talk to those guys at headquarters, we might get some compliance. We're set up to operate as a branch under the direction of headquarters. Being original is not part of the game plan."

"I see what you mean," said Cal, "but things are going to be different on this new job. I'm here for a reason, and the district manager knows it. I can lever the headquarters boys into willing cooperation, but first I have to know what it is you need. Will you prepare me a plan of action so I will know how to back you up?"

"Okay," said Harry. "I can see that this is not a thing that I can just jump into and fly by the seat of my pants. It'll take a little planning. I'll have a plan ready for you in a few days."

CASE 2:
THE SOFTWARE THAT NEVER GOT FINISHED

Jack Daniels was a crackerjack computer programmer for the Scranton Publishing Company. He worked for Hilda Brubaker, who was the manager of management information systems (MIS) for the whole company. One day she got a formal request from the Personnel Department to computerize their record keeping. This seemed like a good challenge to give to Jack. It would be an opportunity to enlarge his experience within the company.

This is how she explained it: "Jack, our buddies down in the Personnel Department want to keep complete personnel records on computer files. They want to be able to print them out in various lists that are sorted by age, sex, surnames, first names, and so forth. You know what I mean. It won't just be a matter of replacing the existing card files. Because computers provide so many opportunities for different sortings and selections, undoubtedly you will have to give them some guidance on what is possible. Basically, that's it. With your experience on various information projects, I know that you can handle it on your own, so go to it."

"Thanks, Hildy," said Jack. "I'm able to get started right away, and you know I'll do my best."

Hilda got busy with the conference season. When she got back, there were meetings about the new inventory control system that was overdue. Then there was a crisis in her family, and it all fell upon her shoulders. So it's not surprising that since Jack didn't come to her, she didn't bother checking with him for a whole month. Finally, she caught up with the work and asked Jack for a progress report. Jack said that he was almost done. He had written a pilot program in code, and he was testing it with the data now. However, every time he presented it to the Personnel Department, they seemed to want something different. He had done several code iterations for them already.

Hilda thought, "Same old story. Here we go again, trying to reinvent the wheel." Aloud, she said, "Jack, have you looked into purchasing software for this job? I know you can create it with any database program, but there are always changes and maintenance problems. This is especially true with people who have never had a computer program done for them before. If we buy something on the market, the originator will have worked out a lot of these problems. It will be complete with manuals and documentation, and it will be off our backs."

"Well," said Jack, "I could have done that, but I know I can write tighter code than the junk that's out there on the commercial market. Besides, if it is our own code, I can integrate it with the files of other programs in the company. In the long run, it will be better."

Hilda said nothing more, and Jack went on with his project. Four months went by, and Jack always seemed to be close to finishing, but never completely finished. One day a bombshell burst. Word had gotten around that the Personnel Department was about to purchase their own software and personal computer. They were going to do this thing on their own. Apparently, they had heard about another company's success in doing it this way. Like a lot of departments, they wanted autonomy. Jack was so angry that Hilda didn't think she could reprimand him or she would lose a good programmer. She realized now that although Jack was a good computer programmer, he really didn't know how to develop a program with people. She hadn't taken the time to show him how to do it. "We can weather the storm," thought Hilda, "but that guy has got to go for training."

THE DYNAMIC PROJECT PLAN

From the foregoing situations, you can see what is needed. First, starting without a coordinated plan is like riding off in all directions. You get somewhere, but is it in the right direction? Lack of direction was the problem in Jack's case.

Second, one needs authority or resources, or both, to carry out a project. One gets these from management. Lack of resources and authority was the situation that hamstrung Harry at the bank.

The Principle of the Dynamic Project Plan

The project manager needs to establish reasonable result, time, and cost targets, considering the available resources and the urgency of the situation. The plan should state when the project will be finished, what the cost will be, what the results will be, and how each of these factors is going to be controlled. The plan may also request the authority that will make it possible to complete the project successfully. Without an approved plan, there may not be adequate resources or sufficient authority to do the job.

A Dynamic Project Plan for a Small Project

Suppose that banker Harry does his homework and presents a plan to Cal that looks like Figure 2-1. Harry could knock it off on a word processor in a few minutes. This plan is very brief. Notice that all we get when the plan is executed is a report. The corrective actions would have to follow, as the next phase. It would make sense for Harry to prepare a rough plan for the second phase and submit it for approval at the same time. If Cal is a little impatient, he might say, "Look, I don't need a report—I need action and follow-through. Let me have more of the follow-through in the plan. Then I will stir the pot to get the authority and funds to do this thing." Harry might reply, "Okay. But I can do this better after I have started the first phase. Let's say we make a revision after one month. I think that would be reasonable." Now the plan includes the possibilities of revision and reapproval.

—The *time target* for completion is 3 months.
—The *budget* for the project is 16 person-weeks of time for myself and headquarters staff. The out-of-pocket expenses are estimated to be $3000.
—The *result* will be a report that analyzes the problems we have and states what corrective measures are necessary.
—We will *control* the time aspects by reviewing the project at the end of each month. We will not attempt to control the total cost, because we don't have a system for charging back staff time to a project. We will control the result by having a review of our progress at the end of each month.
—The special *authority* needed is to be able to give direction to the Bank's Personnel Department regarding who is on our staff. Also, at least for the next year, we need authority to do a mail survey of present and past customers.

Figure 2-1. Harry's dynamic project plan for the bank's Goodwill Project.

A Dynamic Project Plan for a Medium Project

Suppose that Hilda Brubaker is able to convince the Personnel Department that she can provide them with a better system than they could get on their own. Jack has just come back from a three-day seminar on project management. He and Hilda have drawn up a plan that looks like Figure 2-2. This is an adequate plan at this early stage, but it might be too much to expect from a beginner in project management. Hilda should guide Jack through his first plan or have him take a course for the needed training. (She did both.)

A Medium Project as a Contract

If a project is contracted out, the project plan can be part of the contract. The contractor may have its own project leader. The "owner" (the company letting the contract) may also have a project leader for internal coordination. In the foregoing Personnel Records Project, much of the actual work could be done by an outside consultant. In that case, the owner's project leader, Jack, would guide and coordinate with the contractor. He probably would also authorize progress payments.

The owner's project leader may require that the contractor submit a project plan similar to the one in Figure 2-2. In addition, he or she may require weekly reports on the person-hours consumed and on the progress against the original schedule. The owner's project leader should be in control of the progress reviews by the Personnel Department and the contractor. As a consequence, any decisions would be in accordance with the requirements of their master computer system and within manageable contract terms. You can see that the project leader's involvement in contracted projects is much less than in a project the organization does for itself, so the project leader can handle many more projects. Project leaders often handle multiple projects. Some they do in depth; for others, they are mainly coordinators or contract administrators.

In contracted projects, one may put *milestones* into the plan. They are inserted to provide reviews of the progress toward the results.

—The *time target* is 6 months. After that, the new hiring program will begin and the database should be ready to use.

—The *cost* to us will be the equivalent of 6 person-months or a purchase price of $50,000. This is what Personnel feels it is worth to them if they have to buy it.

—The *performance* requirements (results) will be developed in consultation with the client. No system design or coding will begin until they have signed off on this document. After the signing-off, if they request any additional features that impact the cost or time, we will resubmit the plan for approval.

—In order that this database program *interfaces* with our other databases, the files will be exactly as our computer requires them. Otherwise, a conversion program will be written in the case where a purchased program creates the files.

—*Authority* is needed for two things: (1) The Personnel Department will be required to discuss the requirements in a timely fashion. Their co-signature on this plan should be required. (2) If we develop our own program, we need a priority 5 on the time-shared computer system in order not to be unduly delayed.

—Additional *control* of the results will be exercised by extensive review prior to coding. This will include the services of a consultant in this field.

—Some of the data in the file will be confidential evaluations of personnel performance. It is essential that we set up a password and hierarchical *security procedure*. A company procedure will need to be written and authorized before doing the coding. This should be done by the Personnel Department.

Figure 2-2. Jack's dynamic project plan for the Personnel Records Project.

Milestones can also be used to make payments in accordance with progress, rather than according to the actual hours expended. This is a neat tie-in of project management principles with the contracting procedure. At any milestone, a contract might be revised, certainly by the owner but sometimes by the contractor also. With the milestone approach, exploratory techniques can be commenced, providing a better definition for the phase that follows a milestone review.

PURPOSES OF THE DYNAMIC PROJECT PLAN

The dynamic project plan is like a contractual agreement between the project manager and the management, customer, or client. It states what is to be accomplished in exchange for specified resources and authority.

By virtue of having checkpoints for revisions, the plan ensures that neither results, nor time, nor cost will be overemphasized. Although these are independent factors in the plan, they become related in the implementation of the project because of necessary trade-offs between them.

The plan can be used to develop awareness of the overall project goals. The team members can be encouraged to read and study the plan. In some cases, they may participate in the development of the plan.

The plan defines the end point of the project. When the goals or objectives are reached, the project is over.

The plan is dynamic. As experience is gained, the objectives for results, cost, and time can be refined and improved. This is especially true of a project that includes an exploratory design phase where the outcome cannot be precisely specified. One can get a fixed price for the installation of a new copy machine or the design and construction of an ordinary bridge. Some projects will be of this nature. However, most projects can benefit from what is learned in the early phases. In other words, the dynamic project plan should not be chiseled in stone. It should be changeable.

DETAILS OF THE DYNAMIC PROJECT PLAN

The Time Objective (T)

Timing is the element of the project that requires the most effort. Although it need not be the first item in the written plan, it is frequently the first item that is worked on.

When will the project actually be finished? You need to make up a list of activities and then analyze their relationships. Find which ones must be done in series and which ones can be done in parallel. This is usually done with a PERT/CPM diagram (more details in Chapter 4). The diagram helps you work out a practical sequence of activities. Then you need to get estimates of the times necessary to complete the tasks. From those, you can work out the earliest finish of the project (EFp). In some cases, this is all the scheduling that is done for the preliminary plan. This is especially true if there will be a significant time lapse before the plan is approved.

You must also grapple with the realities of resource availability. There is seldom an inexhaustible supply of people for a project. A project may include an activity that has a limited resource availability—for example, a specialty contract or the supply of unique equipment. The resource unavailability can make the final completion date later than the optimum date, which assumed that the resources would be available when needed.

Small and medium projects are frequently undertaken by organizations that are reluctant to use outside resources. If so, the completion time for a project will depend on the availability of internal resources. These resources may be assigned to other projects, as well. If all projects have equal priority, then a new one is just "next in line." Each resource manager can tell you approximately when his or her department can do the tasks for your project. You can use these figures to work out a completion date. If this date is so far off the mark that you know you will not get approval, you must go again to the resource managers to see what can be done by setting aside other work, taking on additional people, working overtime, or whatever is practical in order to meet the project needs. Sometimes the schedule can be tightened up by giving the project a higher priority rating than the others. (We will devote a chapter to this topic.)

For now, let us assume that you can get reasonable commitments of resources to the project. You are able to predict a completion date that could be reached in the normal course of events. Such a time objective might look like this: "The time target for this project is 32 weeks. If started in one week, the project will have a completion date of September 24."

If the deadline for the project is already very tight, you can work backward to find out what is required to achieve the deadline. This process implies that resources can be made available to meet the required date. In any case, if you have a plan, you can find out where the special effort needs to go. If all goes well, you can reach the tight target. If it doesn't, you can revise your plan at some milestone along the way and then take into account the experience gained during the project.

Success in a project does not always mean meeting an apparent deadline. You have to consider the results that are to be obtained and the cost of getting there. Thus, the success of a project is not judged solely by whether it was completed on time. A successful project is one in which the balance of time, cost, and results is known and understood and these factors are the best possible under the circumstances. When a project is retargeted for a completion date, it is once again under control. You need this opportunity to revise the plan and seize control again. Without it, a project that is starting to get late will most likely get even later. It may get completely out of control.

It is customary to include a schedule with your project plan. You may also include a PERT/CPM diagram to show that you have done the necessary analysis. For a small project, this diagram could be included on an additional page attached to the plan.

The Time Control Plan

As you will see in the next chapter, it is necessary to monitor your progress according to your plan. Update the plan after taking whatever actions are necessary and possible. If project planning is new to your organization or if the project is much larger than what you have been accustomed to, be prepared to answer: "How are you going to control the time aspects of the project?" Briefly, you do this by having monthly or weekly progress reviews, at which time you make forecasts of the completion dates of the remaining tasks leading up to completion. This is what is meant by *updating*.

If your organization has been doing project planning, you may have existing procedures for controlling the time aspects. Then you can simply state that you are going to use them. Beware, though, that existing procedures may not be adequate for a unique, or larger, or more difficult project than has been tackled before.

The Cost Objective (C)

How much will the project cost from beginning to end? (We will devote an entire chapter to this topic.) For the preliminary plan, you may use some guesstimates of the project cost. Break it down by phases. In the final plan, you have to estimate in more detail. If you have prepared a schedule, you will already have a list of activities against which you can put a dollar figure for labor plus overhead. Do this also for the out-of-pocket funds and materials needed to complete each task. The sum of these costs will always be a little bit short of what will be needed, because no one can think of everything. It is customary to add a cushion of 5 or 10 percent. This contingency fund allows for minor unforeseen costs that will inevitably surface sooner or later.

A cost objective might look like this: "The estimated completed cost (or budget) is $35,000 plus or minus 10 percent."

The Cost Control Plan

Cost control is easy if you are able to use existing procedures. Basically, you should insert some cost milestones into your plan at points where significant budget funds will be committed. When a milestone occurs, you need to add up your expenditures to date and estimate any remaining payments due on the work completed. When you compare this "committed cost" with the budget for that milestone, you will see whether the costs are high or low. Your organization may have to set up to prepare cost data so that you can get a figure on the committed cost even though all the money is not yet paid out. Thus, a project plan may put requirements on another department to supply information on your committed cost at a milestone. It becomes your right to obtain this information by virtue of approval of the dynamic project plan.

The Performance (Results) Objectives (P)

You cannot really develop a good schedule and a good budget without knowing what results are to be achieved. This is an iterative process. You must go back and forth between desired additional features and the costs in money and time to do them. The results you are going to achieve are a compromise (tradeoff) with the time and budget available to achieve them. It is also a learning process. As you get into the details of the necessary activities, you are able to better define and clarify what is to be achieved. In contracted technical work, the performance objectives are frequently called the *requirements*. This should not be confused with the "statement of work," which indicates how to meet the requirements.

In a technical project, a performance objective might be something like: "Equipment to pump 1000 liters of fluid per hour to a head of 5 meters." The objectives of nontechnical projects do not have so many numbers; they are more likely to have a statement like: "This new product is to compete successfully with competitor's product X" or "Computerization of our database should result in faster and better service to employees when they claim benefits." Again, we will have an entire chapter on performance objectives. Suffice it to say here that the preliminary or final project plan is a good place to clarify the objectives with your management, customer, or client. This book will continue to use the word *performance* to describe the results achieved, whether the results be technical or nontechnical. To repeat, *performance* is any attribute of the end result, other than time or cost.

The Performance Control Plan

Progress toward the specified results is not easy to measure in business projects, in research projects, and even in many technical projects. Still, the project plan should state how you are going to estimate progress toward the objectives. Otherwise, you will not have balanced control. For instance, too much effort might go toward achieving the time and cost targets at the expense of the results portion.

You can always use what is called a *narrative forecast* (both words are significant). The *narrative* states what has been done to date and then makes a subjective *forecast* about its impact on the final results—for example, "The work completed to date indicates that all performance objectives can be met except the efficiency, which might be lower by about 10 percent."

If a project progresses into a hardware or software phase, there is something tangible to measure. You might be able to quantify the expected result by some major parameter—for instance, "dollar profit expected per unit of sale" or "The efficiency will be about 25 percent" or "The new financial product will be deployed in the field by two to three offices per month."

Beyond this point, you may be ready for a *parameter range forecast*, whereby an estimate is made of the best and worst cases for a dominant parameter (measurement). This estimate should improve as you progress through the project, and the range should narrow. An example might be: "Based on measurements made to date, the efficiency should lie in the range of 20 to 30 percent." A graphic form of this parameter range forecast is shown in Figure 2-3. At milestones, the parameter range forecast is revised, usually to a narrower range.

Once again, the emphasis is on forecasting the final result rather than on reporting in detail on what has been done to date.

Decision Reviews

Your plan should include major milestones, checkpoints, or design reviews to take place at the completion of significant work. There may be one to five of these milestones in small to medium projects. At a milestone, the progress against the plan is reviewed thoroughly. One of the following decisions should be made:

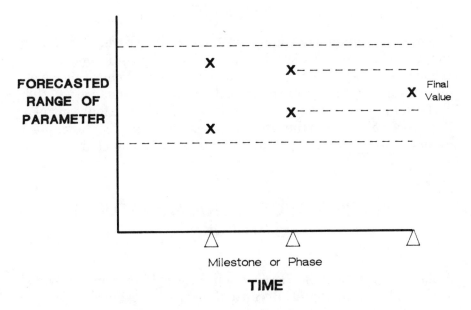

Figure 2-3. A parameter range forecast.

The Decision

1. Continue with the same targets for P, T, and C.
2. Revise the targets on the basis of experience.
3. Do the previous work over again. (This would be a major iteration; it is important that a plan allow for this to happen.)
4. Terminate the project. (Managers with the responsibility to screen out trial projects must make sure that this option is considered.)

Thus, we see that the dynamic project plan is indeed dynamic. It includes its own amending formula. When the plan is approved, the major milestones at which the plan may be revised and reapproved are also approved. If this hasn't been the practice in your organization, the plan is a good place to bring it up.

Other Factors

Other enhancements to your project plan will be covered in a later chapter. The foregoing details are usually sufficient for most small or medium projects. The enhancements include such things as establishing the priority for the project; deciding in advance whether performance, cost, or time would be favored in a revision; control of the interfaces between the different subprojects; an acceptance plan; human resources development; and an organization chart.

THE PROJECTICS* DYNAMIC PROJECT PLAN FORM

A blank copy of the Projectics Dynamic Project Plan form is provided at the end of this chapter. Because this form is designed for a wide range of uses, it may include more than you need for a small project. The form is very compact; it can be done on two sides of one sheet of paper. Larger projects may require addenda to back up some of the summary data included in the plan. Two completed forms for the projects discussed in this chapter are included as Figures 2-4 and 2-5.

SUMMARY

Many people at my seminars have said that they thought the work of planning a project was going to be heavy. They didn't know where they would find the time. During the workshop portion of the seminar, they would prepare a plan for one of their projects. This usually took from three to five hours for a team of four or five people. When they were asked how long it would take to prepare such a plan the next time, they usually estimated from one to three hours—much less than the first time around. Thus, their concern about not having enough time had vanished.

---

* Projectics is a service mark of the Advanced Professional Development Institute in Los Angeles (registration applied for).

DYNAMIC PROJECT PLAN

Name of project **GOODWILL PROJECT**   Its computer filename **Goodwl**

Brief description and overall benefits **A program to get back disgruntled customers and to attract new ones.**

Project/account no. **A-36**   Priority rating **N/A**

Request date **June 1, 19__**   Other ref. dates _____

TIME ASPECTS

Time targets: Start **July 1**   Finish **Sept. 15**   Accuracy **± 1 month**

Milestone descriptions and dates: #1 **Round one complete**

#2 **Round two complete (End)**   #3 _____

Plan for Time Control: Existing controls [ ], or **Review with bank manager at milestone #1**

COST ASPECTS

Budget or estimate **16 person-weeks & $3000** Its accuracy **N/A**

Cost (budget) milestones and dates: #1 **Round one complete**

#2 **Round two complete (End)** #3 _____

Financial benefits to be obtained **None**

Target product cost _____ Cost per day of delay _____

Costs include: All external? **Yes**   All internal? **Yes**   Other? _____

Plan for Cost Control: Existing controls [ ], or **Review at time of milestone #1**

Figure 2-4. Dynamic project plan for the Goodwill Project.

RESULTS

Specific objectives/results expected, in order of importance

1. Of the customers who left the bank in the past 2 years, 75% of those available will return to this bank.

2. New customer accounts to be increased by 20% within one year of the completion of the project. (Note: the project will be over when this measurement would be made, but it is at least a definition of what could be done.)

For further detail, refer to documents N/A

Constraints on solutions Corporate procedures that cannot be waived.

Plan for contol of results: Existing controls [ ] , or Milestone review

Tradeoff guidelines

APPROVALS

Harry.............	Cal.....................	N/A
---------	-----------	----------
Project manager	Project manager's manager	client(s) (optional)

(Figure 2-4 continued)

DYNAMIC PROJECT PLAN

Name of project __PERSONNEL RECORDS__   Its computer filename __Persrd__

Brief description and overall benefits __Computerized Employee Records__

Project/account no. __DP-117__   Priority rating __3__

Request date __Oct. 1, 19__   Other ref. dates __New hiring, starts Jan. 1, 19__.

TIME ASPECTS

Time targets: Start __Oct. 15, 19__   Finish __April 15, 19__   Accuracy __$\pm$ 4 weeks__

Milestone descriptions and dates: #1 __Analysis Complete, Nov. 1__

#2 __Approved Design, Dec. 15__   #3 __Finished Program, Feb. 15__

#4 __Completed Installation, April 15__

Plan for Time Control: Existing controls [ ] , or __Weekly progress reviews.__
__Schedule revision with new forecasts at each milestone.__

COST ASPECTS

Budget or estimate __6 person-months & $15,000__ Its accuracy __$\pm$ 30%__

Cost (budget) milestones and dates: #1 __Same as for Time__

#2 _____   #3 _____

Financial benefits to be obtained __N/A__

Target product cost _____   Cost per day of delay _____

Costs include: All external? __Yes__   All internal? __Yes__   Other? _____

Plan for Cost Control: Existing controls [ ] , or __Milestone review by comparing committed cost with budget at a milestone.__

Figure 2-5. Dynamic project plan for the Personnel Records Project.

RESULTS

Specific objectives/results expected, in order of importance _____

- Data storage, selection and sorting for alpha-numerical employee data

- Text storage with indexing

- System to be better in use than the existing manual system

- Data files and coding to be compatible with our major DP system on the computer so that files can be uploaded and downloaded.

_____

_____

For further detail, refer to documents_____

_____

Constraints on solutions Compatibility with our major Data Processing system

Plan for contol of results: Existing controls [ ], or Review of progress and expected final results at the milestones indicated in the Time Aspects

Tradeoff guidelines The quality of the data program is preferred over time, and both of these over the cost.

APPROVALS

Jack............	Hilda.................	Personnel Manager
Project manager	Project manager's manager	client(s) (optional)

(Figure 2-5 continued)

SUMMARY

A few hours is a reasonable investment of time, at least for a preliminary plan. If you are going to do a detailed plan for a medium project, you are going to have to put in more time and effort—at least a couple of days. You should also consider that you will need time to discuss the plan with management, customer, or client.

There is no question that this effort will have a high payback. If you don't plan a project carefully, you will waste much of your time trying to get it back on track later because of the things that you forgot and the fact that the project isn't really in control.

A survey of Midwestern managers showed a three-to-one gain for any time spent on planning—and they were not project managers. The gain for project managers is more like ten to one. That is, you stand to save 100 hours of execution time for 10 hours of planning.

I have noticed, however, that some people simply do not take to planning. Sometimes they are very fast on their feet in solving problems. It's almost as if they like the action. Having to deal with crisis after crisis means that they are really needed—that they are important people. I suspect that some people have an addiction for adrenalin, which they satisfy by putting out brushfires all day long—brushfires that happened because of a lack of planning. On the other hand, if they don't succeed with the projects, the adrenalin addiction becomes stressful and even life-threatening. Really, it's not worth dying for a project. Besides, there is a better way.

Don't worry about life being dull if you prepare a good project plan. No plan can be perfect, and things are bound to be different during the execution than in the planning. With a good plan, the project will run much more smoothly, but you will still have plenty to do. The difference will be that you will feel that you are in control. In fact, because you planned, you won't have nearly as many problems as you otherwise would have had. You will then be free to handle problems in a methodical way as they come up.

People who are not used to planning seem to have some difficulty believing in planning. Those who do plan—and succeed—are convinced. I am convinced. However, it may be your job to encourage subordinates or other team members to do more planning than they have been doing, and they will give you excuses, such as: "What's the use of planning around here? Everything gets changed daily anyway." Instead of arguing the point, try saying this: "I will give you a few more reasons for not planning: (1) As you say, everything changes around here, and that's true of the world. No day is actually the way you think it will be. So what's the use of planning if it's going to be out of date shortly after you've done it? (2) Since nobody knows the future, why should we try to predict the future? (3) Since planning is about the future—do it in the future!" Then have a good laugh and then get down to the important job of planning.

To get people into the planning habit, managers should give them easy planning jobs to start with. Help them out. Assist them in filling out a form or in developing a schedule, as I do in my seminar-workshops. Then, when they see how easy it is, they are more apt to do it again. The second point to make is that a plan *is* soon out of date; that's why it must be updated. By using the Projectics forms and their associated techniques, you will have plans that are easy to modify. Finally, use a pencil with an eraser to prepare your plan. This is better than doing it in ink as if the future could be forecasted accurately. A pencil with an eraser is known as "the project manager's iteration tool." Of course, the project plan that you send to management, customer, or client will be neatly typed or lettered—as they would expect from a professional project manager.

QUESTIONS FOR ASSIGNMENT OR DISCUSSION

1. Why is the project plan called *dynamic*?
2. Write a 25-word telegram that states the purposes of a dynamic project plan.
3. Refer to the dynamic project plan for the Personnel Records Project (Figure 2-5). Suppose that it falters at the end of the design phase because the designer says that alterations must be made to other company programs in order for him to integrate the design with other databases. These changes could be done in parallel with the coding of the personnel records system. They would require at least four weeks of elapsed time for development, testing, and debugging. They would consume about two person-months of resources. Assuming that the company will go for these additions, make a revision to the dynamic project plan. Imagine that you are going to submit it to the project manager's manager and client for their reapproval.

QUESTIONS FOR ASSIGNMENT OR DISCUSSION 51

(You may find it convenient to add your revisions in pencil to the plan in Figure 2-5.)

4. Develop a dynamic project plan for a small project of your own that involves work done mostly by yourself and possibly two or three co-workers in the same department. (Use a copy of the planning form provided at the end of this chapter.)

5. Make up a dynamic project plan for a medium project of your own or one of a member of your study group. It should include the coordination of two or three other departments and the work of 5 to 15 people. Include a provisional schedule. Also include a rough budget. (Use a copy of the planning form provided at the end of this chapter.)

6. Group exercises for question 4 or 5 can be assigned for workshop teams of practicing project managers. In this case, the selection of the project should be guided by the following criteria: (a) it is ahead of the team or is in progress; (b) it is understandable to the team members so that they can contribute; (c) a team member can act as an information source and make decisions on approximate values of data that are at hand; and (d) it has 10 to 20 activities at a workable level of breakdown. (*NOTE:* The projects that have worked well in my workshops have frequently been in the early stages. It often helps if the real project manager takes the role of consultant rather than leader.)

DYNAMIC PROJECT PLAN

Name of project _____ Its computer filename _____

Brief description and overall benefits _____
_____

Project/account no. _____ Priority rating _____

Request date _____ Other ref. dates _____

TIME ASPECTS

Time targets: Start _____ Finish _____ Accuracy _____

Milestone descriptions and dates: #1 _____

#2 _____ #3 _____

Plan for Time Control: Existing controls [ ] , or _____
_____

COST ASPECTS

Budget or estimate _____ Its accuracy _____

Cost (budget) milestones and dates: #1 _____

#2 _____ #3 _____

    Financial benefits to be obtained _____

    Target product cost _____ Cost per day of delay _____

    Costs include: All external? _____ All internal? _____ Other? _____

Plan for Cost Control: Existing controls [ ] , or _____
_____

RESULTS

Specific objectives/results expected, in order of importance _____

_____
_____
_____
_____
_____
_____
_____

For further detail, refer to documents_____
_____

Constraints on solutions _____

Plan for contol of results: Existing controls [ ] , or _____
_____

Tradeoff guidelines _____

APPROVALS

_ _ _ _ _ _ _ _ _   _ _ _ _ _ _ _ _ _ _ _   _ _ _ _ _ _ _ _ _ _
Project manager   Project manager's manager   client(s) (optional)

CHAPTER
three

DEFINING THE PROJECT OBJECTIVES AND TASKS
pinning them down

> **Key Idea**
>
> The objectives and tasks for projects are to be written in a way that guides the effort toward the desired results.

Projects are specific sets of tasks designed to bring about change or improve unsatisfactory situations. The first vision of the happy results desired at the project's end, however, will not always reveal the best solution. The project manager must determine and clarify the objectives at the beginning of the project. The consequences of not doing so are illustrated in the continuing cases of Harry at the bank and Jack at the computer.

CASE 1:
THE BANKER CREATES NEW PROBLEMS

Cal, the new manager of a small bank, assigned Harry to solve the problem regarding the bank's lost customers. Since Cal had always given Harry a loose rein, Harry went ahead and set up the Goodwill Project.

Suppose that Harry had jumped into action without clarifying what it was that they wished to achieve. Harry might have been working on an objective that went like this: "The objective of the Goodwill Project is to get the bank's customers back." This is a good starting point, but it hasn't really pinned down the overall end results. For example, Harry might solve the problem by offering himself as a personal account executive for each of the lost customers. This approach would get many of the customers back, but the work would overload him. Besides, the other loyal customers might complain if they didn't get the same attention. Another solution might have been to move the offensive teller, "Cranky Mary," to ledger work. Then someone else would deal directly with the public. Such a move, however, could have led to other problems with Mary. Besides, the Personnel Department would be clearly on her side if she filed a grievance over being moved to another job.

Thus, if Harry and Cal don't take the trouble to pin down all the characteristics of a satisfactory solution, it's possible for one problem to lead to another.

CASE 2:
THE SOFTWARE PROJECT FOR PERSONNEL RECORDS

Hilda Brubaker assigned Jack Daniels the task of computerizing the record keeping for the Personnel Department. Suppose that Jack then set off to do just that. One solution could be to purchase a program and install it. That would fulfill the assignment as stated. However, the purchased program might not have enough file space to take care of future data, such as blood test results, health records and family information. Many things are likely to happen in the future that would need space for recording. In other words, it is possible to concentrate on the short-term results and not look at the overall long-term needs. Inadequate project results are frequently due to not pinning down all their attributes early in the project.

SETTING OBJECTIVES

> **The Principle of Setting Objectives**
>
> Objectives should guide the effort by defining the results to be achieved, rather than saying how the results are to be accomplished.

The problem with setting project and task objectives is that we tend to think of the future in terms of something we can already visualize—invariably, something close to what we already know. For example, in the bank case, Harry could visualize a former customer coming back and reopening an account. Likewise, for the software project, Jack and Hilda could easily visualize installing a purchased program, as they have done in other cases. In other words, it's not possible to state what is to be achieved by a project without having some kind of solution in mind. However, when we start clarifying the problem and pinning down all the attributes of a successful solution, the solution that comes to mind usually develops from what we can easily visualize. In order to open up our thinking to new and better solutions, we need to state *what is to be achieved* by the solution we have in mind, rather than just giving further details about the originally perceived solution. To some extent, this is a "means-and-ends" problem. The solution we have in mind is a means to the end. As most projects are intended to bring about new and unique situations, we need to concentrate on the "ends." Then we can go back to the "means" with an open mind, so that we can come up with better ways to achieve the end results.

APPLICATION TO A SMALL PROJECT

Here are some suitable statements that would pin down the results for the bank's Goodwill Project:

—The main objective of this project is to get the lost customers back to the bank. A measure of this would be that 80 percent of the lost customers return.
—A subobjective is that the main objective be achieved with a minimum of disturbance to the operations. A measure is that the loss of existing customers should not exceed the normal attrition by more than 10 percent. Another measure is that employee morale should not be adversely affected.
—Another subobjective is that the main objective be achieved with a minimum of conflict with headquarters. While this is difficult to pin down, one measure would be that the district manager is satisfied with the level of cooperation and the associated conflict.

Cal and Harry should sit down and visualize the *attributes* of a successful outcome, rather than a specific outcome itself. Then, they will likely come up with workable and satisfactory results. This would be better than wrapping their efforts around the solution that first comes to mind.

It is not even necessary to actually measure the outcomes. The statements clarify what is to be achieved and help guide the effort in the direction of satisfactory completion. For the small Goodwill Project, a subjective evaluation of the results would be satisfactory. It would be guided by the statements about measures. Naturally, if the same scheme were to be expanded across the country to all bank branches, the management might very well require that these measures be made. They would probably expand the project to several districts before extending it fully across the nation.

THE DELPHI STUDY PROJECT

This is a project I did for a client. It involved the coordination of four people on the project team and the collection of data from about 25 other people. Since there were no subteams or subschedules involved, this was a small project. Even so, the effort and the systematic methodology were more extensive than the bank's Goodwill Project. The following are two of the ten objectives and some of the measures we set up in the beginning to guide our efforts. The symbol O is used for objectives, and S is used for a specification (or measure). Thus, *O1S1* is the first specification (or measure) for objective number one. This notation shows how the objectives and specifications are related.

> —*Objective O1:* To produce forecasts for northern development that will affect hydrology, in order to develop alternative recommendations for meeting the overall objectives of the XYZ Department.
> —A criterion or specification for the measurement of this objective is *O1S1:* The forecast is to be a median date and its interquartile range. The range should not exceed one-third of the median date minus the base date.
> —Another criterion for the same objective is *O1S2:* The median date minus the base date is to lie in the range of 2 to 20 years.
> —*Objective O2:* To actively encourage the involvement of the XYZ personnel in the development and use of the forecasts.
> —A criterion for this objective is *O2S2:* 75 percent of the respondents should agree that they were truly involved.

The project went very well. We knew subjectively that we had met the second objective within the criterion specified, so we did not find it necessary to take any measurements. However, I recall that pinning down the objectives with these measures impressed the client favorably. Moreover, the objectives did alter our solution-finding on many occasions. For example, whenever one of the survey respondents expressed a reluctance to cooperate, we made an effort to talk to him or her and find out if there was a "burr under the saddle" that we could remove. We did this because one of our measures of objectives, or criteria for achieving an objective, was that 75 percent of the respondents would agree that they had been truly involved.

APPLICATION TO A MEDIUM PROJECT

Let's develop some objectives for the Personnel Records Project and try to pin them down with measures, which are referred to as criteria or specifications: There could be more objectives, such as those about

APPLICATION TO A MEDIUM PROJECT

the compatibility with existing data systems and the possibility of making additions or expansions.

You will notice that we again must deal with subjective measurements of items, such as "future needs" and "user-friendly." We have, however, indicated some of the criteria measurements that could be used. They determine the intensity of the effort to satisfy the objectives. Keep in mind that satisfying the criteria alone may not fully satisfy the objectives. Take "user-friendly," for example. There might be 100 ways in which a program could be considered user-unfriendly. We might have to pin this down with a few more

---

—*Objective O1:* The principal objective is that the new system should carry all existing files and their data as well as the data that may be required in the next 10 years.

—A criterion or specification for measuring this objective is *O1S1:* The number of data fields should be at least twice those currently in use.

—Another criterion or specification for this objective could be *O1S2:* Up to 10 sortings or selections should be possible on any character in a data field. (For example, all surnames beginning with Mc could be selected.)

Another criterion could be *O1S3:* The personnel manager should sign off for agreement with whatever data fields were finally provided.

—There should be more objectives or subobjectives for a project like this. *Objective O2:* The program in use should be user-friendly.

—A criterion or specification for this objective could be *O2S1:* Nine out of ten personnel officers should be capable of being trained in eight hours to use the program. The relearning time after one month's absence from the terminal should not exceed 30 minutes.

—*O2S2:* Operators should not require assistance from the data processing department for more than one out of 100 uses, after a learning period of one month.

—*O2S3:* The data entry errors due to cognitive misunderstandings of instructions or screen prompts should not exceed one in 10,000 fields.

statements. Imagine a case in which we were developing software for automated teller machines that were going to be installed across the nation. That would involve an investment of millions of dollars. It would be worth more effort in that case to pin down the criteria for "user-friendly."

In small to medium projects, we must try to get a handle on what the criteria measurements would be if we wanted to apply them. This is especially useful if the objectives are going to be carried out by others, working on their own. For example, in the software project, Jack Daniels might work on part of the software and contract out another portion. Both parts would be guided by the statements about the program being user-friendly. Thus, the project leader who develops the objectives and criteria would do well to discuss them with other people who are assigned tasks on a project, so that all involved have a common understanding of what the words mean. Because words can have multiple meanings, it is far better to discuss the statements than to leave them open to individual interpretation.

OBJECTIVES FOR THE MULTIPLE-PROJECT INSURANCE FIRM

In a multiple-project environment, we need to consider the interaction of one project's schedule on another. This interaction is in addition to statements about the short-term and long-term objectives of each project.

Consider the ABC Insurance Company project that was assigned to Mary-Helen: to develop and deploy a new insurance policy directed at teachers within the state. Clearly, there should be objectives pertaining to the kind of insurance to be offered, which must fit a narrow niche of the market. There should also be objectives pertaining to the position to be achieved in that market. No doubt there would also be profitability objectives.

In a company that has a line of insurance products, one product can affect another. At ABC, for instance, some teachers may drop existing insurance plans in order to take on the new one. Success with the new teachers' policy might be accompanied by equal losses on other insurance policies. The net return would be zero. So it would behoove Mary-Helen and her boss to add an objective something like this: "The new product should not have a serious impact on the sales of our existing and continuing products."

A criterion for achieving this objective would be: "The losses to other products should not be more than 10 percent of the gains in the new product." Another criterion could be: "In achieving this objective, alterations to save other products should not exceed 1 percent of the policies in existence."

Once again, it would not be necessary to take actual measurements of these criteria. Their existence alone would contribute to a balanced effort on Mary-Helen's part. Then the focused effort applied to one project should not have a negative affect on the rest of the product line.

COMPREHENSIVE AND BALANCED OBJECTIVES

As the cases illustrate, a project usually has more than one objective, and some objectives are more important than others. This importance can be signified by a simple rank-ordering of the objectives. (This means that the first one on the list is more important than the second, and so on.) If necessary, a better result in the number-one objective might be gained at a small expense to the number-two objective. Take, for example, the Personnel Records Project. The more data fields that are available to the operator, the more he or she has to skip fields. This is less user-friendly. So, in fact, there is a tradeoff here between objectives, and we have to know which one is more important. Likewise, in the bank's Goodwill Project, getting customers back might be a tradeoff with not ruffling the feathers of the staff at corporate headquarters. Clearly, getting the customers back is number one.

Comprehensive objectives, therefore, tend to cover the whole field of what's to be achieved by the project, rather than focusing only on a single objective. Thus, although the bank project started with a simple objective to "fix the problem," it ended up with three interacting objectives. The software project, which started with a simple objective to "computerize the personnel record keeping," could have ended up with several pages of objectives and criteria. Naturally, this process requires a little effort by the project team, but it pays off by producing fully satisfactory results at the end of the project.

TIME AND COST CONSIDERATIONS

There is another aspect of project objectives that needs to be addressed. What you get in results depends on the resources allocated and the time taken to get the project finished. Therefore, the results should be coupled with the cost and time objectives, whether those objectives be for the total project or for a single task.

Because project sponsors are frequently changing objectives, you need to be able to do a balanced assessment of the impacts on cost and time. A balanced set of objectives is what you use when you present them to management, review them with the client, or revise the project after a design review. When the project sponsors try to change one objective, they are encouraged to look at the impact on the others, because the objectives are always presented together.

PINNING DOWN THE OBJECTIVES

Whenever objectives can be pinned down by numbers, we can get agreement on whether the objectives were achieved. For example, an objective "to increase sales by 10 percent" can be measured. On the other hand, desirable qualities such as "customer satisfaction," "user-friendly," "workmanlike manner," and "professional standards" are highly subjective. Can these intangibles be measured? The answer is yes—to some extent. To the extent that we can get agreement on the achievement of objectives, we have "objectivity" in the measurement of objectives.

There are two ways to pin down intangible objectives: by *scales* and by *opinion* (see Figure 3-1).

The Ratio Scale and the Interval Scale

The most common scale in use is the *ratio scale*. It is so common that it hardly needs definition, but an inch ruler is a good

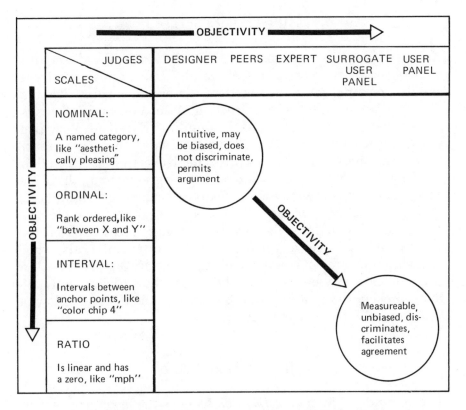

Figure 3-1. Objectivity scales and opinions.

example. The measures are in proportion to the ratio of the numbers on the scale. In other words, zero is nothing, and 16 is 4 times as much as 4. This is also known as a *linear scale*. Because money and elapsed time are subject to precise measurement, they can be measured on ratio scales. Calendar time, however, cannot be measured on a ratio scale because there is no zero in calendar time. (When did time begin?) There is an arbitrary calendar zero, fixed by society at the birth of Christ. It is a useful reference point, but the zero doesn't matter in our day-to-day measurement of such things as "five days from now." For such measurement we use an *interval scale,* in which the intervals are equal, but the zero is not a zero measure. Other examples of interval scales are the Fahrenheit and Celsius scales for measuring temperature.

The Ordinal Scale

Another useful measurement scale is the *ordinal scale,* or *rank-ordering scale.* Each point on such a scale is more important, larger, smaller, or different by degree than the previous point. The scale always changes in the same direction. A good example of this is a semantic-ordinal scale, such as the familiar "Excellent, Very Good, Good, Satisfactory, and Poor." The intervals are not necessarily equal, and there is no zero on the scale. Nevertheless, "Excellent" is a long way from "Poor." We tend to get agreement on this difference, although there may be some disagreement as to whether an item is "Excellent" or just "Very Good." Another example of an ordinal scale is a paint scale, such as the ones you see in a paint store. Yellow, for example, might be divided into ten intervals, which, although they are not equal, enable us to specify a degree of yellow. A paint scale may not be perfectly precise, but it is certainly a lot more precise than saying that something should be "yellow" or "harmonize with the surroundings."

The Nominal Scale

The *nominal scale,* or *classification scale,* is the least precise of our scales. It is usually the name given to a similar class of items, but it is a measurement, nonetheless. For example, if something is to be "rough textured," that differentiates it from a "smooth finish." Also, "blue" is certainly different from "yellow" on a nominal scale.

Using the Scales to Go from Objectives to Specifications

To make use of these scales, we usually start from the wish or want of an objective. Then we go progressively to nominal, ordinal, interval, and ratio scales, where possible. An example is shown in Figure 3-2. The wish or want, as expressed in the objective, would be that the colors harmonize. Out of the universe of colors, we choose a nominal scale of yellow. To further pin it down, we go to an ordinal scale, which puts it between two samples of yellow-orange and yellow-green. We might go further and develop a set of paint chips that are perceived to be of equal color differences. Then we could give

OBJECTIVE:	To harmonize with surroundings
NOMINAL SCALE:	Yellow
ORDINAL SCALE:	Yellow–orange ☐ to Yellow–green ☐
INTERVAL SCALE: (Equal color changes)	5.0 ☐ ☐ 5.4 ☐ ☐ ☐ 6.0 ☐

Figure 3-2. Using scales to go from objective to specification.

each color a number. This would provide more precision for people who are comparing the colors; they can be more objective about which colors meet the criterion and which do not. Color, by the way, is not a trivial matter in regard to products. For example, plastic computer parts must match on the exterior. Even matching colors on a company logo can become quite a problem to printers, embossers, engravers, sign painters, and so forth.

The Use of Opinion

The other way to get some agreement on the interpretation of the criteria or specifications is to use opinion. In the long run, whose opinion really counts? The most unbiased opinion about a project result would come from the end *users*. For example, whether or not the Personnel Records Project is satisfactory would be better judged by the Personnel Department (the users) than by the MIS Department (the deliverers of the system). Likewise, the achievement of "user-friendly" would be best judged by the users themselves.

During the design phases of a project it's not always possible to have users on hand for their opinion. In some cases, they cannot yet be identified or have not yet been trained. Therefore, a *surrogate user panel* would be useful. Some of the office workers in Jack's department could be asked to give their opinion about the readability of the various screens that have been simulated. These opinions would be much more valid than the opinion of the program designer. The designer may be in love with his or her own ideas, so bias is to be expected. Therefore, the program designer should give a lot of weight to what a surrogate panel says about whether the screens are user-friendly or not.

Between the extremes of opinion bias—designers and users—we could have an *expert* who is highly specialized. An expert could say what the end users would give as an opinion. In the Personnel Records Project, for example, a person with a lot of experience in judging software systems might be called in for an unbiased opinion.

Another opinion, closer to the actual designer, would be that of a *peer designer* who is not currently involved in the specific project. Another designer would have a less biased opinion, so this opinion is set between that of the designer and the expert. You can see from Figure 3-1 that both scales and opinion (judges) can be used to increase the agreement on criteria.

Examples

Scales and opinion can be used to improve the measurement of illusive attributes. Here are some examples.

For the Personnel Records Project, objective O2 is: "The program in use should be user-friendly." A measurement criterion could be O2S4: "After three months of experience using the program, 8 out of 10 users should agree that it was user-friendly." This is a combination of ratio scale measurement and unbiased opinion.

Another criterion could be O2S5: "In the event that there is a disagreement on the quality of a screen message or keyed function in the program, the item would be adjudicated by a committee of three persons: the project manager, the personnel manager, and a third person agreeable to both parties. The decision to accept or reject would be based upon a majority vote." This approach starts with opinion and ends on a scale of numbers.

Another objective might be O3: "The furniture should harmonize with the office decor." A criterion for this, O3S1, could be: "The furniture is considered satisfactory if the regularly employed interior decorator for the company agrees that it is so. However, this decision must be made prior to installation of the furniture." This is what expert opinion can do.

Another criterion for this objective could be O3S2. "The color will harmonize with surroundings if it lies between the samples X and Y, which are agreed upon at the start of the project." The use of limiting color samples puts this criterion on an ordinal scale.

Actually, most small projects will not get bogged down in disputes over whether or not a criterion is met. Disagreements are more likely when various departments must agree on the quality of the outcome or on whether a contractor is to be paid whenever a dispute arises. Thus, the use of opinion and scales to pin down criteria is more applicable to medium to large projects than to small projects. I have shown you how to go about it in the early stages of the project. If you take care to define *satisfaction* in the beginning, you'll have fewer time-consuming disputes in the end.

Many nontechnical projects for business and government have rather soft definitions of what would constitute a satisfactory outcome. However, this is no reason for backing off and not trying to define acceptable results. By combining opinion and scales, you can go a long way toward pinning down the desired outcomes.

QUESTIONS FOR DISCUSSION OR ASSIGNMENT

1. Why is it that objectives should state the "what" instead of the "how"? Explain why we tend to include too much of the "how" in stating objectives.

2. What is the point of setting up objectives and criteria at the beginning of the project if they are of the kind that you will not likely measure at the end of the project?

3. Using the chart in Figure 3-1, mark the vertical and horizontal locations for the criteria in this text for the Personnel Records Project. Consider the degree of scaling and opinion involved for O1S1, O1S2, O1S3, O2S1, and O2S3.

4. For a small project of your own, or one assigned to you, develop a set of objectives that are oriented toward the "what" and away from the "how." Ask a noninvolved class member or coworker for an opinion of the quality of these objectives.

5. For a medium project that belongs to you or to a member of your class group, develop a set of objectives and criteria that would pin down the results.

CHAPTER
four

SCHEDULES FOR BEING ON TIME

you need them for control

Key Idea

To be on time with a project, you must produce a detailed schedule. You will use it to monitor and control project progress.

Timing is everything. In project management, good timing means getting activities done in the proper sequence. Before the work starts, the project manager should prepare a detailed schedule as part of the project plan. By monitoring the schedule and getting revised commitments, the project manager can maintain control of the progress of the project.

Our ongoing examples of the bank's Goodwill Project and the Personnel Records Project illustrate the ill effects of poor scheduling.

CASE 1:
THEY RAN OUT OF LETTERHEAD

The bank's Goodwill Project was under way, and things seemed to be going smoothly. Cal had approved Harry's plan. One of its components was to send out a special form letter to past and current clients. At the same time, the bank was going to run an advertisement in the newspaper, thus using a multimedia approach.

Harry's secretary had built a large file of over 2000 names and had entered it into the word processor. The team intended to send 2000 individualized letters on company letterhead. Then Harry was notified that there was not enough letterhead on hand to cover this sudden high demand. All they had on hand was 300 sheets. As it happened, company procedures required that stationery orders be placed with headquarters. The Purchasing Department would reorder with the contractor who had the negatives, the special ink, and the watermarked paper that the company preferred.

Harry soon found out that headquarters was not set up to supply him with letterhead in a hurry. A bank transaction could be done in minutes, but getting a new letterhead supply by due process would take three weeks.

Harry tried to get immediate action by Purchasing but met with obstinate resistance. They sniped: "When your stock is low, why don't you reorder? Our normal reordering time is three to six weeks. Besides, nobody ever orders 3000 sheets at a time. That would last you about six years." Harry decided to take what he could get. He was trying to stay on good terms with the Purchasing Department. As an alternative, he had looked into the possibility of getting some letterhead done by a local printer. Although it could be done in a week, the ink would not be a good match and the paper would be a substitute. Besides, there would be a one-time setup charge, which would be hard to explain to the bank auditors.

A week later, someone called into the office in response to the bank's ad in a local newspaper. It was then that Harry realized that although the ad and the mailing were to be synchronized, they now would be out of step by at least three weeks. Harry had just learned a project manager's lesson: When something gets delayed, check your schedule to find out what else will be affected.

CASE 2:
DUE PROCESS IS NOT FAST ENOUGH

Hilda Brubaker was pleased with the progress on the Personnel Records Project. Jack Daniels had written his software and had thoroughly tested it. The Personnel Department had witnessed the demonstration and they were looking forward to getting the system installed. The reason Jack had done so well was that he had scheduled himself in detail at the working level. In other words, instead of just having one activity for coding, he had broken it down into smaller tasks at the next level of detail. For example, he included such detail as "Verify screen details with client." No problems here. Jack was good at planning.

Where Jack's team ran into trouble was with another department. They didn't find out about the problem until near the end of the project. Jack had been told that the lead time to purchase office furniture was three weeks. Since there was plenty of time, the Purchasing Department did not rush to place an order until three weeks before the due date. That was when they started getting the bad news. First, the computer-styled furniture was in high demand, and the specialty houses that made it were jammed with orders. Second, since the furniture was to be customized, the vendor would have to make drawings. These would have to be approved by Jack Daniels before the vendor would proceed to cut the materials. Because Jack's company was a big buyer of furniture, the Purchasing Department was able to pressure the vendor into the best possible delivery—but that was now nine weeks instead of the planned three weeks. This meant a six-week delay in installation of the equipment.

When Jack thought about it, he realized that he should have asked Purchasing to prepare a detailed schedule for their activities. If they lacked the skill to produce such a schedule, he should have worked with them to produce one. This would have brought up such items as lead time for customized furniture, checking of drawings, and so forth. The Purchasing Department would have been alerted to the problem long before it got serious. Jack had learned a valuable lesson, one he had learned in a training course but had overlooked: You need to schedule in the detail necessary to control the activities. Special activities require more detail in scheduling than activities that can be done by due process.

> ## The Principle of Scheduling
>
> **If the time plan is prepared before the work is started, the activities will take place in the right order. Schedule progress can be measured relative to the plan. Corrective action can be taken while there is still time for it to be effective.**

THE PROJECTICS METHOD OF SCHEDULING

Before you can actually produce a detailed schedule, you first need to learn something about the techniques of scheduling. These techniques were developed for large-scale projects. In the Projectics method, they have been scaled down for managing smaller projects.

Originally, management scientists put together a method called PERT (Program Evaluation and Review Technique). It was developed in 1957 for the Polaris missile program. At about the same time, the Critical Path Method (CPM) was developed by the Du Pont Company for use in the construction of its facilities. These two early techniques have been improved over the years. I have combined the best elements of both in the method described here.

Steps for Establishing and Meeting the Time Targets

1. Make a list of activities (things to be done, steps, or tasks)
2. Make a logic diagram to find the best sequence of the activities.
3. Produce a bar chart schedule and do a critical path analysis.
4. Adjust the schedule for available resources and fixed dates.
5. Identify milestones for monitoring by management, client, or customer.
6. After approval of your Dynamic Project Plan, get commitments on completing the activities.
7. Monitor and update periodically, as appropriate.
8. Report to management, customer, or client, on forecasted completion dates of the milestones. Revise the schedule, budget, and expected results if necessary.

The Basics of Logic Diagrams

The Projectics method includes the construction of a logic diagram composed of symbols representing the activities and the events.

Figure 4-1 is a *precedence diagram.* Each activity (or task) that needs to be done on the project is represented by a box. The left-hand side of the box is the start of the activity, and the right-hand side is the end. The starts and finishes are "events," and they may have calendar dates. The time between the start and finish is the "duration" of the activity.

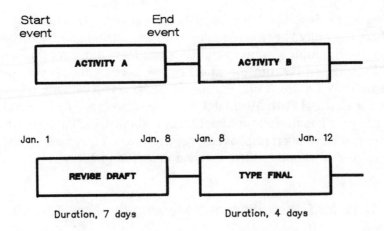

Figure 4-1. A precedence logic diagram.

The relationships of a set of project activities are shown by joining the boxes with lines. Each line goes from the finish side of one box to the start side of another. In Figure 4-1, for example, activity B "depends on" the completion of A. An easily understood example is shown in the lower part of the figure.

Let's add *milestones* for monitoring project progress at the management level (see Figure 4-2). In a precedence diagram, we create a milestone by adding an activity of zero time duration. The method shown here is consistent with the screen graphics of some software programs for personal computers. These are the ones where the logic

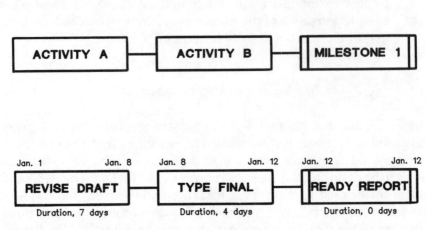

Figure 4-2. A precedence diagram with a milestone added.

THE PROJECTICS METHOD OF SCHEDULING 77

diagram is composed on the monitor screen. (See Chapter 11 on computer use.) Some organizations and some computer programs use what we call *arrow-node logic diagrams*. Appendix A provides a comparison of arrow-node and precedence logic diagrams. In my opinion, precedence diagrams, as discussed in this chapter, are best for small to medium projects, whereas arrow-node diagrams are well suited for large projects.

Parallel Activities. In Figure 4-3, activities A and B are to be done in parallel (generally at the same time), and both are required before the start of activity C. In other words, activity C depends on the completion of A and B. Note that the joining lines go to the ends of the boxes, not to the top or bottom. Moreover, a joining line always goes from the end side of one activity to the start side of another. In this case the line from B to C overlaps part of the line from A to C.

Parallel and Series Activities. In Figure 4-4, activities A and B must be completed before C and D can start (that is, C and D depend on the completion of A and B). The joining lines are squared off and overlapping, but you can always trace the relationships from end to start.

Different Relationships. Watch out for this one: In Figure 4-5, activity C depends on A and B, but D depends on B only, whereas in the relationship shown in Figure 4-4, D depends on both A and B, not on B only.

Predecessors and Successors. In Figure 4-5, activity C has *immediate predecessors* A and B; that is, it depends on them. Ac-

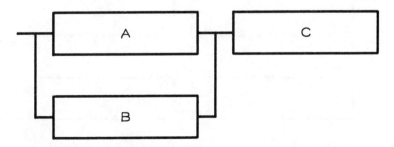

Figure 4-3. A precedence diagram with parallel activities.

78   SCHEDULES FOR BEING ON TIME

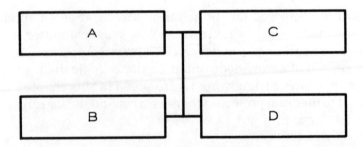

Figure 4-4. A precedence diagram with parallel and series activities.

tivity D has the predecessor B. Note that we dropped the word *immediate*. There are likely other predecessors to D also. Henceforth, however, we will use the word *predecessors* to mean only immediate predecessors.

In the same figure, activity C is the *successor* to A and also to B, whereas D is a successor to B only. You should now understand what we mean by *predecessor* and *successor*.

Exercises

In Figure 4-6, label the activity boxes and join them with lines so that the table of activities and predecessors is fulfilled. (*Note:* A joining line must always join the end side, or right side, of one activity to the start side, or left side, of another activity.)

After completing the diagram (and checking the answer in Appendix A), answer the following questions:

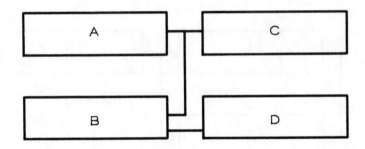

Figure 4-5. A precedence diagram with different relationships between activities.

THE PROJECTICS METHOD OF SCHEDULING

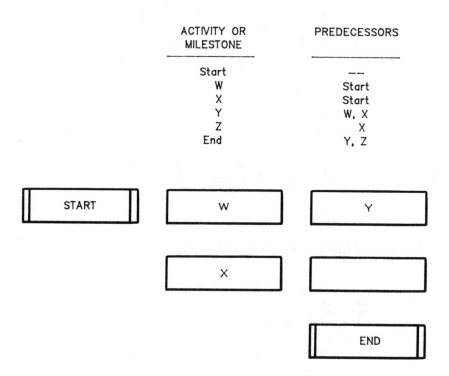

Figure 4-6. A logic diagram exercise.

1. What is the successor to W?
2. What are the successors to X?
3. What are the immediate predecessors of the End milestone?

(All answers are provided in Appendix A.)

Note that there are milestone symbols for the Start and End of this project. These are optional when you produce diagrams and schedules by hand, but many fine computer programs require them. So if you plan eventually to use computers for scheduling (which is likely), adopt the practice of having Start and End milestones.

As another exercise, compose a logic diagram for the set of activities in Figure 4-7. First list the predecessors for each activity. The sequence of activities should be obvious to you.

Now you are ready to do a more extensive exercise. Figure 4-8 is a logic diagram for an opinion survey project of 14 activities and 2 milestones. Information about predecessors is on the diagram, but the connections for some of the activities have been deleted. Com-

80 SCHEDULES FOR BEING ON TIME

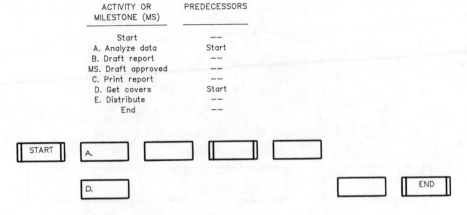

Figure 4-7. Another logic diagram exercise.

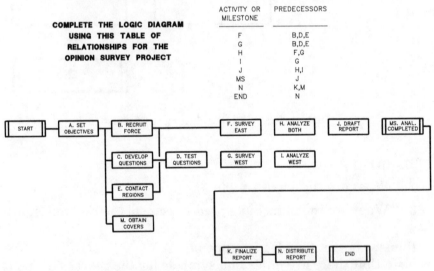

NOTES: 1. A line always goes from the right side of an activity to the left side of another.
2. If two lines cross but do not intersect, leave a gap in one of them.

Figure 4-8. A more extensive logic diagram exercise.

plete the diagram. Note that when two lines cross without connecting, one must have a gap, such as in the line from the right of E to the left of F. Imagine that the line is really continuous but does not intersect the line it is crossing.

Although the answer is provided in Appendix A, there is a way to check for yourself. For each activity, go forward in the diagram to verify successors. Is anything else to be done after the activity and before the indicated successors? Next, go backward in the diagram and check predecessors. Does the activity depend on every one of the indicated predecessors? Are they all there?

Labeling Logic Diagrams

Activities and Tasks. An element of work for a project may be large or small. Unfortunately, there is no standard terminology for the authors of books or software. I like to use the following hierarchy: Project–activity–Task–Subtask.

In this book, I have used the foregoing terminology when convenient and advantageous. Think of an *activity* as something that a functional department does. A *task* is something done by one person within that function; for example, "Type draft" is a one-person task within the activity "Prepare report," which is done by the whole department.

Verbs, Nouns, and Adjectives. An activity requires action and produces something. To label an activity, use an action verb–noun combination whenever possible (for example, "Draft report"). A milestone usually indicates the end of an activity, and an end item has been produced. You can label a milestone with an adjective–noun combination (for example, "Drafted report"). (Exceptions are usually the Start and End milestones.) See Figure 4-9 for an example of the difference in labeling activities and milestones.

The boxes in diagrams and computer fields often have limited space, but brevity in labeling should not destroy the action or end-item concept. If you need to shorten labels, use abbreviations or drop vowels. For example, "Draft and check annual sales report" can become "Draft report," "Draft rep," "Drft rpt," "Dtrt," or "A6." Naturally, you will lose some definition in order to get compact diagrams and computer screen displays. You can provide a table or glossary if you are really pressed for space. Overall, I have found verb–noun labels good for activities, tasks, or subtasks; and adjective–noun labels are good for milestones.

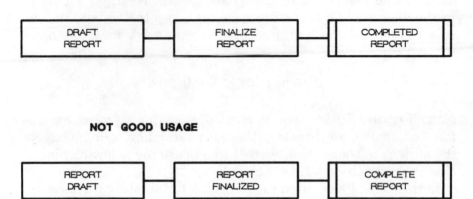

Figure 4-9. Examples of diagram labeling.

PRODUCTION OF A SCHEDULE WITH THE PROJECTICS METHOD

We will now develop an easy-to-use method of bar chart scheduling for small to medium projects. (A medium project would have subschedules as well as a master schedule.) For a small project, you will probably be able to complete a schedule and its calculation in less time than it would take to enter the data into a computer. For medium projects, you can still do the scheduling by hand, but the computer has a decided time advantage. Meanwhile, master the Projectics method of manual scheduling. It will be your backup when your computer is not working or not at hand. The symbols used in the Projectics method are given in Figure 4-10.

Exercises

Complete the exercise in Figure 4-11, indicating all arrow feathers and points. This is called the *forward pass*. Also insert the x's for the latest finishes by doing the *backward pass*. Note that there are Start and End milestones. (As mentioned earlier, these are optional for hand-drawn schedules, but they are needed for some very fine

PRODUCTION OF A SCHEDULE WITH THE PROJECTICS METHOD 83

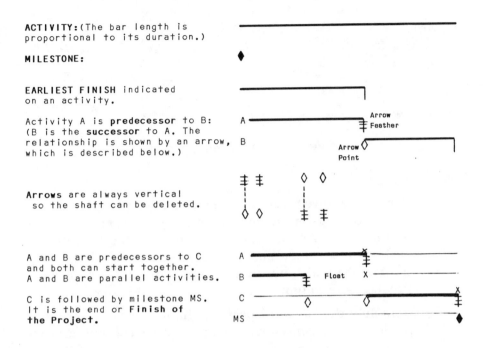

Figure 4-10. Scheduling symbols for the Projectics method.

computer scheduling programs. Besides, the milestones can be used for summary reporting to your management, customer, or client.)

When you have completed this exercise, you will have just learned to do a *critical path analysis*. Activities for which the earliest finish and the latest finish are the same make up a "critical path" through your network or schedule. That's basically all there is to it. In the exercise, only A and C are on the critical path. A critical path comes about when you make the earliest finish of the project (EFp) equal to the latest finish of the project (LFp). In this case, it was four units of time.

Now you are ready for a more extensive exercise with a schedule for 14 activities and two milestones. Use the partially completed schedule in Figure 4-12 for the Opinion Survey Project.

84   SCHEDULES FOR BEING ON TIME

ACTIVITY OR MILESTONE (MS)	PREDE-CESSORS	DURATION	TIME 0　1　2　3　4
MS: START	---	0	
A	START	3	
B	START	2	
C	A, B	1	
MS: END	C	0	

Figure 4-11. A scheduling exercise.

1. Part of the third column, Immediate Predecessors, is blank. Complete it, using the logic diagram you worked on earlier (Figure 4-8). Verify that it is correct by the forward and backward technique, ensuring that the activities in the Code column are truly the successors of those in the Immediate Predecessors column.

2. Complete the "forward pass" of the bar chart, showing all predecessor finishes (arrow points) for each of the activities.

3. Find the earliest finish of the project (EFp), and make it equal to the latest finish of the project (LFp). Then do the "backward pass" and mark the latest finish of each activity with an x.

4. Do not calculate the float on the right-hand side until you have had the lesson on it.

When you have finished, check the answer in Appendix A. Did you have the correct location for the latest finish of each activity?

The Float

If an activity is scheduled to finish before its successor is scheduled to start, there is "float" time on the first activity—in this case, *free float* (FF). There is no delay in the project if the float is used up. Usually, the predecessor is waiting for something else to finish. Thus, free float on an activity is the time it can be late in finishing without affecting the start of a following activity. If the successor has free float of its own, then, provided that it can start later, its float becomes available to the predecessor. This is *total float* (TF), which is often more than the obvious free float. Total float on an activity

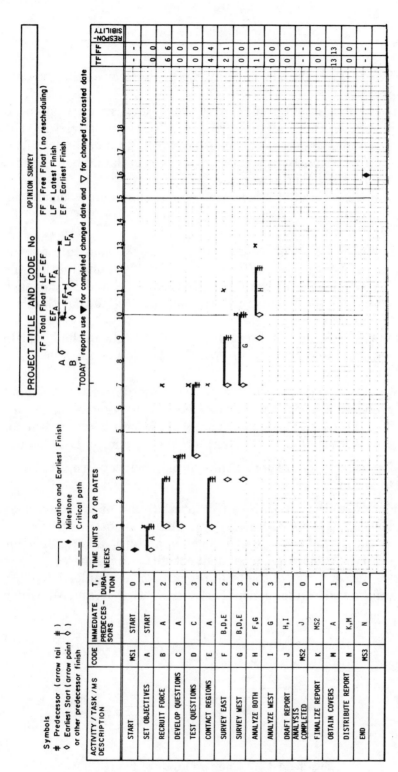

Figure 4-12. The Projectics method of scheduling.

is the time it can be late in finishing without affecting the end date of the project.

Suppose that a subproject, ABC, includes three sequential activities—A, B, and C—which are scheduled as in Figure 4-13. The starts of B and C are delayed because of waiting for other activities (not shown) or because the resources are not available soon enough. In the figure, the FF on A is x and the FF on B is y. The TF on A is $x + y$, because B could start later. (Note that many scheduling systems use the word *slack* instead of *float*.)

Float Exercise. On the right-hand side of the schedule for the Opinion Survey (Figure 4-12), there are two columns marked TF and FF (total float and free float). Calculate TF and FF for each activity and put the values in these columns. (Note that the float *follows* an activity.)

You may check your answers in Appendix A, but in the long run you must learn to do it on your own. Try the following steps:

1. Check successor relationships; for example, if B, D, and E are predecessors of F, then F must show up as a successor to each of B, D, and E. You should have arrow points on the line for F that correspond to the feathers on the ends of B, D, and E.

2. Recheck the durations. The Opinion Survey Project should finish in 16 weeks.

3. One usually determines the latest finish of an activity by looking at the schedule graphics, but it is possible to double-check. To get the latest finish of an activity, add up the time to do the remaining dependent activities and subtract it from the latest finish of the total project. For example, activity F is followed by a sequence of activities—H, J, K, and N—which

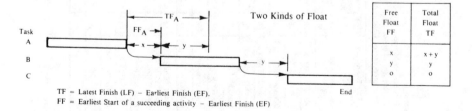

Figure 4-13. The two kinds of float.

together require a total of 5 weeks of work. (G and I are not successors of F.) Since the project must finish in 16 weeks, the latest finish of F is 16 − 5 = 11.

4. There are also ways to double-check the float. First, TF = LF − EF (latest finish minus earliest finish) for any activity. Second, the TF is greater than or equal to FF (that is, the free float cannot exceed the total float.) Third, the TF is the sum of the floats in a dependent string of following activities. For example, for activity F, TF = LF − EF = 11 − 9 = 2. However, the FF—the time between activity F and its successor G, is only 1 week. Yet G itself has 1 week of float after it. If G can start a week later, its float becomes available to F, making a total of 1 week of FF plus 1 week of FF, or 2 weeks of total float. Getting this correct on the float exercise will help you understand the relationship between the free float and the total float.

5. Show your schedule to any other team members who have done the schedule exercise with you. Explain any differences to each other. In my experience in hundreds of workshops, any four people who compare answers usually end up with the correct one.

6. Use team participation in the planning itself. Invite your key project team members to help you develop an activity list, logic diagram, and schedule.

APPLICATION TO A SMALL PROJECT: THE BANK'S GOODWILL PROJECT

Suppose that Harry had obtained approval from Cal for his project plan by promising to follow up with detailed planning. Harry had previously made a rough schedule before submitting his plan in order to set his time targets. Afterward, he prepared a detailed schedule. First, Harry made a list of the activities he needed to do to get the right end result. Then he gave code letters to the activities and indicated the predecessor relationships. From these he drew a logic diagram (see Figure 4-14).

After a few revisions to the logic diagram, Harry estimated the

88 SCHEDULES FOR BEING ON TIME

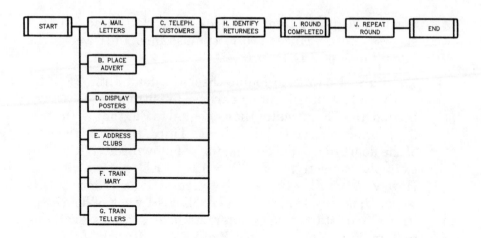

Figure 4-14. A logic diagram for the Goodwill Project.

duration of each activity, in weeks, and inserted his estimates in the last column of his activity list (Figure 4-15). Then he prepared the schedule shown in Figure 4-16.

There are a few points about this schedule that you should understand. First, it is an idealistic schedule because it assumes that the people will be available when required. If vacations interfere, the schedule would have to be adjusted accordingly. Second, activities A, B, D, E, F, and G can all start at time zero, but can Harry handle them all at once? The schedule shows that activities A and B must be started at the beginning because they have no float. However, activities F and G, for training, have plenty of float and so could start later. This would reduce the start-up load on Harry.

APPLICATION TO A MEDIUM PROJECT: THE PERSONNEL RECORDS PROJECT

Suppose that Jack has obtained approval for his project plan. In order to get the finish date for his project plan, he had to prepare a schedule at level 2, which is one level of detail over the project as a whole. Once the plan got under way, he would do subschedules for himself and for other departments at what we call level 3. Levels 2 and 3 are indicated in the project activity list (Figure 4-17). Level 2 consists of phases A, B, C, O, I, D, and CP. Under each of them is the level 3 breakdown of activities. The logic diagram (Figure 4-18) and schedule (Figure 4-19) are done at level 3.

The logic diagram and schedule for the Personnel Records Project show increasing levels of detail. To do this, you increase the detail of the schedule to the point where you have control of the project time aspects. When in doubt about the detail needed, ask yourself, "What would happen if I did not control this small task?" If the task is vital to project success, include it in your schedule. If the project result would be more or less the same if you did not control that task, you can leave it off your schedule; it will get some control at a higher level. For example, if the documentation for the Personnel Records Project is being done by an outside consultant on a cost-plus basis, Jack may have a task called "Prepare draft of operator instructions." If he is going to do it himself, he may have it on his list but not on his schedule, because the consultant doing the documentation would be controlling it.

USES OF FLOAT INFORMATION

Once you understand how to calculate the float, you have a wonderful tool for managing projects.

Activity Name	Activity Code	Immediate Predecessors	Duration In Weeks
Milestone: Start	MS:START	—	0
Mail Letters	A	Start	1
Place Advertisement	B	Start	1
Telephone Customers	C	A, B	3
Display Posters	D	Start	1
Address Clubs	E	Start	4
Train or Move Mary	F	Start	1
Train Other Tellers	G	Start	1
Identify Return Accounts	H	C,D,E,F,G	1
Milestone: Completed Round	I	H	0
Repeat Round of Promotion	J	I	4
Milestone: End	MS:END	J	0

Figure 4-15. Goodwill Project activity list.

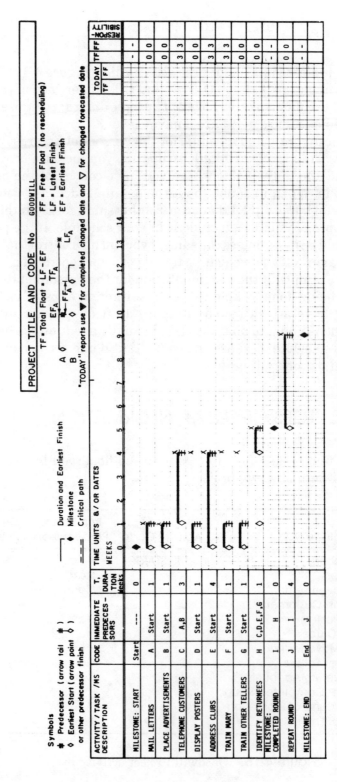

Figure 4-16. Projectics method schedule for the Goodwill Project.

PHASES and ACTIVITIES	ACTIVITY CODE	IMMEDIATE PREDECESSORS	DURATION IN WEEKS
Analyze Needs	A	Start	--
Milestone: Start	Start	---	0
Meet & define data fields	A1	Start	2
Define future requirements	A2	Start	1
Define hardware requirements	A3	Start	1
Milestone 1: Analysis Completed	MS1	A1,A2,A3	0
Design Systems	B	A	--
Develop Flow Chart	B1	MS1	1
Draft monitor screens	B2	B1	2
Test model	B3	B2	2
Revise Design	B4	B3	1
Prepare layout for system	B5	MS1	1
Get approval by client	B6	B4, B5	1
Milestone 2: Approved design	MS2	B6	0
Code Program	C	B	--
Initialize program	C1	MS2	1
Code main routine	C2	C1	1
Code subroutines	C3	C1	1
Test code	C4	C2,C3	1
Milestone 3: Finished program	MS3	C4	0
Order Hardware	O	B	--
Order furniture & await delivery	O1	MS2	3
Order terminals & await delivery	O2	MS2	6
Order peripherals & get delivery	O3	MS2	6
Order cables and await delivery	O4	MS2	2
Milestone 4: Delivered Hardware	MS4	O1,O2,O3,O4	0
Install System	I	C,O	--
Install furniture	I1	MS3,MS4	1
Install hardware	I2	I1	1
Install software	I3	I2	1
Milestone 5: Completed Install'n	MS5	I3	0
Debug System	D	I	--
Debug station 1	D1	MS5	1
Review & debug other stations	D2	D1	1
Review system	D3	D2	.5
Milestone 6: Ready System	MS6	D3	0
Close Project	CP	D	--
Train operators	CP1	MS6	1
Brief executives	CP2	MS6	.5
Finalize Documentation	CP3	MS6	1
Check out backup system	CP4	MS6	1
Integration with main frame	CP5	MS6	2
Milestone 7: End of project	MS7	CP1,CP2,CP3,CP4,CP5	0

Figure 4-17. Level 2 phases and level 3 activity list for the Personnel Records Project.

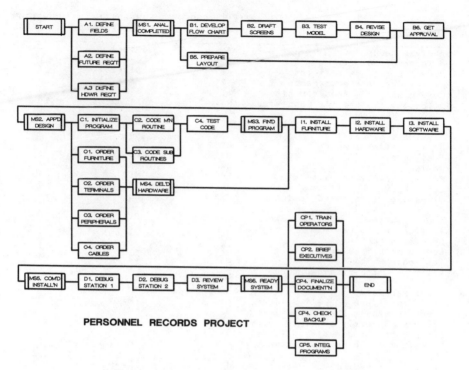

Figure 4-18. A logic diagram for the Personnel Records Project.

1. If TF = O (the total float is zero), the activity is on the so-called critical path. That is, the EF and LF are the same. If this activity is finished late, the whole project will be late.

2. If the total float is small, the activity is still critical. Any significant delay in its completion will probably exceed the TF, thereby causing a delay in the project completion.

3. Activities can be sorted by the amount of TF. This gives a degree of time criticality.

4. Free float (FF) is what I call the "teamwork term." It is the time between an activity and its earliest successor. If the person doing an activity is late and exceeds the FF, then the successor must be rescheduled. This is not conducive to good teamwork. In addition, the project manager will not look good. Rescheduling is not always easy to do. Worse still, the person doing the successor activity may have other commit-

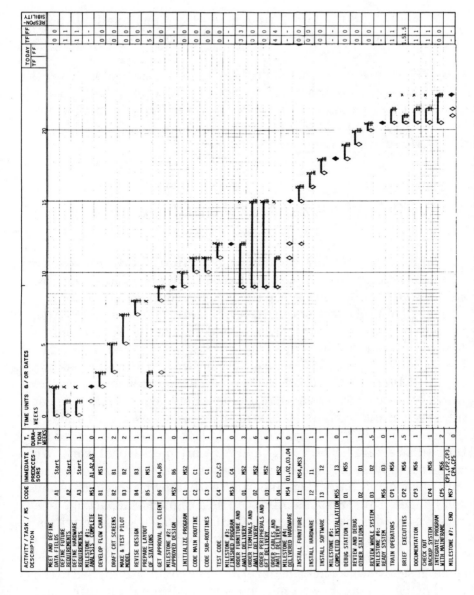

Figure 4-19. Projectics method schedule for the Personnel Records Project.

ments, and the loss of time may exceed any available float, thereby putting the end date of the project in jeopardy.

5. There are other uses of float information, some of which will show up in other parts of this book. If you wish to really go into it, there are many uses shown in an adjudicated paper I wrote, "Save Time and Money on Projects by Using Float," *Project Management Quarterly*, December 1983.

THE WORK BREAKDOWN STRUCTURE

In a large project, a Work Breakdown Structure (WBS) is developed when the activity list is prepared. Each activity is given a code that ties the work to be done to the skills required to do it.

A small project does not require a WBS. Medium projects often do, because they are carried out by several departments. The Personnel Records Project, for instance, has a WBS, but I called it "levels." Level 1 is the project name. For a one-level project (such as the Goodwill Project), there is but one account number for all project work. Whenever we have subaccounts, or subdepartments, we get into levels 2 and 3. Figure 4-20 is an example of a Work Breakdown Structure for constructing a hi-fi set. At level 3, codes are added for the skills required. Thus, A1.4 and A2.4 are mechanical work. We can group all the mechanical activities into a *work package* for the supervisor of mechanical engineering, with its own subschedule and sub-budget. Thus, responsibility can be assigned as a package to a supervisor, who acts as project leader for a defined set of activities.

The schedule for the Personnel Records Project (Figure 4-19) is a bit short of requiring a formal WBS at this point. Activities O1 to O4 come close to a work package (level 3). They could be assigned to the purchasing manager, who may do some additional planning and control at a more detailed level (level 4). You will see how this can be formalized into a WBS and a code of accounts when we get into budgeting. However, unless a project is larger than the Personnel Records Project and requires tight control of costs, it is sufficient to use the codes shown. Skill codes are probably not needed unless many projects are to be done by the same department. This will be covered in the chapter on multiple projects (Chapter 12).

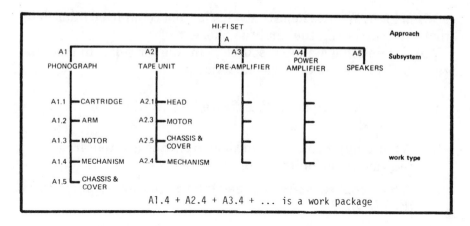

Figure 4-20. Work breakdown structure for constructing a hi-fi set.

ADJUSTMENT OF SCHEDULES FOR RESOURCE AVAILABILITY

Resources of people, machines, equipment, and facilities are needed to do a project. In our scheduling examples thus far, we assumed that the resources would be available when required. Is this always so? What about vacations? Other projects? Prior commitments? As soon as you set an actual calendar date for the start or finish of a project, you must cope with resource availability.

In the Goodwill Project, the scarce resource turned out to be letterhead stationery. It's doubtful that Harry would have planned to this level of detail for his first project. Besides, a delay of a few weeks can be accommodated—there are no deadlines.

For the Personnel Records Project, there are no deadlines that cannot be changed. However, the MIS department's reputation must be considered, so a little resource planning would be appropriate. On the right-hand side of the schedule in Figure 4-19, we could put in the initials of the resource persons. Jack's initials would be put opposite the analysis tasks. We would discover, however, that three activities—A1, A2, and A3—are to be done by Jack at the same time. Jack could get some help or just add a week to the schedule. However, suppose that the analysis work falls during his vacation period. Too bad. He must either stretch out the project or take his vacation later. We also hope that Jack has not committed himself to other projects during the analysis phase.

You can do some simple resource planning for small to medium projects. For each task, check the following:

1. Who is going to do the task? Are they available on the dates required?
2. What equipment, machines, or facilities are required? Are they available on the dates required?
3. What supplies, materials, and information are required to do the activity?

PUTTING IT ALL TOGETHER

Let's review the steps in scheduling a project:

1. *Make a list of activities.* You saw how this was done for a small project at level 2 and how the levels can be developed further for a medium project. You saw also how reporting milestones can be added at the completion of significant work.
2. *Make a logic diagram.* A box represents an activity. It is joined to predecessors and successors. A double-walled box represents a milestone. Logic diagrams can be extended from level 2 to more detailed levels.
3. *Prepare a bar chart schedule.* For this, you need activity durations. Approximations are good enough for a rough schedule. However, when you find out what is timewise critical (that is, no float), you need better time estimates. In my experience, the best time estimate is the one given to you by the person who is to do the work and agreed to by the supervisor. This estimate becomes a commitment. People will control themselves to meet their commitments whenever possible. If they fail to keep a commitment, or are unable to do so, get new commitments from them and revise your schedule. You can see why I advise people to use a pencil for schedules. Make it easy for yourself—changes are inevitable.

4. *Adjust the schedule.* Fortunately, when you use a pencil, you can easily revise your schedule for resource availability and fixed dates. A computer program is easy to change, too. Using computers will be the subject of a chapter later in this book.
5. *Identify milestones.* Management needs to know how the project is doing, but not in the same detail as the project manager needs. If you insert milestones at the completion of significant work, you will be able to review and revise your project plan and get approval for any major changes. If you do your job well, you'll be reporting good news at the milestones (more about this later in another chapter).
6. *Obtain approval.* Sometimes getting the approval to go ahead takes a long time. When it does come through, you may need to get new commitments from project team members.
7. *Monitor and update.* This will be the subject of a later chapter.
8. *Report to management.* You need an organized way of reporting by week, month, and milestone. Reporting is covered in other chapters.

QUESTIONS FOR DISCUSSION OR ASSIGNMENT

1. Preparing and implementing detailed schedules require time. This effort should be offset by some advantages. What are they? List three advantages of detailed scheduling, and explain each with a short paragraph. (This may also be a group exercise.)
2. Explain the usefulness of the "forward pass" and the "backward pass" for (a) logic diagrams and (b) schedules.
3. Examine the schedule in Figure 4-16, prepared for the Goodwill Project. Suppose that the duration of the "Mail letters" activity is increased from 1 week to 3 weeks. All other durations remain the same. However, because of the heavy load on Harry in the first week, he decides to start the training—activities F and G—3 weeks after the start of the project. Modify the schedule to accommodate these changes; then recalculate the latest finish and the float for each activity. What is the new finish time for the project?

4. Examine the schedule in Figure 4-19, prepared for the Personnel Records Project. Suppose that activity O1, "Order furniture and await delivery," is found to take nine weeks after its earliest finish. As there were three weeks of float at this point, the net delay to the project is six weeks. Modify the schedule to show this, and designate the latest finish for the activities affected. Recalculate the total float and the free float and mark it next to the original values. The end of the project should now be at 32.5 weeks.

5. From a practical point of view, is it necessary to delay the completion of the Personnel Records Project by six weeks? Why not substitute other furniture until the new furniture arrives and the "Review and debug other stations" is complete. Modify the logic diagram (Figure 4-18) to accommodate this change. Assuming that it would take a week to install the new furniture, modify the schedule (Figure 4-19) to show this change. When would the project finish?

CHAPTER
five

BUDGETING AND CONTROLLING THE COST
how to avoid overruns

> **Key Idea**
>
> Cost control requires milestone budgets. Cost is a tradeoff with time and results.

The success of a project is judged not only on what it accomplishes but also on how much it costs and how long it takes to complete. Project managers should institute a series of budgets, linked to phases of the project (or to milestones) that can be assessed periodically. These budgets help control the cost of the project as it progresses. The information they provide is the basis for making tradeoffs between time, cost, and results. The following familiar cases show Harry and Jack learning this lesson through hard experience.

CASE 1:
THE BANKER LOSES MONEY

Although the bank's Goodwill Project was small, Cal thought it wise to have an accounting of the total completed cost. He wanted to know if Harry could control the cost as well as get the results. Besides, unusual expenses sometimes had to be explained to the auditors.

When the project was over, Harry collected the information he had and totaled up the expenses. (He did not include the person-weeks involved.) Harry's figures indicated that the project had cost $4000, instead of his budgeted $3000. The overrun had many causes. There were extra artwork costs on the posters, traveling expenses to headquarters, and a hike in the postage rates. The big expense item was for outside office services to make up time in the production of the personalized letters. If Harry had been able to produce all the letters with his own staff over a longer period, the cost would not have been significant. Moreover, he was forced to pay for the outside office services from the office expense account. It came to about 10 percent of his total annual budget. Another item was the advertising costs. The local newspaper was very cooperative and helped Harry design a large display ad, which was placed in the business section of the paper. However, Harry had not asked the newspaper about the cost in advance. He was surprised by the size of the bill. "It's too late to do anything about it now," thought Harry. "I should have been watching the cost as I went along. The only way I could have done that was to have a budget for each item. Then I would have known if there was going to be a high or low on the total. Also, it seems to me that there is always some extra cost that we don't think about. I should have added a contingency fund as well."

Later, after explaining this to Cal, Harry was assured that a $1000 overrun on this project was not really a big deal. The branch operation budget was about $500,000 per year. Harry thought that Cal had taken the news rather quietly. What Harry didn't know was what was under that pleasant face mask. Cal was wondering if Harry would be able to handle a really big project, such as opening up another branch office.

CASE 2:
THE PURCHASING DEPARTMENT DID THEIR OWN THING

The Personnel Records Project was being run with cost control techniques. Jack had budgeted the person-weeks for all tasks under his direction—primarily, analysis and coding. For the ordering tasks assigned to the purchasing manager, he had budgeted a ballpark figure.

The people working in the Management Information Systems Department reported to Jack weekly on the hours charged to his project when they turned in time cards. These hours were entered into a computer, and Jack got a weekly summary report. He was thus able to compare the budgeted person-weeks per task with the actual usage. One of his new programmers was slow, so the actual cost in person-weeks of his first task was well above the budget. The summary reports gave Jack an early warning signal. He took the time to give the slow programmer some special training to get him up to speed.

The weekly reports were summarized at each milestone. At the end of the "Analyze needs" phase, the actual cost versus the budgeted cost ($3500) was not too bad. Consequently, Jack spent very little time scanning the subsequent weekly cost reports. He was working heavy overtime on the "Code program" phase. Also, he was away for a week to attend a conference. When the coding was complete, he got busy with other projects. He didn't get around to scanning his cost reports until the "Order hardware" phase was over. He found that the actual person-weeks was far, far in excess of anything he had planned for, so he asked for an explanation. Jack was told that because of the delay in acquiring the computer furniture, several trips to the vendor had been necessary, as had trips to other potential vendors. In all, it had required a full-time buyer for the whole period. Jack had budgeted only a half-hour a day for a buyer. Tough luck. Because of his company's internal charge-back system, all of the person-weeks and travel expenses were being charged to his project.

"Too late now," thought Jack. "To be in control, I need to be close to the action. I should have delegated the cost control to the purchasing manager. He would have submitted a detailed list of tasks and the associated person-weeks beforehand. We would have negotiated a reasonable budget. Then he would have controlled it. It seems to me that the purchasing manager would have pulled in the reins if he had been committed to a budget. I don't need the best computer furniture in the world. I just need something that works and is on time."

What was happening here was that the Purchasing Department was making a tradeoff in favor of a high-quality job, even if it cost extra. They had decided on the tradeoff on their own.

Principles of Cost Control

1. Cost control depends on having budgets by tasks and by departments. At the end of a task or at a milestone, the actual cost is compared with the budget. This gives feedback on how the project is doing with respect to cost.

2. Cost control is interrelated with control of the schedule and of the results. Tradeoffs between them are used to guide the project to the best combination of time, cost, and results that can be achieved under the circumstances.

APPLICATION TO A SMALL PROJECT

Many small projects are not subject to cost control, because they may be peripheral to the main operation. On the other hand, many organizations are set up solely to run groups of small projects. Examples are a new-products group in a pharmaceutical firm, fulfilling unique orders in a small job shop, and an advertising agency. If the cost is not controlled on the individual projects, then the cost is really not controlled on the total. Cost overruns will be likely.

Suppose that the bank's Goodwill Project is going to be subject to project management cost control techniques. Figure 5-1 shows the budget by activity for the project. For each activity, we have estimated the person-weeks and the out-of-pocket expenses. There are totals for the person-weeks and for the expense items; these are the milestone budgets and the project budget. Even if this breakdown is not used for detailed cost control, this is the way to estimate the resources needed. For example: Can the bank handle the person-weeks without scheduling paid overtime or hiring temporary staff? Will the annual budget for expense items include enough to cover this project? Should Harry seek authorization for additional expenditures for the year?

ACTIVITY NAME	DURATION IN WEEKS	PERSON-WEEKS	EXPENSE ($)
Milestone: Start	0	–	–
Mail Letters	1	2	1000
Place Advertisement	1	0.5	200
Telephone Customers	3	1	100
Display Posters	1	1	100
Address Clubs	4	1	100
Train or Move Mary	1	0.5	0
Train Other Tellers	1	1	0
Identify Return Accounts	1	1	0
Milestone: Completed Round	0	–	–
[Subtotal is Milestone Budget]		[8]	[1500]
Repeat Round of Promotion	4	8	1500
Milestone: End	0	–	–
[Total is Project Budget]		[16]	[3000]

Figure 5-1. The Goodwill Project budget.

At the only milestone, Harry would assess his costs for the first round and forecast the final cost of the project. It is better to forecast a high cost after the milestone cost is evaluated than to surprise management with it at the end. First, it gives time for acceptance of the higher figure; second, it gives management the opportunity to take corrective action.

In the bank's case, there is no regular recording of person-weeks used on any particular project. They are not set up to do that; their primary business is operating a bank. Thus, the initial value to them of this project budget is to assess whether or not the bank will have the resources available when they are needed for the project.

This technique of budgeting (and its use for cost control) is very important when there are multiple projects. The resources needed in person-weeks and expenses for all projects can be summed up. Then we can look in advance for potential overloads and high expenditures. Alternatively, management can staff up and get the necessary expense money to cover the planned program.

Suppose that, with this budget before him, Harry is at the point of deciding whether to use outside services. He would get an estimate on the increase in expenses and decide whether he can cover it or not. Thus, he would be deciding on a tradeoff between cost and time.

APPLICATION TO A MEDIUM PROJECT

Most medium and large projects are subject to some type of formal control—at least an overall budget for the total project. However, this is not actually control, because you cannot find out how you are doing until after the project is over. On the other hand, if you have a budget by the month, week, or milestone, you have benchmarks for measuring cost progress.

Figure 5-2 is a list of Personnel Records Project activities and their budgets. Person-weeks are transformed to dollars at $1000 per week. The dollars are summed up for each task and for the milestones.

Note that in addition to the sub-budget for the entire "Order hardware" phase, there is a detailed budget for each of the tasks involved. If the estimating is done in cooperation with the purchas-

APPLICATION TO A MEDIUM PROJECT

PHASES and ACTIVITIES	DURATION (WEEKS)	PERSON-WEEKS	LABOR ($)	EXPENSE ($)	BUDGET TOTAL ($)
Analyze Needs	—	—	—	—	—
Milestone: Start	0	—	—	—	—
Meet and define data fields	2	2	2000	0	2000
Define future requirements	1	0.5	500	0	500
Define hardware requirements	1	1	1000	0	1000
Milestone 1: Analysis completed	0	[3.5]	[3500]	[0]	[3500]
Design Systems	—	—	—	—	—
Develop flow chart	1	1	1000	0	1000
Draft monitor screens	2	2	2000	0	2000
Test model	2	1	1000	0	1000
Revise design	1	0.4	400	0	400
Prepare layout for system	1	1	1000	0	1000
Get approval by client	1	0.5	500	0	500
Milestone 2: Approved design	0	[5.9]	[5900]	[0]	[5900]
Code Program	—	—	—	—	—
Initialize program	1	1	1000	0	1000
Code main routine	1	1	1000	0	1000
Code subroutines	1	1	1000	0	1000
Test code	1	0.5	500	0	500
Milestone 3: Finished program	0	[3.5]	[3500]	[0]	[3500]
Order Hardware	—	—	—	—	—
Order furniture and await delivery	3	0.2	200	4000	4200
Order terminals and await delivery	6	0.6	600	4000	4600
Order peripherals and get delivery	6	0.6	600	4000	4600
Order cables and await delivery	2	0.2	200	1000	1200
Milestone 4: Delivered hardware	0	[1.6]	[1600]	[13000]	[14600]
Install System	—	—	—	—	—
Install furniture	1	0.2	200	500	700
Install hardware	1	0.2	200	500	700
Install software	1	1	1000	0	1000
Milestone 5: Completed installation	0	[1.4]	[1400]	[1000]	[2400]
Debug System	—	—	—	—	—
Debug station 1	1	1	1000	0	1000
Review and debug other stations	1	1	1000	0	1000
Review system	0.5	0.2	200	0	200
Milestone 6: Ready system	0	[2.2]	[2200]	[0]	[2200]
Close Project	—	—	—	—	—
Train operators	1	1	1000	0	1000
Brief executives	0.5	0.5	500	0	500
Finalize documentation	1	1	1000	0	1000
Check out backup system	1	1	1000	0	1000
Integration with main frame	2	2	2000	0	2000
Milestone 7: End of project	0	[5.5]	[5500]	[0]	[5500]
TOTAL PROJECT BUDGET		[23.6]	[23600]	[14000]	[37600]

Figure 5-2. Level 2 and level 3 budget for the Personnel Records Project.

ing manager, then it is possible to get his commitment to his sub-budget.

Suppose that for Jack's project, the furniture buyer suggests to his boss, the purchasing manager, that he go on field trips to the furniture manufacturers. If the purchasing manager authorizes this additional cost, he knows that he will exceed his budget. He is at a point of control. He has some obligation to control the time and cost aspects of his subproject. He could take this change in plans to Jack and ask for an increase in his sub-budget. If he succeeds, he can retarget his subproject and have a new sub-budget approved. He will be in control. Moreover, the total project can be replanned and retargeted, and the whole team will know where they are going. After retargeting, Jack can make a forecast of the final cost. This is called the estimate at completion (EAC). He should do this forecasting at least at every milestone and report it to management. There will be losses, but there will also be gains. Some things will cost less than anticipated. However, the reality of project management is that overruns are frequent. No one is so good at estimating that he or she can come out right on the dollar. Suppose that the EAC of the total project is more than the manager, customer, or client will go for—say, more than 10 percent higher than originally planned. The project manager can submit a new plan at a milestone and get new targets approved. Everyone wins. Whether the final cost is more or less than the original plan is not the point. It is being in control that counts.

APPLICATION TO ANNUAL BUDGET CONTROL OF MULTIPLE PROJECTS

Another mechanism of cost control is the annual budget for the department. Many departments are staffed at an adequate level to do the job on the average. They have an annual budget for salaries and expenses. If the annual budget is met and they are keeping up with the work, then the department managers believe they are in control. Although this form of control is flawed, in that it does not track individual projects, it is used in many places.

Suppose, for example, that an organization is set up to mass-produce refrigerators. The product development group consists of two or three people who work with major department stores. They specify the details needed to give identifiable differences in a basic product for different store brands. There are 250 employees in the company. How important would it be to control a dozen or so individual projects in a year, when the total annual budget for the product development group is less than 2 percent of the total? Not really important, so it seems.

Although I am outlining a form of cost control through annual budgets, this is not really tight control of costs. Most organizations are moving toward combined control of costs on individual projects and control by an annual budget.

APPLICATION TO MULTIPLE PROJECTS

As an example of annual budget control, consider the multiple projects done by Mary-Helen for the insurance company. Her manager has an annual budget for the salaries and expenses of a group of about 15 people. The expense budget includes such items as travel, advertising agency assistance, printing, telephone, office supplies, and minor equipment.

You may recall that Mary-Helen made a forecast of her project load that included a serious overload in February and March. Something has to be done, or some projects will be late. In response to her problem, her manager, Bill, authorizes paid overtime for that two-month period and for some of the time preceding it. To Bill, this looks like a good way to meet marketing deadlines. Further, he considers Mary-Helen's forecasting such a good idea that he has other members of his department do it as well. Soon he finds himself authorizing additional overtime for the others. When the monthly salary reports start coming in, he sees that he is running over the salary budget for three months in a row, with no opportunity to make it up in his annual budget. Although he is meeting his time commitments at the end of the year, someone will rake him over the coals for going over his salary budget. What can he do?

1. He can do fewer projects.
2. He can defer some projects until next year. In this case, his annual budget will look okay.

He can find a creative solution. For instance, if the overloads are temporary, he can offer time off at another time of the year instead of overtime pay.

There are also some other tricks of the trade for managers to use in dealing with annual budgets. For example, if Bill is about to blow his advertising budget, he can ask the agency to delay invoicing until the next fiscal year. This reduction in his expense budget will offset the variance in his salary budget.

If you are subject to the control of an annual salary and expense budget, you can use these techniques. If individual projects are being controlled for cost as well, then you will have two dimensions of cost control. It will take some extra effort to keep projects within budget and also keep the annual budget in control. You can do this only by having detailed budgets and data on your actual costs versus the budget. It sounds like a lot of work, but many organizations are heading this way. Once the process is established, the results are superb.

THE ACTIVITY BUDGET

The budget for an activity or a task should include all costs controllable by the person responsible for it. It should reflect the true cost of getting the task done.

Budgeted cost is primarily in two categories: personpower (manpower) and expense. Typically, the personpower will be budgeted in hours, weeks, or months of actual work on the project. This is not the elapsed time of the task from start to finish but the actual time spent doing the task itself. A common mistake here is to assume that if a task takes one person four weeks to finish, the budget should be four person-weeks. This is not necessarily true, because the person may be working on other projects. On the other hand, a task that takes four weeks may require three persons working on it full time; thus, the budget would be 12 person-weeks.

Personpower is frequently transformed into dollars. This is usually an average rather than the true individual salaries for the persons working on a task. Average salaries vary with skills, so it is important to know the level of skill required for a task. However, you may budget for a low-skilled person and be forced to use a high-skilled person, at a higher rate, because the low-skilled person is not available. This is one reason for using average figures for a department. You lose on some and win on others. When we use an average rate, it frequently includes the overhead.

Overhead is seldom low. It includes the employee benefit packages as well as administrative costs. Assuming that there is one manager for every ten workers, overhead is never less than 10 percent, because a manager is classified as overhead. When you add facilities cost and ancillary services such as accounting, you are lucky to have an overhead cost as low as 50 percent of the direct labor cost. In government services, I have heard of overhead figures of 230 percent of the direct labor cost. Whatever the overhead cost, it's going to be related to the person-hour cost and included in the budget.

Expense items are typically the costs of materials or equipment to do the project. However, in many nontechnical projects, there is no equipment cost, and the paper cost is negligible. Expense items often include the contracted cost of outside services. These out-of-pocket expenses are really labor costs, but by putting them in the expense column, they are kept out of the salary budgets that organizations use for estimating and controlling staff costs on an annual basis.

There are some additional items that you should consider when calculating the true cost of doing an activity. *Paid overtime* is seldom avoidable. *Materials* drawn from stores may be charged to annual material budgets, but they are part of the true cost of the project. By including these materials in the budget, you will have funds to purchase them in case they are not available from your storeroom. *Computing costs,* if charged to a department, are also an item to consider. Any *outside contracted work* on your project is also part of your project cost.

Travel costs require some special mention. Many organizations have an annual budget for travel. Whether the travel is for education or for a project, it goes into the same budget. The problem with this is that travel budgets are frequently cut back, or they may be expended early in the year. Then, when the travel is needed for the project, the money is not there, and it can't be done. It is much better to put travel in your project budget and have it under your own control. It doesn't cost your organization any more, and it puts the travel costs under tight control. The organization's annual travel budget, then, should be for nonproject work, such as attending conferences.

ACCURACY OF ESTIMATES

A detailed estimate for a project, task by task, is likely to be close to the true value. Some items may be high and some may be low, but they will have a canceling effect. Then you need only add something for a contingency fund, and you will have a figure you can live with.

What happens if you don't prepare a detailed estimate or you don't have sufficient time to do it thoroughly? Frequently, projects are launched without a detailed analysis of the cost. Then, after the project is finished, there is a lot of mudslinging and backstabbing about the cost overrun. As one fellow put it, "We are given a half an hour to prepare a capital estimate of up to one million dollars. Then if it doesn't come out right, we are hung by the thumbs."

Financial control is important to a company. It is often a deciding factor in profit or loss. Suppose that a manager prepares an estimate of the annual salaries for his seven subordinates, including the cost of overtime. If, at the end of the year, his actual costs are way out of line with his budget, it's fair to criticize him, because it was possible for him to do a fairly accurate estimate in the first place. Suppose, on the other hand, that a project manager is given a project such as computerizing the accounting function. Experience shows that estimates for such projects tend to be a bit lopsided toward the optimistic side. A 100 percent overrun is possible. You can't apply the same kind of accountability to such a project estimate as to an annual salary estimate.

Unfortunately, we are frequently dealing with people who only have two modes of operation: It's either right or it's wrong. They are binary thinkers. However, there is a solution that I have started many clients on, and it has worked well. When you give an estimate, put a plus and minus on it—for example, $100,000, plus or minus 30 percent. Then, when the project is approved, the $130,000 figure is also approved. If you have bad luck, you are covered. However, if your management is not satisfied with your plus or minus estimate, they can allow you the time to do a more detailed estimate. You may estimate the project again after you have reached a significant milestone. When you hand in budgets with plus or minus percentages on them, you will more often be right than wrong. And the truth is that this technique properly represents your uncertainty about the estimate. Note, however, that some projects should come in on the minus side of their budgets to compensate for the plus side of others.

MILESTONE REPORTING VERSUS PERIODIC REPORTING

I have mentioned weekly, monthly, and milestone reporting of actual costs. Of these, the only one that is important to small and medium projects is milestone reporting. Unfortunately, most organizations are set up for weekly or monthly reporting, and this can't be avoided. With regard to cost control, however, it's difficult to determine cost progress by periodic reporting. For example, consider the milestone at the end of the "Install system" phase in the Personnel Records Project. The sub-budget for this phase is $2400, and the anticipated completion date of the phase is week 18. Suppose that the milestone is reached and we review the weekly report closest to it. Even if the data are timely (and they seldom are), they can be significant only if the milestone is reached on schedule. Suppose that the milestone is delayed by a month. At the original milestone date, the expenses will be less than the milestone budget because much of the work has yet to be done. Management might then assume that the actual cost is much less than the budget, and so think that everything is fine. This false sense of security may continue until the project is closed out—say, about three months after it's finished. Then the bad news comes: It is badly overrun.

Whatever periodic financial reporting an organization has, it should be augmented by milestone reporting. If this is not done by the financial group, it behooves the project leader to do it. At a milestone, a number of tasks have been completed. For each one there has been an actual cost. Part of this actual cost has been paid out, such as salaries. Some of it is still in accrual, such as materials delivered but not yet paid for. The project leader has to take all of these items into account and estimate the final cost for anything that has been done. He or she will then have a figure of the estimated actual cost for each activity, and thus for the milestone itself. This figure can then be compared with the budget for the milestone. Only then will anyone know whether the project is over or under the budget.

At a milestone, we have a true indication of how we are doing. We can then estimate the actual cost at completion of the project—the estimate at completion (EAC). We take into account any tendency to be over or under our original budget as well as any corrective actions or additions that we anticipate in the future. This procedure tells management, customer, or client what to expect at the end, unless some changes are made in the plans. When you forecast the EAC, it may be higher than the original budget. However, when you get good at project control, the EAC will frequently be less than the original budget. The main benefit to you as a project leader is that you will know that you are in control.

COMMITTED COST AT A MILESTONE

Within a large organization that has a number of medium projects, it is not unusual for the project costs to be tabulated by the financial department. Proper accounting procedures are used, and the tabulation is done by people with specialized skills. When such tabulation is done properly and in a timely fashion, it is very useful to the project leaders. It also relieves them of the tedium of cost accounting. Moreover, if the project leaders are not good at financial tabulation, it is better that they work at their own specialization.

Unfortunately, in many large organizations, the financial group is set up to serve overall operations, not to serve project groups. This means that their focus is on getting a figure on running costs each month so that it can be compared with the monthly budget. From this figure, they can estimate the annual profit. With regard to overall operations, costs for salaries are very much the same from month to month, and material costs do not vary much from month to month. Even if the report is two or three months late, it is still useful to the managers who are trying to control the annual budget. The same is not true for project work.

Here is a cost control problem that my seminar attendees often relate: About one-third of the people I've talked to do the cost control themselves; about one-third get accurate data from the accounting group; but about one-third are getting late and useless information from the accounting group. There is a reason for this problem. Suppose that we estimate the cost for some equipment or contracted work. When the order is actually placed and acknowledged, we have a better estimate of what the actual cost will be. When it is delivered, we know better the cost of any extras and the freight. Also, there may be a 30-day or 90-day payment schedule. Thus, at every point, we are estimating what the actual cost will be when the item is all wrapped up.

Some operations-oriented accounting departments report only on cash disbursements—that is, the actual payment for the equipment or service, which frequently occurs long after it has been received. Sometimes a little more sophistication is used, such as accrual accounting. When the invoices arrive, the amount is put into an accrual account. This is appropriate accounting, because the accruals plus disbursements are quite close to the actual cost. If this information is reported back in a timely fashion, the project leader has useful data. To be really useful, however, these data have to be collected with all other costs leading up to a milestone. Then the project leader can compare the costs with the budget for the milestone, even if the milestone occurs in the middle of a regular accounting period. If the financial group is going to give milestone reports as well as periodic reports, they are obviously going to be doing more work and should be staffed to handle it.

Here is another example. Time cards are frequently used in project work. Each person's salary is posted into different projects as well as into a salary account. Before project accounting was necessary, it had to be posted only in the salary account. Now there is at least twice as much posting to be done. If it is done by the accounting group, they must have additional staff to handle it. If they don't have the additional staff to do it in a timely fashion, it must be done by the project group. There is no getting away from it: If it is not done for you, you must do it yourself in order to have the data you need to control cost. You should not agree to be responsible for cost unless you have the necessary information to control it.

CHOOSING MILESTONES

Milestones should be located at the completion of significant work. The examples I have given in this book have been broken down into orderly phases, with milestones at the ends of the phases. Not many milestones are needed in a project to control the cost. Usually, not much money is expended early in the project, so milestones are used for time progress. Later in the project, costly resources have been committed, and milestones are very useful for determining cost progress. Actually, if the cost of every task is compared with its budget, you will be in control, but this involves a lot of unnecessary detail. Moreover, you need milestone data for reporting to management. They don't need reports on every task, but they need summary reports that are meaningful. Milestone reports are designed to meet this need.

For very large projects, with hundreds or thousands of tasks, it is possible to create an artificial milestone every week or every month. At every reporting point, another hundred tasks may have been completed. As long as the cost of doing these tasks is compared with the budget for doing them, you have dependable information for cost control. The outgrowth of this approach is a reporting system known as *C/SCSC*—also known as *C-spec* and *earned value reporting*. The main application of this reporting system is to defense projects of magnitudes running into millions of dollars. You will not use it on small projects. However, if you work in a large organization, you may be required to report to the higher level in an earned value format. Management will take your data on a per-task basis and aggregate it for the higher-level reports on thousands of activities. This does not concern the project leader at the lower level. Much variety in reporting techniques can be permitted at the lower level, as long as the required format is met at the higher level.

COST IS A TRADEOFF

Being in control does not always mean having the cost right on target. To bring a project in early will generally require more funds. So cost and time are tradeoffs. Another possible tradeoff is between the results and the cost. If we find ourselves running high on costs halfway through a project, we may trim off the optional features of the results. This is a form of tradeoff. Cost, time, and results are juggled according to the circumstances.

Ultimately, cost control is possible only because we have planned it in advance, we have detailed budgets, and we have a recording system for our actual cost. However, the final outcome may be a cost overrun if time or results were more important than cost. Cost control, then, entails making deliberate decisions about these three factors in the final cost. You must have them under conscious control in order to get a quality result.

DELAYS ARE SOMETIMES VERY EXPENSIVE

If your project is part of a contract, there may be penalty clauses for late delivery. If you are bringing out a new product for the Christmas market, for instance, then even a day's delay will cost heavily in loss of profit. As another example, if you are creating the software for automated control of a large refinery, the cost per day of delay may be more than the cost of the project. There are often tangible costs associated with delay. In that case, we can work out a *cost-per-day of delay*. This figure can then be used as a tradeoff for time. If the cost of making up a day is less than the loss per day, then we may spend the extra money to do so. This would result in an apparent project cost overrun, which is allowed in order to avoid another form of loss.

There are many projects for which there is no cost of delay and no deadline. Both the Goodwill Project and the Personnel Records Project are of this type. There is no cost-per-day of delay, and delays will probably be accommodated in order to keep the cost down. In such projects, the price we pay for delay is often lost reputation. Sometimes we may take on a little extra cost to keep our reputation from being damaged. For instance, consultants who get into trouble on a project are often willing to take a loss just to keep their reputations intact. You may find yourself doing this, too.

WAYS TO KEEP THE COST UNDER CONTROL

1. Prepare a good cost estimate for the total project at the beginning. If it's not accurate enough, put a plus or minus on it.
2. Have a budget for all significant tasks.
3. Learn from experience. At a major milestone, revise your estimate at completion (EAC) of the final project cost. You should be able to indicate a tighter plus or minus on your estimate as you progress through the project.
4. Get personal commitments from the people who will be doing the tasks. Also get commitments from their supervisors; they are the ones who exercise control at the level

where it counts. When you get commitments, you push the level of control downwards.

5. Have sub-budgets for medium projects. These subprojects will be under the control of the department managers who will provide services to the project. This gives you additional control points.

6. Expedite your major purchases and contracted work. The people doing the work may be several levels away from you, so you need additional control. Delays in delivery of material or services usually result in additional makeup cost to your project. Offer to pay on receipt if materials are delivered early; suppliers will see an advantage in getting paid early.

7. If your original cost is too high, take the time to explore all alternatives. Many a project has come in at half the cost because a lower-cost alternative was found.

8. When a task is done adequately, terminate the work on it.

9. Exercise scope control. Project leaders who give in to all requests for extras are running a risk. It's hard to say no, but if you first request new funds for the extras, you will appear reasonable. Many extras will not be approved under those circumstances.

10. Have a contingency fund for correction of errors or omissions. Nothing ever goes perfectly; there will be corrections, revisions, overtime, unscheduled travel, and so forth, in a project. The contingency fund should not be used to finance increases in the scope of the results. When extras are added to the work, you should get a revision to your plan that allows more money and more time for doing them.

QUESTIONS FOR DISCUSSION OR ASSIGNMENT

1. At the beginning of this chapter are two situations in which the cost is out of control. State one reason why the bank's Goodwill Project is out of control for cost. Do the same for the Personnel Records Project.

QUESTIONS FOR DISCUSSION OR ASSIGNMENT

2. For a medium project, such as the Personnel Records Project, cost control is exercised by the project manager, who compares committed cost with budget and then takes appropriate action. Who else is exercising cost control on the project? Describe how it would be done, using an example drawn from this project.

3. The cost data for a milestone are used to control the cost. Why is it necessary to have the committed cost at this point instead of only the expenditures to date?

4. Why should a project manager get a new budget and schedule approved when there is a significant scope (results) change?

5. In Mary-Helen's multiple-project case, suppose that she is unwilling or unable to work continuous overtime without payment. What alternatives are open to her manager in order to control his annual budget for salaries?

6. In the Personnel Records Project, suppose that the purchasing manager is unable to authorize travel and extra work for purchasing the computer furniture. What could be the effect on the overall project results? What tradeoff considerations are involved?

7. Refer to Figure 5-2, the budget for the Personnel Records Project. For the task "Order furniture and await delivery," the budget was 0.2 person-weeks at $1000 per week, plus $4000 expense. Suppose that because of the difficulty in obtaining custom-made furniture, the actual cost was 9 person-weeks, plus an additional $500 for unplanned travel expenses. Develop or find the figures for:
   (a) The original sub-budget for the "Order hardware" phase
   (b) The actual cost of this phase
   (c) A revised EAC for the whole project
   Write your answers on figure 5-2, next to the budget values. How many extra columns would be needed if Figure 5-2 were modified to show actuals as well as budgets?

8. Prepare a detailed budget for a small project of your own or one that is assigned to you.

9. This is a group project: For a medium project belonging to a member of your group, or for one that has been assigned, prepare a detailed budget and explain how you would use this budget to control the cost.

CHAPTER
six

ENHANCEMENTS TO THE DYNAMIC PROJECT PLAN

items that need attention

ENHANCEMENTS TO THE DYNAMIC PROJECT PLAN

> ## Key Idea
>
> You should plan to control items that can affect the success of the project.

The balance of a project can be upset by a number of secondary factors. The project manager must create a plan to control these factors, and the plan should be approved by his or her superiors. The project manager must have guidelines in place that will help preserve the desired balance between time, cost, and results.

The following cases demonstrate how Harry, Jack, Mary-Helen, and their supervisors needed to make the right choices to keep their respective project on track.

CASE 1:
THE METICULOUS BANKER

You may recall from previous chapters that the bank's Goodwill Project was a promotional program to get back former customers. The first round of the project was well under way when Harry noticed some change in Cal's attitude. Whereas previously Cal had given Harry a free hand, he now had a nit-picking attitude. Cal had read about the connection between high-quality work and profit in the book *In Search of Excellence,* and he had decided to apply it to Harry's project. The first evidence of the change to high quality was Cal's interception of the design for the posters that were part of the project's multimedia campaign. He didn't like "this" and he didn't like "that." He made quite a few changes. The artwork had to be done over. However, there was some time float on that task, so it didn't matter. Cal's attitude took him from one thing to another until he was also criticizing the quality of the mailout. He insisted that the first names of the addressees be put on the letters. This revision took extensive telephoning and retyping. Nor was Cal satisfied with metered postage; he insisted on the use of the latest post office issue of a commemorative stamp. Harry went along with Cal's sudden mania for perfection, but he could foresee a serious delay in the project. It was time to draw the line.

Fortunately, Cal and Harry had worked together for years, so Harry felt free to bring up the subject. During a quiet moment, while sitting in Cal's office, Harry said: "There is something I want to tell you, Cal. I know we've been friends long enough so I can speak my mind. Look, I can go along with this search for excellence up to a point, Cal, but your nit-picking attitude is getting to me. However, that's not the main reason I'm bringing this up."

Cal looked a little surprised and replied, "Okay, Harry. I'm glad you got it off your chest. Now, what's the main reason?"

"Well" said Harry, "this search for excellence by having perfection in our posters and our mailout is slowing down the project. It's going to be even later than the last date I gave you. A project that is perfect in all respects is going to take too long. Can't you see that, Cal? I think you should back off for a while."

Cal's eyes flashed in anger for a brief moment and then softened as his face drifted into a sheepish grin. "Harry, you old son-of-a-gun, you have punctured my balloon. I can't say I'm sorry, though. I didn't realize that pushing up the quality of the work will delay the project. You didn't plan it that way. Go ahead and get the show on the road. I'm not giving up, though, on my search for excellence. If we're going to turn this bank branch around, we've got to give our customers the very best."

CASE 2:
THE PERSONNEL MANAGER BLOWS THE WHISTLE

The Personnel Records Project had a number of minor problems. The six-week delay in the installation of computer furniture was one of them. The personnel manager blew his top. He felt like a wild horse with a burr under his saddle. This event—the latest in a long series of irritations with the Management Information Systems (MIS) Department—spurred him to action. He went over the heads of both Jack and Hilda and complained to the chief executive officer (CEO), who felt obliged to look into the matter and asked Hilda to do something about it. Hilda wanted to be compliant. Since the personnel manager had demanded overtime on the project, she knew she could authorize it, so she called Jack into her office. "Can you speed this project up, Jack? I understand you're going to be six weeks late. That's on top of other delays that we've had with the Personnel Department. Can you and the others work some overtime to make up time on the schedule?"

Jack thought for a moment. Another project manager might have been annoyed by the personnel manager's complaint to higher levels. Jack was not that type. He opened up his project folder and laid the schedule in front of Hilda. "Hildy, look at this activity: "Order the computer furniture." That is the main holdup, and no amount of overtime on our part is going to bring it in any sooner. A bit of overtime after the furniture comes in might pick up a few days, but basically this is something we've got to live with."

"Well," said Hilda, "I see your point, Jack. I wish we could offer something to the Personnel Department. They think it's important to come in close to the original schedule. Besides, we need the goodwill of the personnel manager when it comes to recruiting new programmers. Can't you think of something?"

Jack sat, lost in thought. After a minute, his face beamed, and he said, "I've got it! Why don't we rent some substitute computer furniture and install it on the original schedule. Then, when the nice, new stuff arrives, we can have it replaced. What do you think of that, Hildy?"

"Jack, I think you have something there. What do you think it would cost?"

"Off hand, I would think about $2000. Being as it's furniture instead of services, it's going to be charged to the Personnel Department. Let's see if they want to do it."

The personnel manager felt good about the fast response he got and Jack's positive attitude toward his demands. However, when he realized he would have to trade off $2000 for six weeks of earlier implementation, he had second thoughts. After all, they did have a manual system in operation. Being six weeks late with the new system was not worth that much money. He thanked Jack for the effort and even apologized for going over his head. "I should have dealt with you in the first place" was his final comment. After this comment, Jack felt inclined to do something about the six-week delay. He wasn't sure yet, but maybe the Purchasing Department could get one furniture unit in early, and the rest would follow as scheduled.

CASE 3:
YOU GOT IT, BOSS

Mary-Helen was working hard on her project for the Teachers' Life Insurance policy. She was giving time to some of her other projects too. However, the target date for completion of the insurance policy was slipping out of reach because of unforeseen circumstances. For one thing, the actuaries and the lawyers were having a dispute over rates and wording. In her monthly report, Mary-Helen had forecast a two-month delay in completion of the project. This worried her boss, Bill, because he had heard that the competition was bringing out the same policy. Bill put the pressure on Mary-Helen to get the project caught up. "This project is very, very important," he said. "We've got to get it out on schedule."

As Mary-Helen was already working overtime, she did the only thing she could do. She dropped all her other projects and concentrated on this "very, very important" one. She did not realize it at the time, but she was responding to a rule of thumb for employees: "Whatever interests the boss fascinates the hell out of me." She delivered the project on time, and the boss commended her for it.

A few days later, he came storming into her work area and asked for the report on the Liability Project. Mary-Helen was embarrassed. She had put it aside because the other project seemed more important. She would now devote all her energy to the Liability Project. Too late—the report should have been ready. The state legislature was going to vote on an important bill concerning liability. The lobbyists should have had this report by now. Mary-Helen became a little defensive and said, "But, boss, you told me that this other project was most important, so I gave it my top priority. I did what you wanted me to do, didn't I?"

Her boss gritted his teeth. He felt trapped. He couldn't look Mary-Helen in the eye. He slowly and deliberately said, "When you gave top priority to the Teachers' Insurance Project, I didn't think you had to drop everything else. I can see that you were trying to be compliant when I put the heat on. If I do that again, please let me know the consequences to the other projects as soon as you can."

OTHER PLANNING CONSIDERATIONS

In the Goodwill Project, you can see that too much emphasis on excellence had an adverse impact on the time and cost.

In the Personnel Records Project, too much emphasis on the completion date could have escalated the cost. It would have been nice for Jack to have had an agreed-upon guideline at the beginning of the project. A guideline like this would have sufficed: "In this project, the results (performance) are number one, the cost is number two, and the time is number three. Use this guideline if you need to make tradeoffs when the original targets cannot be met." Then, Jack could have settled the furniture delay problem by himself, because he would have known that cost was preferred over time.

In a multiproject environment such as Mary-Helen's, people need to know the priority of one project over another. This is especially true when resources are strained. In this case, the resource was Mary-Helen herself. Had she known that the Liability Project had more overall value to the company than the Teachers' Insurance Project, she could have governed her actions accordingly. As it was, she did not have priority ratings for her projects, so she did the next best thing and decided for herself on the basis of the limited information available. She merely responded to the pressures of the day. We can now make a statement about this in the form of a principle:

Another Principle for Planning

Anything that is likely to affect the balance of the time, cost, and result targets should have a plan for its control.

Example for a Small Project

Suppose that the Goodwill Project was to be planned in a more formal way. The original plan could have included such clauses as the following:

OTHER PLANNING CONSIDERATIONS 125

> *Tradeoff guidelines:* If the original targets for results, time, and cost cannot be met, tradeoffs should be made as follows: In round 1, completion time can be traded off for results, because it's necessary to get the information soon in order to do the project better in the next round. In round 2, the targeted results would be preferred over the time aspects, meaning that a slightly better result could be traded off for a small delay in the time of completion.
>
> *Close-out guidelines:* The project will be finished when 75 percent of the customers have returned or two rounds have been completed. (Beyond this point, we would have to start a new project. This avoids repeating a promotion endlessly without reconsideration.)

Although such guideline clauses are probably too sophisticated for the Goodwill Project, you can see that the items covered deserve some attention.

Example for a Medium Project

The following items could have been included in the Dynamic Project Plan for Personnel Records Project.

> *Balanced reporting:* The results, time, and cost factors are to be reported together on one project status report. This is to be done weekly by the project manager.
>
> *Tradeoff guidelines:* If it is not possible to meet the original targets, the preferred tradeoffs should favor results over cost over time. (Thus, if the results are in jeopardy, we could increase the cost or take more time.)
>
> *Interface control:*
> 1. If the software development is contracted out, the hardware is to be agreed upon by the designer and the contractor immediately after the pilot test.

> 2. In the event that there is to be a capability to upload o download with the mainframe computer, the designer must specify the file formats before coding begins.
> 3. In case it is desired to link the systems to branch offices and to portable units, the protocols should be specified in the design phase.
>
> *Close-out guidelines:* The project should be considered completed and handed over to the users when the following criteria are met: (1) the operators can enter the data at a rate of 20 names per hour; and (2) all specified functions can be performed by 8 out of 10 operators, each having six hours of training.

I have tried to include in the plan those things that are likely to affect the balance of results, cost, and time. Balanced reporting ensures that the three major targets are considered together. The tradeoff guidelines will save time when the project objectives need to be altered. Interface control is very important in software projects. It is also important when different departments work on different parts of a project. Interface control is sometimes necessary on medium projects and is almost always required on large projects. The close-out guidelines are especially important for developmental software projects. No software is ever perfect, and bugs will inevitably arise at some future date. The original project team may be called upon to make corrections. However, the charges should not go into the old project account, which must be closed off at some point. Management will assign new work orders or new projects to take care of things that happen beyond that point. If the end point of the project is not defined, it will be hard to determine whether or not the project came in within the budget.

Example for Multiple Projects

Although each of Mary-Helen's projects is small, taken together they constitute a medium project. Here are the things that need attention in the Teachers' Insurance Project:

> *Balanced reporting:* The project manager should show the status of all projects together on one sheet. The results, the forecasted completion date, and the estimated cost at completion should be included. Once-a-month reporting would be adequate in this case.
>
> *Tradeoff guidelines:* For this project, time over the overall result. (Early completion is so important that a small reduction in the results could be traded off for a gain in time. A cost tradeoff is not mentioned because there is no cost budget for this project.
>
> *Priority:* This project has priority rating 6 among the department's projects.
>
> *Close-out guidelines:* The project shall be considered completed and belonging to the Sales Department when the following criteria are met: (1) the sales trainer has been briefed; (2) all policy documents are in stock; and (3) camera-ready promotion material has been provided.

I've introduced here the notion that a project has a priority relative to other projects. (Mary-Helen's project is priority 6.) This is important when the people, material, or facilities resources are limited and there are multiple projects. Relative priority will be treated in more detail in a later chapter.

SMALL TO LARGE PROJECTS

The following are things to be considered in the Dynamic Project Plan for medium and large projects:

Balanced reporting is required for all projects. This means that the management gets reports about the results, the time, and the cost in one document at one time. None of these targets can be changed without recourse to the others. (See Chapter 8, Figure 8-2, for an example of balanced reporting.)

A *priority rating* for the project among other projects is required if the resources are fixed. If the project manager can increase the resources to suit the workload, priorities are not required. Also, if an organization is working on only one project, relative priorities are obviously not required.

Tradeoff guidelines are optional for all sizes of projects. One may presume that the targets will be met and that no major tradeoff will be necessary. The big advantage of having tradeoff guidelines for a medium to large project is that a major tradeoff can be started while waiting for a decision.

Interface control is needed for medium to large projects that are multidisciplinary. In large technical projects, this is known as Systems Engineering.

A *training plan* is required only if the success of the project depends on learning new techniques or new technology. Even though training may be done outside the project budget, it is part of the plan for eventual success. Training plans are most likely to be necessary on medium to large projects.

A *correspondence control plan* is needed only on very large projects, such as large defense systems. Such a plan is used mainly to determine who can give information on behalf of the owner or contractor. It is also related to secrecy.

A *manufacturing plan* is found only in some large projects. For example, a new facility may be required to implement the project; that would require a manufacturing plan.

A *quality assurance plan* is often found in large technical projects. Because of the relationship between excellence and quality, one may also find such a plan in some medium projects. (For example, a document may describe how the Quality Assurance Department is to participate in the early stages of a project.)

A *distribution plan* would be required for selling to a new market.

A *close-out plan* is usually attached to medium and large projects. Without it, it is difficult to wind up the project and free the project manager for other work.

This book is concerned chiefly with small to medium projects. When you are planning, you should give some consideration to balanced reporting, priority, tradeoff guidelines, interface control, and close-out. You may need to include some of these items in your Dynamic Project Plan. If they are not relevant, you can skip them, but not before you consider the consequences of not including them.

SUMMARY

A Dynamic Project Plan includes objectives for the results, time, and cost of a project. It also includes plans for controlling all of these factors. However, as I have shown, many things can affect a project and cause distortion of the results. Remember that a project does not go along in the due-process mode, which is how routine operations are managed. Instead, it is organized in detail, it is compressed for time, it has a budget, and it has tight controls.

Situations that can affect normal work cannot be tolerated in project work. You should have plans to offset whatever you think can have a serious impact on your project. When all items discussed in this chapter are considered, you will have many more factors under control than just the basics of schedule, budget, and results.

The biggest impact on projects is made by people. Their personalities affect the results. Did you notice that I have not mentioned a people control plan? Is it possible to control people? The answer is yes and no. People control themselves when they get feedback on the consequences of their actions. Our reporting system can detect changes in the targets. It can forecast the changes that would occur if personality factors dominate the situation. The reporting that comes from having a good project plan has a stabilizing influence on the personality factors. If wackos, psychos, and nit-pickers are affecting your project, you are not alone. These terms often apply to people in management positions who are not getting good feedback on their actions. So what *you* must do is this: Plan, plan, plan—and report, report, report.

QUESTIONS FOR ASSIGNMENT OR DISCUSSION

1. List three factors that can have a negative impact on the success of a project. Identify them from the text of this chapter.
2. When would tradeoff guidelines be of benefit to a project manager?
3. Refer to a small project of your own or one that has been assigned to you. Take the basic project plan, as modeled in

Chapter 2, and expand it to include some of the factors in this chapter.

4. For a medium project of your own or of a member of your group, expand the Dynamic Project Plan with additional factors that need control. Include those that might seriously affect the overall targets.

5. Why does a multiproject environment usually require priority rating of the projects?

CHAPTER
seven

RESOURCES AND MOTIVATION
assignments become commitments

> **Key Idea**
>
> When your project is launched, you need to get firm commitments on resources.

People are an organization's most important resource. But that truism is incomplete. Project managers need more than people's time and talents; they need commitment to schedules. Workers at all levels will commit to a project and thus be motivated to do timely work if they are involved early in the planning process. As Harry's and Jack's experiences (detailed below) attest, commitment from resource people is one of the keys to a successful project.

CASE 1:
DIFFERENCES IN MOTIVATION

Recall that the bank's Goodwill Project was a bit rushed during the mailout period. As it happened, Harry had put two secretarial typists to work on the job. One of these typists, Betty, worked not one minute beyond quitting time, was frequently late, took long breaks, and chatted a lot. The other one, Margaret, worked energetically at her job of typing up special letters. When the project was running behind, she volunteered to work overtime on evenings and weekends without any pay.

During a long drive to another town on business, Harry was running the project through his mind. He thought about the difference in motivation between Betty and Margaret. On regular bank work, they were about the same; but on the project, they were completely different. He did recall that he had consulted with Margaret about how the work was to be done, and they had discussed how she could fit it in with her other work. He had done this before he had given her the assignment. As for Betty, he had simply assigned her to the work. In regular bank work, that procedure was fine. It seemed to Harry, however, that motivation on project work was a different matter, especially when the project work was a departure from people's regular assignments. Harry made a mental note to involve more people next time in the planning of project tasks.

CASE 2:
OFF TO A BAD START

A Dynamic Project Plan was developed at the beginning for the Personnel Records Project. Hilda thought that it was a good idea to get the approval of the personnel manager, so that there would be better acceptance of the final results. Jack took the plan to the personnel manager.

"Why should I sign this?" asked the personnel manager. "You never asked me to sign for any other project work in advance, did you? Besides, when we recruit people for your department, we don't require you to sign off in advance."

Jack went away quietly. The personnel manager had bullied him, and he really didn't know how to counteract it. Besides, the signing off was a new idea. He wasn't sure himself that it was necessary.

Nevertheless, Hilda insisted that the project could not go forward until the personnel manager had signed. So the plan sat on the personnel manager's desk while he went away to a conference. Jack eventually let him know that the project was being delayed week after week by his intransigence. Reluctantly, the personnel manager signed it, but the project had experienced a three-week delay before it even got started.

To make matters even worse, Jack's programmers had taken on other assignments in the intervening time. They were now tied up on very high-profile projects elsewhere. A few weeks ago they could have been doing the Personnel Records Project, but not now. These difficulties notwithstanding, Jack felt that his first obligation was to try to get the project finished on the original schedule. He got out his bar chart schedule and noted that it wasn't just his own commitments that had to be reorganized. The ensuing work by the Purchasing Department also had to be rescheduled. Jack thought, "Those people who hold up approval just aren't aware of the problems they cause."

> **A Principle on Resources**
>
> The availability of resources affects the completion time of the project.

> **A Principle on Motivation**
>
> A personal commitment works better than an assignment from the boss.

APPLICATION TO A SMALL PROJECT

There was no delay in the implementation of the plan for the bank's Goodwill Project. Consequently, there was no need to do any rescheduling and get new commitments. However, Harry needed some people for the project over whom he had no direct authority. He therefore had to depend on getting personal commitments from them for the completion of their tasks. Such arrangements put the onus on the individuals to fulfill their commitments or provide an explanation. As Harry realized, when project work is loaded onto operations, it may require some additional motivational techniques on the part of the project manager. One important motivational technique that Harry could use entails getting the people involved in the planning of the work. Not only is involvement motivating, but it also allows participants to make their own time estimates and thus be committed to them.

APPLICATION TO A MEDIUM PROJECT

On the Personnel Records Project, Jack is the personnel manager, so he is the one who must try to reschedule it. In terms of resources, he may use more people, he may schedule more overtime, or he may contract for additional short-term professional help. Another possibility is to delay other work that is less important. He could also try fast-tracking the tasks—that is, starting a task before its predecessor is finished. Frequently, a task can be started without full information from the preceding task. However, there is some small risk of having to do the work over. Let's suppose that Jack proceeded as follows.

In examining the project schedule (see Figure 7-1), Jack noticed that the task "Define data fields" was scheduled to take two weeks and that he would be doing it. He also would be doing other work. By bringing his designer into the project sooner and having him work in place of Jack on the "Define hardware requirements" task, he could probably get the analysis phase done in one week instead of two, thereby picking up one week. Looking further down the schedule, there didn't seem to be a possibility of saving much time.

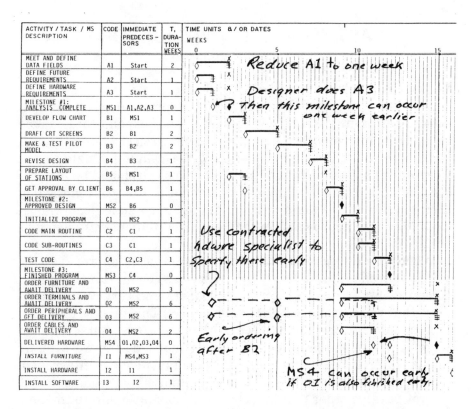

Figure 7-1. Jack's attempt to save time by fast-tracking the tasks.

The tasks were rather short. However, he noticed that the ordering phase stretched out to six weeks because of the time required to get the terminals and peripherals. If he could get these items specified in detail earlier, the purchasing cycle could be started sooner. By contracting to bring in a hardware specialist, the preparation for purchasing could be expedited. This meant that the terminals and peripherals would be ordered after "Draft CRT screens." The designer could be prevailed upon to release the terminal and peripheral information at that point. Jack also realized that he would need a new commitment from the Purchasing Department for them to go along with the new dates. (Of course, Jack did not yet know of forthcoming delays on the computer furniture.) He had now picked up as much as four weeks on the schedule. By using similar techniques, he might pick up still another week later on.

ASSESSING THE NEW SITUATION

Personal commitments to the schedule are very important to your project. There are often delays in getting approval to go ahead with projects, especially when they involve capital expenditures. Some delays run into months. Are the original project estimates still valid? Are you still committed to the same completion date as you were when you submitted the plan? Perhaps you should have made the completion date so many weeks or months after the approval of the plan. If you are faced with an almost impossible deadline because of a late approval, you may be forced to trade off money or results for time.

When your project is approved after a significant approval delay, you are forced to start over in some respects. You must now get firm commitments from the resource managers and service organizations that you need to complete your project. This process may also reoccur later on in your project. Although people make commitments early in the project, they may actually do the work many months later. In the meantime, many factors could have intervened. The future is never quite what we thought it was going to be. Therefore, give other people a chance to commit again to the best they can do on the schedule. In the next chapter, we will see how to do this at proper intervals.

MORE PEOPLE, LESS TIME?

Overtime is the easiest way to increase project resources, since no new skills are required and no startup time is required. If you have 25 percent more overtime, you will have 25 percent more resources. However, sustained high levels of overtime will make your resources less efficient.

If you put more *people* on a task, will it take less time? Yes and no. If the project is a construction job with 5 carpenters and you put on 10, it probably would speed the job up proportionally. If a scientist is doing a research project and another scientist joins in, the project may actually take longer; together, they will consider more possibilities, each of which has to be submitted to validity testing by dichotomous arguments. Another case in which adding more people will not help is if there isn't room or facilities to accommodate them.

Startup time may increase the cost of adding people to a project, because they may not know the specific details of the project. If they are responsible for a three-day task, then startup time needs some consideration. By the time the new people could get up to normal working speed, the task time would be nearly at its scheduled finish. If their time on the task is scheduled for a month or more, startup time will probably not be significant.

Additional resources may be available in the form of *ancillary services* to aid the people you already have. For example, even a "go-fer"—someone who goes for materials—can be helpful. Many professionals and specialists have inadequate support from secretarial services. Often, a lower-skilled person can be assigned to do tasks that the professionals would otherwise have to do. In other words, if professionals and other highly skilled persons are provided *additional support persons,* their specialized output can be increased.

Outside resources from a contracting agency are frequently overlooked as additional project resources. There are often specialists available who are very familiar with the type of work being done for the project. It is true that hiring specialists by the day can be costly, and there may be travel and accommodations expenses as well. But consider this: Contracted persons can be put to work immediately, because they have good skills. Moreover, they don't have to attend meetings and do other administrative work. As a consultant myself, I have found that I can turn out surprisingly large amounts of work in short periods. The clients are amazed. While they are being interrupted for this and that and trotting off to unnecessary meetings, I am sitting quietly in an office and working at 100 percent efficiency. I normally do in a week as much as a regular employee is able to do in two weeks. The point is: Given the right kind of consultant, the cost per day may be high, but the cost per unit of work may be very reasonable.

ALLOCATION OF ACCOUNT NUMBERS

In some organizations, the issuance of a project account number is a signal to start a task and charge the cost to the account. In fact, some departments insist on an account number before starting on a task. A rigid account number system is usually necessary in a large organization to control the use of budgeted project funds, and is certainly necessary on large projects. It is not found so often on medium projects, and it is seldom found on small projects—unless, of course, there are multiple small projects.

When an account number is issued or requested, it is a good time to discuss the cost of doing a task. This is a prime opportunity to get a commitment on the budget for the task.

When a task is done, it's wise to close out the account. Any additional charges to that account would then require the authorization of the project manager. This would guarantee that they were warranted.

WHOSE ESTIMATE IS BEST?

At one time in my career as a manager, I took on a very important new project. The technology was new, and I didn't know how long it would take to do the project. I did my homework, though. By talking to other specialists in the field, I found out that the project would take about one year. However, since we were not first to do it, and since our company was rather small, I thought it would be great if we could do it in nine months. I therefore set out to convince my project leader, John Sennik, to do the main development and design work in nine months. Just before I discussed it with him, however, it occurred to me that he might have his own ideas about time requirements. When I asked him how long it would take, he said he could do it in six months. It seemed impossible at the time, but you can guess the outcome: He did it in six months because it was possible to do it in six months and he had committed himself to do it in six months. True, he worked overtime, he worked weekends, he stopped reading magazines, and he did not linger at meetings. But he met the challenge, and he did a good job of it.

Thereafter, when setting a time for a task, I first asked the people involved how long they thought it would take. Invariably, they gave me tighter estimates that I would dare force upon them as their manager. That's been my experience, and many, many people in my seminars have told me this has happened to them also. The reason that it works is because of the personal commitment. Naturally, we do not take advantage of anyone in this situation. If the persons are green and don't know how to estimate, we urge them to talk to senior people before giving their final estimates to us.

The best estimate is the one to which the involved person has given a personal commitment. Suppose that it's much longer than you think it should be. If you coerce the estimator into a tighter time target, what do you suppose will happen? The actual time will probably come closer to the original estimated time than to your requested time—because the estimator wants to prove that he or she was right. This attitude can work to your advantage, also. Suppose that people set targets that are a little too tight. Will they come crying for more time? No, they will knuckle down and get it done, even if they have to do it on their own time. They like to be right, and it's a win-win situation. This also holds true for the budgeted hours and expenses required to do a task.

COMMITMENT AND MOTIVATION

The best commitment you can get on a task is from the person who will actually be doing the work. Sometimes, however, that person's supervisor is more skilled at estimating. In that case, you should get a personal commitment from the supervisor. For example, if you require the services of a typing pool, you don't necessarily need a personal commitment from the word-processing specialist for a couple of run-of-the-mill reports. The supervisor's commitment will suffice, because he or she has more than one person available to do the job. For specialized work, however, you should get commitments from both the specialist and the supervisor.

Thus, the best level of commitment is actually a joint commitment from the person doing the work and from that person's supervisor. The joint commitment is important, because the supervisor controls the resources. Unless the supervisor is also committed to you, he or she may put the tasked person on other work.

If people are really committed to the work, they should not mind signing a task form (see Chapter 10, Figure 10-5). For now, suffice it to say that written commitments can be given by people who are serious about their commitment. In a large organization with many demands on each person's time, verbal commitments may be hard to keep, but written commitments can be used by tasked people to fend off additional work that would overload them.

SUMMARY

This chapter introduces the *controlling* part of project management. Planning was covered in the previous chapters. Now you are dealing with the future, which is always different from whatever you thought it was going to be. Because the future has changed, you must adjust your plan to accommodate the changes. In the techniques discussed in this chapter, we have dealt with the need to readjust the plan and get new commitments after it has been approved. In the next chapter, we will talk about further adjustments and corrections to the plan.

QUESTIONS FOR ASSIGNMENT OR DISCUSSION

1. Under what circumstances are you likely to have to revise your schedule after the Dynamic Project Plan has been approved?

QUESTIONS FOR ASSIGNMENT OR DISCUSSION 141

2. How is true commitment to a schedule obtained?

3. You are going to make an additional revision to the schedule for the Personnel Records Project. (You can mark over Figure 7-1 in pencil to do this. Disregard Jack's attempt at fast-tracking.) Take the task called "Draft CRT screens" and put two people on it. Assume that it will be done in half the time. Redraw the schedule accordingly up to milestone 2. (It should then be one week earlier.) List two or three factors that have a bearing on your assumption about doubling resources and halving the time.

4. For one of your own small projects or one assigned to you, state what would need attention if there were a significant delay in the approval of its plan.

5. For a medium project of a member of your class group or work group, assume that there would be a one-month delay in getting approval (or whatever delay would be significant). State the effects on the project and what new commitments would be needed.

CHAPTER
eight

REPORTS, ACTIONS, AND SOLUTIONS
you seize control again

> **Key Idea**
>
> You seize control of your project again by tracking differences from the plan, taking corrective actions, getting new commitments, and forecasting the end points of the project.

One test of managerial competence is the ability to learn from experience. Preparing reports at designated project milestones is part of the process of evaluating and learning. By comparing the current status of the project with the original (baseline) plan, a project manager should be able to plan corrective actions, make new forecasts, and keep superiors up to date.

The following cases describe how Harry and Jack were able to deal with this aspect of project management.

CASE 1:
THE BANKER LEARNS FROM EXPERIENCE

The bank's Goodwill Project reached the first milestone and was now ready to go into round 2. Harry made a reasonable assumption that things should go more smoothly because of the team's experience with round 1. He repeated the schedule detail of round 1 and began round 2. Unfortunately, although things didn't get worse, they didn't get much better, either. The team ran into a shortage of paper, as before, and they had costly advertising, as before. Harry was away for much of the project time, and he had assigned the work to his staff. It just so happened that his scheduled vacation came during the crucial period of round 2, but he took it anyway. When he got back, he found that his highly motivated secretary had moved on to a better job in another branch. Not only that, but the boss was meddling in the project again! Cal had directed the staff to include news of improved bank services with the letter that was going out. In other words, the problems had not gone on a holiday.

Things weren't going great with his Goodwill Project, but it would get finished. After his vacation, Harry was seeing the world through rose-colored glasses, and everything looked good. One evening, he came across an article on project management that set him to thinking about his own project. Thought Harry: "It seems to me that the essence of project management is to plan, and then replan when things have changed. Everything changes. The future is never the way I think it's going to be. Still, I can't be changing the plan every day. What makes sense is to review the total project plan at a major milestone. I guess I missed out on the opportunity to do that at the end of round 1. Why do we need special reviews for a project? We don't do it in our routine work. A short weekly or monthly meeting is all that is needed to keep the routine work running smoothly. We make an annual business plan and maybe revise it once during the year. What I'm finding out is that project work is different from operations. We are trying to squeeze something special into our routine operations. We run into situations that are different, and we have no experience or procedures for them. It seems to be a learning situation. Yes, that's it! We learn as we go. If we don't replan our project at a milestone, we're not learning from our experience. Well, if I ever get to be in charge of projects at headquarters, I'll know what to do."

CASE 2: THE CEO GETS WHAT HE ASKS FOR

After the complaint by the personnel manager about the delay in the Personnel Records Project (see Chapter 7), the CEO (Chief Executive Officer) thought he should be informed about what was going on with all projects. He reasoned: "If there was a complaint on one project, there were probably two others in trouble, too. My managers are reluctant to complain, because they want to keep good relations with the other departments. Well, whatever it is, I want to know what's going on." The CEO picked up his dictating machine and sent a directive to his department managers: "When you are in charge of a project that affects the operation of another department, inform me regularly of its status. Please send me weekly status reports of any such project."

When Hilda got the letter, she knew exactly what to do. Jack was already sending her a weekly written report. She would just send copies to the CEO of those projects that affected other departments. She was glad for the opportunity, because she felt that her department was understaffed. Some of these reports would lead to discussions of how much new staff would be required to do better.

Jack did his weekly reports on his word processor. They occupied about three pages. He dealt with the schedule progress on the first page. On the next page, he dealt with the expenses to date versus the budget. Most of the third page was a list of technical problems and what the team was doing to solve them.

When the CEO received a copy of the first report, he felt a bit frustrated. He couldn't figure out the report, but he put it in a reference file. He also got reports from other departments, but they were all different. The CEO's thoughts went like this: "I've got the reports I asked for, and if I need the information, it's in my file. Frankly, I wish they would get together and use a common reporting style. The truth is that I don't know what a good project status report would look like. For one thing, it should be considerate of my time, so that I can get the key points right away. I don't have a lot of time to read and study these things. I want summaries. I'll table this for discussion at our next monthly meeting."

Principles for Reports and Actions

1. After comparing project status with the baseline plan, you should take corrective action.
2. You seize control again by getting new commitments.
3. Senior management needs a summary report that includes the forecasted end points of the project.

APPLICATION TO A SMALL PROJECT

The bank's Goodwill Project is an example of a small project. Harry and Cal, as managers, do not need weekly reports. They are close to the action and will not benefit much from the formality of weekly reports. However, as you can see, as the months pass, both the resources and the objectives are likely to change. They can change significantly when a project runs for more than three months.

Thus, it would be helpful to replan the Goodwill Project at the end of round 1. Let's call this a *milestone review*. At this point, Harry would review the past progress and use the experience gained to replan the remaining part of the project. Harry could do this on his own. There is no need to resubmit a new plan to Cal unless there are significant changes in the time, cost, or result targets. In this case, the changes are not significant to the bank's overall operations. (Small projects with low impact on routine operations will eventually get done without project management, but they will likely be late. If you have many small projects, you may be short of time, especially if you have operations work as well. Even a small project on a tight schedule can divert you from important operations work.)

Milestone reviews are useful for projects that may be affected by routine operations. For example, if Harry's Goodwill Project worked so well at that branch that headquarters adopted it for deployment to many other branches, the situation would be different. The other branches would face different futures, and they would not necessarily work with the same enthusiasm as a branch that had originated its own project. Milestone reports from each branch would be good for headquarters, to see whether the project was under control. They should get the forecasted completion date (FCD) and the (cost) estimate at completion (EAC). Figure 8-1 is an example of a summary milestone report, that was used to tie projects in with an organization's existing system of management by objectives (MBO).

APPLICATION TO A MEDIUM PROJECT

For reports and actions on the Personnel Records Project, Jack should hold brief, weekly progress meetings with his team. The team should include the personnel manager and the purchasing manager or their delegates. The agenda would include the following topics:

MBO OBJECTIVES AND PROJECTS	RESULTS EXPECTED		FORECASTS OR ACTUALS		Date of report: Jan. 1 Schedules, Milestones, Forecasts							
	Milestone Date	Budget $1000's	FCD	EAC	Dec	Jan	Feb	Mar	Apr	May	Jun	
PROJECTS TO IMPROVE QUALITY Q								◆				
Q1: New Procedure	Dec 15	--	Jan 1	--		▽ ⚑						
Q2: Competitive Evaluation	Mar 1	5	Apr 1	6				⚑	▽			
PROJECTS TO REDUCE ERRORS E												
E1: Train Operators	Feb 1	1	Feb 1	1			▽⚑					

Figure 8-1. A summary milestone report for managers using MBO.

> **Agenda for a Project Progress Meeting**
>
> 1. What have we accomplished since the last meeting?
> 2. What should we start on next?
> 3. What problems need action?
> 4. Who will take action, and by when?

Jack should take the information gathered at each meeting and compare project status with his plan. To take action, he may have to do a few "what if's" on the schedule. He can make trial plans involving increasing resources, fast-tracking, and the like. He may even have to recalculate the completion date of the project. At the same time, he should recalculate the final cost. If a milestone has occurred between meetings, he can assess his committed cost versus the budget for the milestone. Jack's final summary report to Hilda should include an FCD and an EAC. He should also accompany this information with a brief report of the forecasted final results, plus any changes to the scope of the work. An example of such a project status report is provided in Figure 8-2. This one-page summary report is also suitable for submitting to the CEO. For passing upward in management, the information can be reduced by highlighting the EAC and FCD for the project.

The project status report in Figure 8-2 is a summary of the progress analyses of schedule, cost, and results. The details of these analyses are developed in the rest of this chapter.

THE CONCEPT OF A BASELINE PLAN

When you have your project plans approved, you have approval of the start and finish dates. This may require some adjustment as you launch the project and get new commitments from the resource managers. Shortly after approval, you should produce a feasible schedule, which can be designated the *baseline schedule*. All future progress will be measured against this approved baseline. If you later revise the plan at a milestone and get approval of a new finish

PROJECT STATUS REPORT

COMPANY CONFIDENTIAL: YES ☐ NO ☒
PROJECT MANAGER __Jack Daniels__

PROJECT TITLE __PERSONNEL RECORDS__
ACCOUNT NO. _____
DATE OF ISSUE __3/14/88__ APPROVED BY __H. Brubaker__

SCHEDULE

PHASE	MM-DD-YY 0 1 2 3 4 5 6 7 8 TODAY = 3/14/88 9 10 11 12 13 14 15 16 17 18 19 20 21 22 23 24 WEEKS FROM START	Original Completion	Current Approved Completion	Forecast Completion Date (FCD) Or Actual
ANALYZE NEEDS		1/15/88		1/15/88
DESIGN SYSTEM		3/4/88		3/4/88
CODE PROGRAM		3/25/88		3/25/88
ORDER HARDWARE		4/15/88		5/30/88
INSTALL SYSTEM		5/1/88		7/1/88
DEBUG		5/23/88		7/20/88
CLOSE		6/6/88		8/3/88

SCHEDULE NOTES: [1] Six-week delay in obtaining computer furniture

PREVIOUS UPDATE __2/1/88__
"TODAY" = DATE OF CLOSE OFF __3/14/88__ (DASHED VERTICAL LINE)
NEXT UPDATE __4/1/88__

COST NOTES: [2] Anticipated extra time and expense for furniture buyer

COST

PHASE	Original Budget	Current Approved Budget	Unapproved Additions	(EAC) Estimate at Completion
ANALYZE NEEDS	3500			3500
DESIGN SYSTEM	5900			5900
CODE PROGRAM	3500			3500
ORDER HARDWARE	14600		6000 [2]	20600
INSTALL SYSTEM	2400			2400
DEBUG	2200			2200
CLOSE	5500			5500
TOTAL	37600			43600

$ UNITS IN 1000's

RESULTS

ORIGINAL SCOPE: __As in the Dynamic Project Plan__   PROGRESS INDEX FOR PROFESSIONAL SERVICES _____
SCOPE AT LAST REPORT: __Same__
CHANGES SINCE LAST REPORT: __None__   POTENTIAL PROBLEMS NOT INCLUDED IN FCD OR EAC _____

LEGEND: DATE CODE: MM-DD-YY   NO CHANGE: NC   NOT APPLICABLE: NA   Changed Forecast: ▼   Actual Date: ▽   Estimate at Completion: EAC   Forecast Completion Date: FCD   Total Completed to Date: TCD

Figure 8-2. A project status report.

date, you will then have a new baseline schedule. It makes no sense to continue with a baseline schedule that shows months and months of delay for reasons beyond our control. It only makes the whole project team appear bad, and it probably will get worse before it gets better. However, when the plan is retargeted to a new baseline schedule, the team has a chance of winning again. Motivation and morale will be much better.

We could extend the concept of the baseline schedule to a baseline results (or technical) plan and a baseline budget. This would be more suitable for large projects than for small to medium projects.

SCHEDULE PROGRESS

You should review the schedule at weekly or monthly meetings. Try to fit it into your current system of reporting. You should take care not to hold too many progress meetings. A project that is in the development phase would not usually require weekly meetings for review of the schedule. However, it may require weekly problem-solving meetings. Usually, when a project reaches the finishing phases, there is a lot of action because the deadline is approaching. You might then go from monthly to weekly schedule reviews.

In projects such as long-term research, quarterly updates of the schedule are adequate. Because most organizations are tied to monthly reporting, one might end up with a quarterly report repeated three times. Keep in mind that a schedule update involves some calculations, analysis, and new commitments. The effort has to be proportional to the results we can see. Basically, if you have about ten updates during the project, there will be enough corrective action to keep it in control. Some projects, such as a maintenance shutdown, a move to a new facility, or a sales conference, could benefit from daily updates of the schedule.

The result of a review of the schedule should be a forecast. You should determine when each altered task will likely be completed and calculate when the overall project will be completed—the forecasted completion date (FCD). An example of a planning schedule that has been updated to show schedule progress is shown in Figure 8-3. The actual starting dates and forecasted finishing dates are indicated by filled and open triangle markers. Note, also, the *now*

152 REPORTS, ACTIONS, AND SOLUTIONS

"TODAY" reports use ▼ for completed changed date and ▽ for changed forecasted date

ACTIVITY / TASK	CODE	IMMEDIATE PREDECES- SORS	T DURA- TION	TIME UNITS &/ OR DATES : WEEKS
DESIGN QUESTIONNAIRE	A	St.	3.5	TODAY FCD for A — 1 2 3 4 5 6 7 8 9 10
CONDUCT SURVEY	B	A,D	2	
ANALYZE & REPORT	C	B,E	1	
OBTAIN RESPONDENTS	D	St.	4.5	
WEIGHT RESPONDENTS	E	D	4	

A started ½ week late and is forecasted to finish ½ week late.

Figure 8-3. A periodic report on schedule progress.

and *today* line, which is a vertical line at a given date. The form in Figure 8-3 is an easy way of periodic reporting. The original schedule is simply marked up in pencil and copied for the persons involved. In doing the update, you must get new commitments for any task affecting the completion of the project.

BUDGET PROGRESS

In your project plan, you develop budgets for each milestone. At a milestone, you must take the expenditures to date plus accruals and estimate the committed money. Only then can you make a reasonable judgment of how the project is doing financially.

Much of the financial data, such as hours charged to a project, is accumulated on a weekly basis. You can have a weekly budget and a record of the weekly expense. This is fairly useful for calculating the person-hours worked on a project, because it is close in timing to the payroll disbursements. However, weekly periodic reporting is not so useful for calculating costs of purchased goods and services because of delays in payments. In contracted work, there are often holdbacks. If a project has a serious delay, and you total up the disbursements, you will appear to be underspent compared to your budget. You may therefore think you are doing well, but the bad news will come sometime after the project is closed off. This is a common experience, and you should try to avoid this pitfall. You should realize that for small to medium projects, you can make a

BUDGET PROGRESS

judgment at a milestone only when the budget for the milestone can be compared with the committed money for the work done. Figure 8-4 shows a budget report that has been manually altered to show the actuals to date. (Note that the duration can be different from the person-weeks budget because more than one person may be involved.) To make it easy for yourself to report, leave blank columns next to your original budget data when you prepare the budget.

If the date of the report coincides with a true milestone, you can make a good judgment on the budget progress and use it for the project status report (Figure 8-2). Although this report is periodical, the EAC can be estimated at a true milestone. Between milestones, you may make minor adjustments to the EAC, but the values are most meaningful when a milestone has occurred.

ACTIVITY NAME	DURATION IN WEEKS	PERSON-WEEKS		EXPENSE $	
		BUDGET	ACTUAL	BUDGET	ACTUAL
Milestone: Start	0	–		–	
Mail Letters	1	2	3	1000	1200
Place Advertisement	1	.5	.5	200	400
Telephone Customers	3	1	1	100	50
Display Posters	1	1	1	100	95
Address Clubs	4	1	.5	100	50
Train or Move Mary	1	.5	.5	0	0
Train Other Tellers	1	1	0	0	0
Identify Return Accounts	1	1	0	0	0
Milestone: Completed Round	0	–		–	
[Subtotal is Milestone Budget]		[8]	[6.5]	[1500]	[1795]
Repeat Round of Promotion	4	8	6	1500	0
Milestone: End	0	–		–	
[Total is Project Budget]		[16]	[6.5]	[3000]	[1795]

Figure 8-4. A budget and actuals report.

RESULTS PROGRESS

This is the most difficult aspect to report on, and it is often neglected. As explained in Chapter 3, there are practical ways for showing progress on results. The emphasis is on what the future results will be.

Early in a project, you can use a *narrative forecast*. Here are some sample statements for a research project: "We have completed the pilot experiment and the data have been analyzed. Based on this, our laboratory test method should be able to measure the impurity content to an accuracy of plus or minus 5 percent" or "We will meet standard tests (meet government standards, get agency approvals) for the project results."

As mentioned in Chapter 2 you can use a *parameter range forecast* when you have quantitative parameter measures. (There are no suitable parameters for the projects used as examples in this book.) For some kinds of nontechnical projects, you could look at quantitative measures such as the number of sales expected, the quality level, the impurity level, or the error rate.

BALANCED REPORTING

In the Personnel Records Project, you may recall that the personnel manager complained about the project being late. The chief executive officer acted only on the information regarding time, whereas the final solution involved a time and cost relationship. This is an example of unbalanced reporting and resulting unbalanced action. In order to get balanced actions, you must have balanced reporting. This means that you should report on time, cost, and results simultaneously and in the same document, as was shown in Figure 8-2. Decision makers can look at all three aspects at the same time. Hopefully, they will see that if one aspect is altered, the others must be adjusted accordingly.

Another aspect of balanced reporting is that reports should direct attention to the right things. Senior management does not need to be encumbered with the details of a project. In fact, it's a good idea not to report on nonessential details, so that management doesn't waste your time by nit-picking on details. The details can be made available if they need them. Senior management only needs to know the three-point prediction: FCD, EAC, and final results.

In most organizations, a number of projects must be reported on to the CEO. A summary report makes a lot of sense. Since alterations to one project may take resources from another, it's important that they be reported together. (This process is covered in Chapter 12.)

MAJOR AND MINOR TRADEOFFS

A tradeoff is defined as major when it requires approval. For example, if you need to make up time on the project by hiring additional people or by having the current staff work substantial overtime, you may require approval from your management, owner, or client. This is a major tradeoff. Typically, more than a 10 percent increase in cost requires reapproval of funds. Another example would be adding to the scope of a project, which can also add significant time. The original plan approver should approve such changes. As mentioned in Chapter 6, it's a good idea to have major tradeoff guidelines discussed at the time of the first plan approval.

You must also watch for minor tradeoffs—those that are decided on by the person doing the task. For example, if an artist or draftsperson joins two surfaces with a smooth line, it's a minor decision, but it might have substantial impact on appearance and cost. If a technical person specifies the next higher quality component once in a while, it wouldn't make much difference. But a perfectionist who tends to make everything better than needed can seriously affect the cost and time aspects of the project. How can you control this? The answer is that you must have some control over the heart and mind of the person doing the work. This can be accomplished by getting a commitment on the three end points of every task: the completion time, the cost of doing the task, and the results to be obtained. Even given that, you may sense that you are going to get a Cadillac when you have actually specified a Volkswagen. Your tasked person needs some guidance on what is best for your project. On one project, a Volkswagen-type job will be more than adequate; on another one, you must have the Cadillac version.

Unless this is discussed and agreed upon at the beginning, you will most likely get what the tasked person believes in. Thus, you must get agreement on the belief system. The people who are doing the tasks should be encouraged to work at the quality level that is best for your project. You should ensure that they are rewarded for performing at the necessary quality level.

MILESTONE DECISION REVIEWS

Some milestones are good points for revising the schedule. Budget milestones might be significant only toward the end of the project. There should also be milestones at which you check on the results. In small to medium projects, you put in whatever milestones you can and select a few for complete reviews of the project. I call these *decision reviews*. The outcome of such a review may result in major changes to the project direction. In contrast, the regular weekly or monthly meetings are intended to solve problems with the current targets, but not to change the targets themselves.

At a milestone decision review, the outcome should be one of four decisions:

Possible Decisions at a Major Milestone

1. Keep the same targets for P, T, and C.
2. Set new targets for P, T, and C and get approval.
3. Go back and revise the work until you can make a decision.
4. Terminate the project.

The third type of decision means going back and doing something over again. In engineering, this is known as a *design iteration*. If you wish to know more about this, you will find it in my book *Planning and Creating Successful Engineered Designs* (Advanced Professional Development Institute, Los Angeles, 1986.) Another reference is a book on design by Dr. Gerald Nadler of the University of Southern California, *The Planning and Design Approach* (Wiley, 1981).

COPING WITH UNCERTAINTY

Some activities or tasks in a project can have very uncertain durations. For example, the duration of original research is somewhat indeterminate, although it would not be done if completion were not expected in the foreseeable future. This is true of mission-oriented research. The time estimate may be something like "between six months and two years." Another highly uncertain activity that is sometimes necessary in small to medium projects is approval by government agencies. For example, pharmaceutical companies must perform elaborate tests before a government agency will approve their products. If such uncertainty happens to be part of your project, you can't say when your project is going to be completed until after you get the approval.

There is a way to cope with this kind of uncertainty; it is based upon statistics:

1. You estimate the *most likely time* to complete the task in the normal course of events—say, six months.
2. You estimate the *optimistic time* to do it; that is, there is 1 chance in 1000 that it would be as early as, say, four months.
3. You estimate the *pessimistic time;* that is, there is 1 chance in 1000 that it would be as late as, say, nine months.

Thus, you end up with three time estimates instead of one, which is a problem, because all our schedule calculations involve working with just one time estimate. The three estimates can be converted to an equivalent time by a formula, but you need not worry about it, because the formula approach has no applicability to small or medium projects. What is important about the estimates is the *range*. You now have data to show that the necessary time lies between four months and nine months. What can you do about it? You can take some *offsetting actions* that will improve your chances of coming in earlier rather than later:

> **Offsetting Actions to Cope with Uncertainty**
>
> 1. Start sooner on the activity, even if the prior tasks are not completed. There is some risk that part of the work will be wasted, but there may also be a gain in time.
> 2. Put more resources on the activity, such as working overtime or adding more people. Spend your money where it counts.
> 3. Save time on preceding or following activities. That's where you may put the extra resources.

For medium to large projects, there are a few other things you can do. If you wish to know more about this, see my *Project Management Course Manual,* published by the Advanced Professional Development Institute of Los Angeles. The Institute also provides other learning materials on project management, including an album of cassette tape recordings of my three-day seminar on project management.

RESERVES OF MONEY AND TIME

It is not unusual to have additional money available in the budget, such as a *contingency fund*. This is certainly true for capital projects, but the idea can be applied to any project. There will be unforeseen costs, such as unscheduled overtime, unplanned travel, rentals to replace broken equipment, and so on. Also, there will be some errors to be corrected. Contingency funds usually run 5 to 10 percent of the total; that is, the project is allowed to run over the budget by this amount without additional approval. Contingency funds have a curious way of being fully spent before the project is over. Because of this tendency, there should be some management approval before these funds are used up. After all, not everything costs more. Some items end up costing less than planned, so we get gains that offset losses. Although all expenditures from a contingency fund should be justified, the contingency money should be available in case it is needed. The project should not get stalled because of the lack of a few dollars.

What about contingency time? We don't have a formal way of allowing for this, but we do have a language that covers it. One of the terms used is a "fudged estimate" of the duration. The catch is that all project team members add a bit of extra time to their tasks, the project may never get approved, because it would take too long or cost too much.

I have observed that since most managers come from the ranks, they know all about fudging and doctoring time estimates. They will be suspicious of any time estimate that looks too long, and they will put pressure on to have it reduced. This is not a good relationship. Honesty and forthrightness are better for the project. Your team members will give more accurate estimates on time duration if they are not severely criticized when they don't meet their targets. You will win on some and lose on others. Time gained by one team member might be useful to another. That's teamwork.

In some organizations, extra time—say, two weeks—is added to every project. Unfortunately, this puts the calculations for float in error. Even critical tasks seem to have two weeks of float, so no one feels any urgency. The two weeks is invariably used up, and then some. There is a better way, however. What I have suggested to many project managers is that they put in a task that they control themselves. For example, you may put in two weeks to get out the final report. You know that, in a pinch, you could do a temporary report in two days, thereby giving you an eight-day time cushion. The calculations on the critical path are then meaningful, and no one is going around with a false sense of time security. You should do this with your manager's knowledge, and you should try to finish early on some projects to show that the time cushion is for unforeseen events, not for neglect in monitoring the project.

ADDITIONAL CONTROL POINTS

For medium projects that involve the work of other departments, you can have additional control points. When subschedules and sub-budgets are developed and managed by department managers, there are additional control points. You will have the commitment of the department managers to their subschedules, thus pushing the control level down closer to the action.

EARNED VALUE REPORTING

Earned value reporting is a system of reporting that is currently making headway on large projects, particularly those for defense systems. It is also known as C/SCSC (Cost/Schedule Control Systems Criteria), or C-Spec. Medium projects often get involved in this when they are parts of large projects. Much of the software that you can purchase includes optional earned value reporting. You can use it if you need it.

In earned value reporting, the schedule variance is shown in dollars instead of time units. In other words, you may have a statement such as: "The budgeted cost for work scheduled (BCWS) was $35,000, and the budgeted cost for work performed (BCWP) was only $30,000." This means that you are $5,000 behind in the work scheduled. In addition, there is a figure for the actual cost of work performed (ACWP). If this is compared with the BCWP, you have the true cost variance. This is exactly what you do at a milestone, anyway. However, on a very large project, hundreds of tasks are completed every week. An artificial milestone is created, and the data can be meaningful. However, in itself, this method is not useful for monitoring small to medium projects. At most, you may be required to submit data on the percentage completion of each task to provide data for higher-level reporting on the C-Spec.

SUMMARY

The first requirement for the control part of project management is to have an approved plan. In your Dynamic Project Plan, you included a description of how you were going to control it. Now you can implement the control portions.

For schedule control, you have periodic (weekly or monthly) meetings and end up with a forecasted completion date (FCD).

For budget control, you compare the committed costs with the budget at milestones. You can then predict the estimate at completion (EAC).

For results progress, you use a narrative forecast or a parameter range forecast. Control is exercised through decision reviews and control of the tradeoffs.

The actions you take are very important. You can reschedule activities. You can shift resources from one part of the project to another. You can schedule overtime or hire additional people. You can also make tradeoffs. For example, if you are running behind in time or over on cost, you can offset it by producing a lesser result at the end. Tradeoffs are a control tool; they involve the art of compromise without compromising overall project goals. You do the best you can in the situation in which you find yourself.

If the accumulation of tradeoffs gets to be serious, you should retarget your plan at one of the milestones and get it reapproved. That changes the baseline. When you revise your schedule or budget, you must get new commitments from the members of the project team, so that they are committed to the new forecast. You have seized control once again, just as you exercised control by obtaining commitments in the beginning. So, to maintain control of a project that is running away from you, grab hold of it and seize control; then let it run for awhile and seize control again.

QUESTIONS FOR ASSIGNMENT OR DISCUSSION

1. For the bank's Goodwill Project, Case 1, prepare a statement of about 10 words that you could send to Harry in a telegram. Tell him what he should have done at the end of round 1 of his bank project. (Refer to the text in this chapter.)
2. For the Personnel Records Project, Case 2, compose a directive from the CEO to all department managers, requiring that they report effectively and compactly on their projects. About 100 words should do it.
3. Name three differences between managing projects and managing routine operations.

4. For a small project of your own, or one assigned to you, prepare a detailed statement of about 200 words on how you would control the time, the cost, and the results.

5. For a medium project of someone in your class or work group, prepare a detailed plan of about 500 words on how you would control and report on the time, cost, and results.

CHAPTER
nine

MOTIVATION
keeping the team enthusiastic throughout the project

> **Key Idea**
>
> Recognition of their accomplishments in solving challenging problems will motivate the team to succeed.

A good project plan will be more effective if the project team feels motivated to carry it out.

Motivation of the project team is more difficult for the project manager when he or she must depend on subordinates of other managers. Without formal authority, the project manager must depend on voluntary teamwork to get the work done. This chapter will show you how to use motivators that work well with nonsubordinates.

In the following cases, you will see that some actions by managers can reduce the team effort on a project. In some cases, the actions may have a serious negative impact on the project's progress.

CASE 1:
A CRITICAL ATTITUDE DID NOT RECHARGE THE BATTERIES

The bank's Goodwill Project had completed round 1, and the results were being assessed. The results were neither good nor bad. Some customers had come back and a few more were expected. It would take a bit more time.

Cal had asked Harry to come into his office to go over the project with him. Cal asked, "How come the mailout and the advertisement in the newspaper were not synchronized? Maybe that caused a problem. Besides, the letters were a bit late getting out." Cal also asked Harry quite a few questions about what else had gone wrong with the project. Cal was unaware that his slightly raised voice was being heard in other parts of the bank's general office. Betty, for example, was working just outside his office, and she got the impression that Cal wasn't too pleased with the way the project team had done the project. When Harry finally came out of Cal's office, he probably didn't notice that everyone had their eyes glued to their work. No one looked up at him. Nobody felt good.

Nevertheless, it had been decided to go ahead with round 2, and Harry set about delegating the tasks to various people in the office. A week later, when Harry was running the project through in his mind, he distinctly felt that the team members did not have the original enthusiasm they had when they started the project. Betty had not volunteered any more overtime. Margaret had taken even longer lunch breaks than before and seemed to have more occasions for sick leave. The project was moving along, but with no spark of life.

CASE 2:
MARVIN SCREWS UP THE PROJECT

The Personnel Records Project had reached the computer coding stage. One of the smart young programmers, Marvin, liked the challenge of writing computer code for a new program. He worked enthusiastically with line after line of code and ran them through his mind as he imagined them working on the computer. After a week and a half of coding, he had something he could run on a real computer, and it seemed quite good. As a whole, the program worked well, but there was an additional feature that the Personnel Department had wanted. Unfortunately, this was the feature which had caused an unusual bug to occur. Just as writers are blind to their own compositional errors and typists are blind to their own typos, so are programmers frequently blind to their own coding errors.

After a couple of days of debugging, Marvin was asked by Jack, his manager, how things were going. He let it slip that he had a bug in the coding. He said he had already spent two additional days on it, and he didn't know just how much longer it would take. He now thought that his original time estimate needed to be increased by a week. Jack did not take this well. He remarked that a bug in the program was something he didn't need right now. Jack was determined to get the coding finished. He even went to the trouble of going over some of the code with Marvin. Jack indicated that, in his opinion, the feature had been introduced in the wrong way in the first place. He tilted his head in a snobbish fashion and gave a little puff of disgust. He mumbled something about not knowing how they could explain this one, and then he walked away. That was on Friday at 4:30 P.M., and as it was quitting time, Marvin left. Jack was busy somewhere else, or he might have wondered why Marvin took off so close to quitting time. Marvin usually spent a couple of hours doing additional programming because he enjoyed doing it.

That was not all. Marvin was gone for the first three days of the next week. When he came back, he gave no explanation for his absence. He also refused to work overtime to get the project back on track. Jack got the impression that Marvin was looking for another job. This was not unusual for new computer programmers, as they frequently changed jobs. Also, Jack was aware that one of the large corporate giants in the area was aggressively looking for new computer programmers.

Unfortunately, nobody asked Marvin what was on his mind. What Marvin was thinking was this: "I should have been praised for finding that bug when I did, rather than not finding it until the program was installed. Everybody gets a bug sometimes in their programs. Not everybody discovers it. I did, and I think I should have been praised for it. Instead of that, Jack left with his nose in the air, as if he knew how to program so well that he wouldn't have had any programming bugs if he had done the coding himself."

Thus, Marvin was a bit miffed. Perhaps he got over it soon and got on with the job. After all, he generally enjoyed finding out the cause of a bug in a program; he took it as a challenge. He usually worked voluntarily in the evenings and on weekends to fix a bug, if only to satisfy himself. So the time lost by Marvin on this project was related to Jack's attitude. Jack's reaction could have been better.

Principles of Maintaining Motivation

1. Praise is more effective than criticism.
2. Praise from peers has special merit.
3. The work itself motivates the team when problems are resolved quickly.
4. Knowledge of the overall benefits of a project will help generate enthusiasm.

APPLICATION TO A SMALL PROJECT

For the bank's Goodwill Project, suppose that Cal, Harry, and the project team had met for a complete milestone review at the end of round 1. They would have discussed the problems they had encountered, with a view to overcoming possible problems in round 2. They would have looked upon the results as something accomplished despite the difficulties faced. In other words, the results would have been assessed in relation to the time taken and the resources used.

Cal would have done well to take a back seat and let Harry lead such a meeting. Cal probably would have seen that most of the problems encountered were due to inexperience. On reflection, he might have recognized that some delays were due to his meddling as well. Actually, the results were positive. Not every promotion works well. Sometimes mistakes are made, and customers may be insulted by statements with unintended double meanings. The whole project could have been a flop.

There are many things that Cal could have done to keep the enthusiasm of the team at a high level. At the end of the review meeting, he could have said something like, "The good news I am hearing is that we are starting to get our customers back. I thank you all for your effort and I'm looking forward to an even more successful round two." Then, back in his office, he could have dictated a memo for Harry's records about what Harry had accomplished for a first-time project. Also, he could have taken time to thank Betty openly, within the hearing of other people, for the extra effort she had put into the project. Later, upon the return of one of their valued customers, Cal could have called across the office to Harry and said, "Look here, Harry, I just got a letter from one of our major former clients. It looks like they are coming back with us very soon. That's good news. Thanks a lot."

One of the consequences of a proper review at the end of round 1 would have been retargeting the project for round 2. Taking their experience into account, the team could have redeveloped realistic time and budget targets on which everyone could win. And winning itself is something that sustains motivation.

The lesson to be learned here is that project management reporting should focus on what was accomplished, not on the measurements of lateness or cost overruns.

APPLICATION TO A MEDIUM PROJECT

Let's give Jack a chance to go back to the point where Marvin informed him of the time-delaying bug he had found. Finding a bug is a design iteration, and it is natural to the process of creating something new. Jack should take the time to acknowledge to Marvin that finding a problem is never good news, but it's better to have it early than late. Research has shown that the cost of a correction in coding is only one-tenth of the cost of correction after installation. Why not rejoice? Jack could say something like, "We're lucky that you found the bug when you did, Marvin. Thank you very much. Let me know if I can be of help." Jack should take the attitude that Marvin is trying to do his best. He should give Marvin a few days to see what he can do to correct the problem. Chances are that Marvin will rise to the challenge and give it all he's got.

Jack should keep in mind that he is Marvin's technical peer. Therefore, he must be especially careful when criticizing Marvin. Criticism from a technical or business peer can sometimes be devastating. It undermines the confidence of the person doing the work. It is much more severe than criticism from someone who doesn't really understand the work. At the same time, if Jack is able to recognize any technical successes by Marvin, his praise will be very motivating. It will give Marvin assurance that, in the view of his colleagues, he can really cut the mustard. Jack might take the opportunity to say something like, "You know, Marvin, I like the way you fixed that up. It took fewer lines of code than I thought it would. We can probably use that idea on another program." Peer praise can be very powerful medicine.

PRAISE AS A MOTIVATOR

You have probably heard of positive and negative reinforcement—based on a theory developed by B. F. Skinner. We shall see that it has a very close relationship to sustaining motivation in a project team.

Skinner's research had three main findings, which I am going to apply to the most difficult area of project management—that is, the motivation of people who work for other managers.

PRAISE AS A MOTIVATOR

First, positive reinforcement is more effective than negative reinforcement. What this means in dealing with people who work for other bosses (nonsubordinates) is that praise is more effective than criticism.

With project management, we set up challenging time and cost targets and then we measure our progress against them. The reporting system points out differences. It is natural that busy managers focus on the late activities and on the cost overruns. However, this tends to emphasize the negative aspects of project progress. Unfortunately, some people take a delight in doing this. Without project management, they would not have such precise measurement and therefore would have less opportunity to criticize. With good project management planning, we set up a number of tasks and develop a tight schedule and a tight budget. Therefore, we are likely to create some problems that might not otherwise be noticed. Consequently, we must turn the reporting system around so that people focus on the positive aspects of achievement, which are being measured at the same time as the negative aspects.

Praise is more possible when people succeed in meeting their time and cost targets. It is essential that they meet these targets so that praise can be forthcoming. They try their hardest when they have made a commitment. Therefore, you should seek to get commitments from the people involved in the project, even if the time targets or cost targets are somewhat higher than you desired in the first place. What they believe in is what you will get.

In my many years of practice, I have noticed that when people are asked to set their own targets and be committed to them, they usually set tighter targets than I would dare set for them. Many other managers have confirmed this experience. Commitment works in favor of the project manager in many ways. Therefore, the time and cost targets for projects should be those which people believe in, are committed to, and are possible. Then you will be able to give praise for a job well done.

Keep in mind that there are three elements of a task to reckon with. You can give praise for being on time, for staying within the budget, and for achieving the right results. You can also acknowledge that the right results were obtained despite unforeseen difficulties in scheduling and budgeting. Always give credit for effort. Most of the minor failures on task accomplishments are due to the failures of other persons, and you should acknowledge this. Do everything to help all project people reach their commitments on a task. Then, when you give them praise, they will feel good and you will feel good.

Second, both positive and negative reinforcement are needed. What Skinner found through his research on programmed learning exercises was that praise should be given in a ratio to criticism of about 20 to 1. That means "Attaboy" 20 times for one "Darn it!" Because project management is set up to identify problems, it is quite possible for this ratio to come out too high on negative reaction and very low on positive comment. Therefore, it behooves the project leader to withhold criticism; let the reporting system do that. You should look for praiseworthy actions wherever possible and give favorable comments. In *The One-Minute Manager,* by Blanchard and Johnson, the authors recommend one-minute praisings in a stylized form. I agree that a one-minute praising is better than no praising at all, although in many cases a 20-minute praising would be warranted. *The One-Minute Manager* also recommends that you give one-minute reprimands close to the action, as well as one-minute praisings close to the action. Unfortunately, with project management, we tend to identify too many problems. If we give reprimands for all of the problems, we are bound to give reprimands for many things that were not caused by the recipient. Be sure to read the counterargument in *The 59-Second Employee* by Andre and Ward. This book gives a more balanced viewpoint to apply to project team members who have special skills or talent, such as professionals.

When you are dealing with nonsubordinates, it is not your job to criticize the way in which they do their work. That job belongs to their direct manager. Leave it at that. This means that when you give an element of praise in an environment that is loaded with implied criticism, it may be 100 times more effective than criticism.

Third, the reinforcement should be close to the action. You are not seeing nonsubordinates as frequently as they are seen by their direct manager. If the task duration is many months, you do not have much opportunity to issue praise close to the action. This means that shorter tasks are better than longer tasks. When I am asked in a seminar: "How short should a task be?" my reply is: "How long do you like to go without praise?" Most people feel that daily praise is a little too often but six months of waiting for praise is too long. It's not surprising that some project managers advocate tasks of two weeks' duration whenever possible. This ties in beautifully with project management, because good project control is obtained through having short, detailed tasks.

Take a look at the diagram in Figure 9-1. The top task is about six weeks long. If it is done on time, you can issue praise by some statement such as "Thank you for being on time" or "Attaboy!" If a task is impossible to do on time, as the second task in the diagram, it will be late, and negative reinforcement is likely. On the bottom two tasks in the diagram, the larger assignment has been divided into shorter tasks. Now, praise can be issued more often. Criticism might also be issued more often, so it is important that these short tasks be achievable.

You can see that if task deadlines are impossible to achieve, you will end up with either direct criticism or implied criticism through the reporting system. That would be perceived as unfair. If the circumstances were difficult, you might modify your response by a statement such as, "It's late, but under the circumstances you did quite well. It's close to the budget and it does work okay." If you are sure to praise the effort that was made, you'll get better efforts in the future.

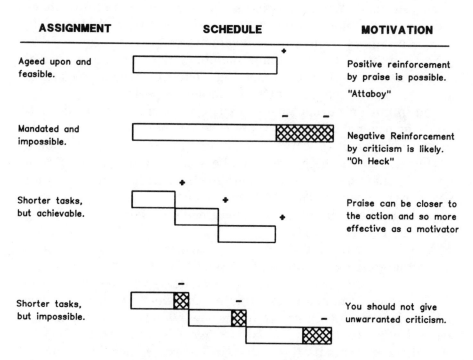

Figure 9-1. Praise as a motivator.

PEER PRAISE AS A MOTIVATOR

There are two meanings to the word *peer*. It sometimes refers to the level in an organization. All supervisors are peers, all managers are peers, and all executives are peers. This is not the kind of peer level that I refer to, unless they have the same occupation. Basically, what I am referring to here is a peer that has the same skills, occupation, or profession—for example, salesman to salesman, programmer to programmer, banker to banker, and so forth. Rank in an organization is immaterial to being this kind of peer.

The reason peer praise is an effective motivator to use with nonsubordinates is that managers tend to neglect this. They probably don't need it because they have three powerful motivators: pay, promotion, and parking space. You have to use other motivators because you cannot give out those tangible rewards to people who work for other bosses.

You may not be the peer of a team member, but as a project leader you probably understand enough of the work to recognize excellence when you see it. When a team member achieves something above average, you should tell his or her peers about it, so that they, in turn, can inquire about the achievement.

You might also have team members describe their special achievements at your project meetings. This gives them exposure to their technical, occupational, or professional peers.

You might encourage them to write a report for other departments or other districts. In some cases it may be appropriate to encourage a person to write for a trade magazine or for a professional journal. When you help team members get exposure of their good works to their peers, you are helping them in a very important aspect of their career. They will remember the project manager who helps them. You will have their sustained enthusiasm for working with you on your projects.

Figure 9-2 depicts a typical unit, consisting of a manager and subordinates. I have indicated a project manager who works for some other manager but, on this project, deals with persons X and Y. The project manager coordinates the work required for the project. It is not necessary that X know what Y is doing, or vice versa. Normally, the functional manager coordinates the work of specialists and puts it all together. In my experience, I have found that people tend to work in small mental compartments. They are

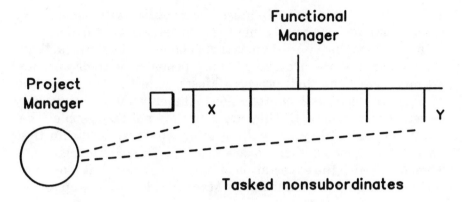

Figure 9-2. Peer praise as a motivator.

either secretive about what they do, or they do not care what the other people are doing. In the case depicted in Figure 9-2, X and Y are working on the same project, and the project manager can pass along information from one to the other. Suppose that X develops a neat way of diagramming for a report. Suppose, also, that Y has to crank out reports, as well, but doesn't know how X has combined two computer programs to get a neat diagram. The project manager may mention to Y what X has done and encourage Y to inquire further. Y then goes over to X and says, "Would you mind telling me about that new way of formatting a report?" and X says, "Sure, I'll be happy to tell you about it, but who told you?" Y replies, "Oh, the project manager told me." So now the project manager is one-up as far as X is concerned. Person X sees the project manager as one who encourages exposure of good works.

THE PROJECT AS A MOTIVATOR

Back in the 1950s, a man named Macgregor came out with a book entitled *The Human Side of Enterprise*. In it, he explained Theory X and Theory Y management styles; this is now part of almost every course in general management. Briefly, if you believe in Theory X, you think that people can't be trusted, that they are naturally lazy and trying to get out of doing work. You then may act like an autocrat with your subordinates. More subtly, with nonsubordinates, you may continually bug them to get the work done.

In contrast, Theory Y assumes that people like doing work. When you believe this, you are likely to trust people to do their work and not bug them about their progress. Most people working on projects bring some special skill or profession to the job. That is why you have assigned them the task. They are definitely not lazy people. They like their work. They are willing to do whatever is within their jurisdiction. Just ask them to do a task and get an agreement on it. Then leave with the expectation of having it done. That may be all the motivation you need to apply. Many people will live up to your expectations.

There are two things that can cause people to act like Theory X people, even though they are, in reality, Theory Y people. If you are frequently critical of their work with regard to schedule, cost, or results, then you are not the most welcome person. They may act as if they are lazy, simply because they are disinclined to work with you. You may have brought to bear, directly or indirectly, more criticism than they think was warranted. You may get comments such as, "I am very busy. Right now I really can't say when I will get it done" or "I'll get it done when I get it done and I can't tell you when that will be." They appear to be lazy and uncooperative toward you, but if you investigate further, you will find that they are doing the work well for other people. Then you must re-examine the relationship you have established. If you somehow got off on the wrong track, it is going to take some extra effort. Before you can get back into praising, they will have to do some more work for you. If your behavior has been bad, you could start by apologizing.

The second way you may cause a person to act like a Theory X person is to be critical of the project itself. Research shows that enthusiasm on a project is related to how people perceive the value of the project itself. A lousy project will get less than enthusiastic cooperation. So don't run down your project, even if you personally believe it's a waste of time. It's assigned to you for some good reason. You should find out what this is and let other team members know about it. It may be that the person who acts like a Theory X person has simply been misinformed about the value of the project. You might begin by asking what he or she thinks of the project.

An informed view of the overall goals and their importance in motivation may be derived from a study of *In Search of Excellence*, by Peters and Waterman. They point out that the executives in excellent companies help their people see the big picture. To some extent, if you are a project manager, you have an ad hoc organization for a project. You can draw attention to higher-level goals of the project. For example, the Personnel Records Project is intended to computerize the record keeping for employee records, but what does this do for the company as a whole? Does better record keeping mean that the Personnel Department will be able to give more attention to other important programs? Does it mean that project team members themselves will receive more prompt attention when seeking employee benefits? A little exploration with the personnel manager may enable the project manager to say something about the higher-level goals. It is easy to make them known to the team members so that they see "the big picture." Their degree of effort will not be anything more than their perception of the worth of the project.

THE PARTICIPATIVE APPROACH

If the project team members participate in the planning of the project, as well as in doing the work of the project, their involvement will be much more extensive. They will be parties to the overall plan and will likely assist enthusiastically in overcoming the types of problems that are often experienced in carrying out a project. In other words, involvement through participation in the planning process promotes a high level of motivation, because people "buy ownership" in the project.

There are three levels of participation:

1. *I plan, you comment.* In this approach, the project manager drafts a schedule, budget, and description of the results. The draft plan is submitted to team members for their comments before it is finalized. This enables the project manager to make minor corrections to the plan and thereby get a better plan. This is good for the whole team, and people are certainly participating in the planning. However, we must consider what happens when the plan goes wrong—and all plans are flawed, because no one knows the future perfectly. When something goes wrong with the plan, and it surely will, your team members are likely to point out that the project

manager did most of the planning and had better fix the problem on his own. They do not feel responsible.

2. *You input, I plan.* At this level, the project team is called together to give their ideas to the project manager at the start of the project. Because the work of scheduling and budgeting requires special skills, the project manager then takes those suggestions and makes up the plan. He or she should incorporate as many of the submitted ideas as possible. If the project manager's idea and a team member's idea are equal in effect but different in method, then the team member's idea should be chosen. It is important to have their support on the project. Later, when the project is in difficulty, as it most surely will be, we may again ask the question about whose project it is. Since the team members have been truly involved in the planning, even before the plan was formulated, they will feel some ownership of the plan. An exception would be any person who submitted some good ideas that were not adopted. Therefore, after the plan is finalized and under way, the project manager should take time to speak to team members whose ideas were not used. A simple list of the ideas submitted, with an indication of which ones were used, would be a good starting point. Then the project manager may say something such as, "Here is your idea. I was unable to use it at this time and place, but thank you for it anyway." By taking these steps, the project manager shows that he has genuinely adopted ideas from the team members and is willing to explain why a particular idea has not been adopted. A detailed justification is probably not going to be necessary. It is important that all team members be satisfied. If they feel they have the best plan that was possible under the circumstances, they will support it even at the end of the project, when their support is most needed.

3. *We plan.* At this level, the project team is called together before any formal planning has been done. The leader of the meeting should not have preconceived ideas of what the outcome should be. Either the project manager should be perceived as neutral, or the meeting should be handed over to a neutral, but experienced, meeting facilitator, who can do it on behalf of the project manager.

At the first meeting, the planning team develops a task list. It is frequently convenient to write the tasks on a chalkboard.

Better still, write them on 3 × 5 self-sticking notes and stick them on the wall in approximate order. After the meeting, a list of activities is provided to all attendees. They are expected to discuss them with subordinates who may be involved in the project and come back to the next meeting with time estimates for the tasks in which they will be involved. They should also define the immediate predecessor tasks. Then, at the second meeting, the time estimates and the sequencing of the tasks are studied. The minimum time to complete the project is worked out. If this is too long, the team members work together to plan the project in more detail in order to reduce the time to complete it. Similarly, they may work together to reduce the budget or change the results. It is important that a decision maker at a higher level than the participants be available to resolve any disputes between team members.

From a practical point of view, this level of participation is most useful for projects in which the cooperation of the team members toward the end of the project is essential for a successful outcome. For example, the participative approach is very appropriate when moving a whole organization to a new facility. Other examples are the institution of a management information system that will affect most departments or the introduction of a new technology that will change the work style of many of the participants.

Clearly, this full participation in planning will require more time to get the project started, and this has to be offset by gains in the implementation of the project. So reserve this level of participation for cases in which there will be a payback at the end of the project. When you choose to go to full participative planning, it's a one-way trip. Once people have participated in the planning, they don't like to go back to a nonparticipative situation. Nevertheless, you may find it necessary to do this on some projects in which there is neither time nor benefit for participative planning. You can cover the bases on such projects by simply telling people the reason you did not have full participative planning. Then you can implement full participative planning whenever there is time and there are benefits to be obtained.

Team planning is the forward thrust of the new management techniques and practices in North America. More and more projects require voluntary cooperation from many jurisdictions. Participative planning has been found to be an effective way to get that voluntary cooperation.

Granted, participative planning contributes much to the initial motivation of the project team, but what does it contribute to maintaining motivation? When major problems face the project and the plan must be altered, the total team should be called together again to replan the project. This maintains their motivation. The appropriate time to do this is when a major problem is faced or at the design review milestones. In this way, a signal is given that the project really belongs to everyone. All team members are needed for its ultimate success.

POWER AND INFLUENCE

The project manager is frequently in a low-power leadership position. His or her authority over team members who work for other managers is small in terms of legitimate authority. As a consequence, his or her leadership style must rely on influence and persuasion, rather than on authority and commanding.

A book that addresses this subject very well is *Power and Influence: Beyond Formal Authority,* by John P. Kotter. To compensate for lack of formal authority he suggests the following:

1. Build a power base of information. Get to know the people and departments that you need. What are their sources of power? Are they being used? Understand and respect their position. It will help you build good working relationships.
2. Find out the personal and career needs of the people and try to satisfy them.
3. Assess the risk for each task. Whose support is necessary? Who could block it? Why and how strongly would they do this?

Kotter presents many more ideas. I suggest you study his book if you are lacking in direct authority.

Here is an application that I have developed by applying some of Kotter's ideas to project management. Figure 9-3 is an example of a Risk Chart, on which you assess the risk to your project for each activity done by a nonsubordinate. (Keep it private.) In Figure 9-3, it is self-evident that items 1 and 3 require some power and influence planning on your part if your project is to succeed.

Suppose that these activities are in a consumer products company. The activity "Collect field data" has been assigned to the Customer Service Department. Will their cooperation be low or high? Their primary function is not the collection of special field data, so that even if they are cooperative, data collection does not satisfy their goals as well as their regular work. What can be done about it? First, find out if the supposition about the degree of cooperation is true. Scout it out. Then, if it is true, consider some strategies such as the following:

1. Present the activity as one that will satisfy the organization's higher-level goals.

2. Find out if there is something they would like in return.

3. Have the Customer Service Department participate in the planning of the data collection method.

4. Move slowly. Discuss it first. Find out their concerns and deal with them. Acknowledge that the data collection is extra work for them. Show gratitude.

5. Put adequate milestones in the activity so that progress can be monitored, because it's a high-risk item for your project.

RISK CHART

ACTIVITY OR TASK	DEPARTMENT OR PERSON	EXPECTED COOPERATION	RISK TO PROJECT
1. Collect field data	Customer Service	Low	High
2. Analyze data	Data Processing	High	High
3. Obtain test equip.	Don	Low	Low
4. Etc.			

Figure 9-3. Sample risk chart.

QUESTIONS FOR DISCUSSION OR ASSIGNMENT

1. State one reason why the initial motivation on a project may not be sustained.
2. Name two ways in which the motivation on a project may be maintained.
3. Under what circumstances would the motivation of the project team tend toward enthusiasm for the project rather than apathy?
4. In about 100 words, explain how the motivation of a project team is influenced by one of the following: praise, peer praise, the project, or participative planning. For the one you have chosen, add another 100 words or more to illustrate your explanation by an example from your experience.
5. As a group exercise, have each member present his or her explanation and an example for question 4 to another person. The second person should then explain it back, to the satisfaction of the first. (This will help members internalize the concepts that have been discussed.)
6. This is a group exercise. Appoint an organizer. Read, again, the two sections in this chapter on the bank's Goodwill Project. Select players to play the roles of Betty and Cal. Have them role-play the situation where Cal thanks Betty for her extra effort on the project within earshot of others in the office. Appoint two monitors to critique Cal's effort. Repeat the role-play so that each member of the group has a chance to try his or her style and get feedback from the monitors. The purpose of this role-playing is to acquire skill in coming across with sincerity.
7. This is similar to question 6, except that it is to be done for the Personnel Records Project. The role-players are to be Jack and Marvin. The situation is where Marvin explains his problem with a bug in the software and Jack responds in a positive way.

CHAPTER
ten

THE PROJECT MANAGER'S SPECIAL AUTHORITY
with it, you can win

> **Key Idea**
>
> To be accountable for the success of the project, you must have appropriate authority.

Most management books state that authority should be commensurate with accountability. However, because project managers frequently must get key project tasks done by other departments, they often lack the necessary authority. This problem is compounded by the inclination of subordinates to take direction only from their own managers.

As shown in the following cases, lack of authority, or lack of its recognition by others, can cause delays on a project. Trying to get the project completed through enforcement from higher managers often results in even less cooperation in the future from the offended parties.

To cope with this situation, an organization should grant project managers the authority they need, without usurping the existing authority of line managers. This chapter shows the ways and means to cope with this situation.

CASE 1:
THE BANKER WHO COULDN'T WAIT

The bank's Goodwill Project had a few delays. You may recall that there was a delay in getting the new letterhead stock. Harry did not want to accept a six-week delay in this project just because of some problems with stationery. He explained his situation to the headquarters Purchasing Department and asked for a one-week delivery of the new stationery. The Purchasing Department simply refused to discuss anything other than their conventional lead time. Harry found their attitude infuriating. He just about blew his top. He was thinking, "Why could they not change their routine for a special project like his? Why do they not even consider giving me a better delivery date? I could go to a local printer and get the stationery in a few days. So why not get this attention from headquarters?" When he mentioned this to Purchasing, they brought up their standard line—preferred supplier, standardization, lowest cost, and so forth. So Harry decided not to go to a local printer. Still, he didn't think he should have to put up with the intransigence of the buyer he was dealing with.

Harry went to his boss, Cal, and asked for some help. Cal telephoned the manager of operations, who in turn had a word with the purchasing manager. The buyer was told to drop everything else and get the stationery in on the one-week deadline instead of the usual six.

The buyer was not pleased when Harry went over his head. He did what he had to do, but Harry anticipated that in the future, the buyer's cooperation would be difficult to get. He wondered if he should have had some authority to deal with this himself, instead of escalating it to a higher level. Either the Purchasing Department would treat his project as a special case and commit to a short delivery time, or else he should be allowed to go directly to a printer. For the general situation of obtaining office supplies, he could see that the headquarters arrangement was good for the bank as a whole, but they were not really set up to handle specials. He concluded that if project managers are expected to get the unusual done, they need some special authority.

CASE 2:
HE DIDN'T ATTEND THE MEETING

The Personnel Records Project had an activity A1: "Meet and define data fields." It was felt that the data fields should be defined before the design could be completed. A subtask of this was defined as A1.1: "Define access rules." This subtask normally preceded the design, but as a last resort, the access rules could be defined just before the coding started.

Why were access rules necessary? Data such as names and addresses could be obtained by anyone with an account number on the computer. However, medical records should be accessible only to the doctor or personnel manager. These people would require a password to gain access to this part of the data. Prior to development of the computer database, this was handled by keeping the file cabinets locked; access was managed by the supervisor of records.

The personnel manager was unfamiliar with computers and could not bring himself to consider the access rules. To further complicate the situation, the software designer planned to have the computer keep a record to show whose account numbers had been used to access sensitive data. The computer would also record the account number of anyone who even tried to access such data. Moreover, he wanted all of the access rules defined before he started the design, and not just before the coding was started. The programmer assigned to this task was Monica. She worked with the supervisor of records to define the data fields. However, the supervisor could not define the access rules, as this was up to her boss, the personnel manager. The supervisor was not inclined to tell her boss what to do and when to do it. So it was up to Monica to persuade the personnel manager to do this key task.

As mentioned, however, the personnel manager was reluctant to get on with it, so Monica contacted the project manager, Jack Daniels. She told him that the access rules were going to be late and that further delays would cause the schedule to slip. Jack requested a meeting with the supervisor of records, the personnel manager, and Monica. The personnel manager put them off, saying that he was too busy with union negotiations. He would not say when he would be available. A week slipped by, and Jack decided to ask for help from his manager, Hilda. However, there was a long-standing feud over recruiting between Hilda and the personnel manager, and she was unable to get his expedient cooperation. As a matter of fact, her calls were not even returned. Finally, in desperation, Hilda asked Jack and Monica to draft an access matrix. She took it to the chief executive officer for approval. The personnel manager was thus persuaded to accept this draft but complained that he didn't really have time to consider it thoroughly. Anyway, the deed was done.

As you may recall, the personnel manager tried to get back at the project team when they had trouble with furniture delays. In other words, when you go to higher authority to get something done by a colleague in your organization, it is likely that hard feelings will result. This does not enhance long-term cooperation. Hilda and Jack knew this, and they wondered why they didn't have more authority with the personnel manager for a project situation. In other words, because the personnel manager was a needed resource on this project, Jack felt he should have had some authority that was recognized by the Personnel Manager.

> **A Principle of Authority on a Project**
>
> The project manager must have some rights with nonsubordinates in order to succeed with the project. These rights should be granted before real work on the project is started. Special rights or authority can be granted by the head of the organization. This is best done with the concurrence of the other managers involved in the project.

APPLICATION TO A SMALL PROJECT

The project plan for the bank's Goodwill Project (see Figure 2-1) had requested some special authority over the headquarters Personnel Department. However, no mention was made of the headquarters Purchasing Department.

Is there a blank statement that would do for all such situations? Let us try:

1. The project manager has the right to request that a project task be completed by a certain date. If the date cannot be met, then a commitment should be made to whatever date is possible.
2. The project manager has the right to go outside the organization for resources if they are not available internally when needed.

If projects were done frequently in the bank, there could be a memorandum of understanding from the chief executive officer. This memorandum would explain the special authority granted to the project manager for the duration of the project. Banks that use project management techniques for the introduction of new products and services have enough projects to make this formality worthwhile. However, the Goodwill Project is a one-time-only event; hence, problems have to be handled as they arise. The completion date of this project was not vital to the organization. In contrast, the completion date on a project for a new banking machine that would be deployed across the nation would warrant the formal granting of special authority.

APPLICATION TO A MEDIUM PROJECT

In the Personnel Records Project, does Jack need any special authority or rights in order to get the project done? After all, most organizations start with a cooperative attitude between departments. Many projects get done without any special authority. When there is goodwill between departments, projects get done—eventually!

Consider this: The Personnel Records Project is not routine to the organization. For all routine work, each department has worked out its own modus operandi. Thus, the people in the Personnel Department have ways of doing their basic functions. They know how to go about arranging union meetings, recruiting, personal development, and so forth—but they don't have a modus operandi for developing a computerized record keeping system. Of course, if they continued doing projects like this, they would learn how to make them go. They would have a way of doing things, formal or informal, that would work.

However, the Personnel Records Project is a one-time occurrence, and it tends to interfere with routine operations. In the view of the Personnel Department, these routine operations are fundamental to the department's existence and should take priority over special projects. That is what happened.

In Chapter 9, we learned how a cooperative attitude can be fostered and how motivation can be maintained. But is this enough? When the crunch is on, Jack's project will compete for attention with important routine operations. Therefore, Jack needs some basic authority to back him up.

I have found it better to use the word *rights* rather than the word *authority,* because it covers a wider range of actions. The project manager has the authority to use resources and authority to sign task forms. The project manager has the right to have a commitment on a task. There is a subtle difference between rights and authority. Rights seem to cover authority as well as things that do not require formal authority, such as the right to communicate directly.

Suppose, for example, that Jack and Monica had the right to communicate directly with anyone who had an assigned task on their project. Then Monica could have asked the personnel manager for a meeting. He would have respected her right to talk with him directly and get a commitment, no matter what their difference in rank. Then Monica could have expected a reply as to when a meeting could be held and when the access rules would be finalized.

There is another right that would be useful in this project. The project manager should have the right to resubmit the project plan and get new approved targets. If things do not go well, Monica and Jack could resubmit a revised schedule for the project at a suitable milestone. This would be their fallback position. Approval of the revision would put them on a winning schedule once again. Their management would also find out about uncontrollable delays and could find out why, if they care to.

In this case, the personnel manager was stalling. However, it could have been true that the personnel manager simply did not have the time to do it, even though, in principle, he was for it. In that case, the resources would not match the original time plan, and the schedule should be revised.

THE RIGHTS OF PROJECT MANAGERS

The following discussion describes the ideal situation. If you have all of these rights, you will be fully accountable for the project being completed on time, within the budget, and with the right results. If not, you will be only partly accountable for the end results. For example, suppose that other departments can charge your project whatever it takes to do a task, without first giving an estimate for your budget. Then you cannot be held accountable for that part of the cost. As another example, suppose that you cannot get time commitments from other departments. Then you cannot be fully accountable for getting the project finished on time. Although you may do the best you can, there are limits to your accountability.

Consider how the project manager's accountability may be affected by the following eight rights:

Eight Basic Rights of Project Managers

1. *The right to state the "what," but not the "how."* As mentioned in Chapter 3, task objectives are much better phrased by what is to be achieved than by how it is to be done. If the project manager states what is to be achieved, then the tasked person can decide how it is to be achieved.

2. *The right to assign tasks and get commitments.* As seen in the foregoing cases, the projects would have gone more smoothly had Harry and Monica had this right and had it been recognized by the others, regardless of their rank. The most important commitment on a small to medium project is the completion date of a task. With nonsubordinates, this is the most powerful motivator a project manager has. If you can't get commitments, then you can't give a commitment for a completion date of the total project. You may end up being only a coordinator, just reporting on the completion of tasks and estimating the final completion date. For larger projects, you should also expect to get commitments on the budget and on the nature of the results.

3. *The right to allocate budgeted funds to tasks, whether they are to be done within the organization or outside.* To be responsible for control of the total cost, the project manager must have the right to control the funds on individual tasks. If cost control is important, budgets should be prepared by the resource managers for the tasks that contribute to the whole. Then they should try to stay within their budgets. If, on the other hand, cost is not a primary target, manpower and materials may be charged to the project as they occur. Without prior estimates, the project manager will not be able to keep the cost under control.

4. *The right to communicate directly with anyone who has an assigned task on the project.* We have seen in the Personnel Records Project that the project would be have been facilitated if Monica had had the right to communicate directly with the personnel manager. This right to communicate, and the accountability to respond, should be recognized by both parties in order for it to work. Going through channels is more polite and courteous, but it often takes much longer than direct

communication. This right gives one big advantage to project management as a way to manage special jobs.

5. *The right to oversee the work in progress.* When a task involves physical hardware, one can assess the progress by seeing the work in progress. This is not so for mental work, which may be encoded in calculations and stuffed away in a file somewhere. For a project manager properly to assess the progress on a task, he or she should be able to see the work in progress. Otherwise, there would be an inclination to make the tasks shorter and have work items delivered frequently by people who must be monitored closely. In the Personnel Records Project, Jack had access to most of the work on the project because of the subordinate relationships. However, for the furniture procurement, the buyer may have been deceived by false promises from the furniture supplier. To assess progress properly, the buyer or Jack would have to visit the furniture factory and inspect the work in progress. On the other hand, a task like "Developing access rules" might be worked over in the personnel manager's mind for weeks, whereas the encoding into a matrix may take only an hour. The right to oversee work in progress would not be of much use on that task. To control it, Jack might have to include some milestones, such as the completion of the first and second drafts.

6. *The right to nominate a person as a team member, and the right to veto a person at any time.* To restate this, we could say: the right to nominate and veto team members. Basically, if the project manager is to be accountable for the quality of the results, he or she should have a say in who becomes a team member. To do so, he or she must know the differences in work quality of those being proposed as team members. In the foregoing cases, there were not many choices. Jack might have had a preference for one buyer over another if he had known their track records. In fact, it's entirely possible that the purchasing manager would reserve his best buyers for the regular work of the corporation. If Jack knowingly got an inadequate person, he could veto the choice at the beginning. If he took an unknown person on the strength of the purchasing manager's designation, he should have the right to have that person replaced if he or she doesn't work out. Given this right, Jack would be ultimately accountable for the results achieved and would be in a strong position to exercise his rights with regard to the time and budget targets.

7. *The right to obtain a priority rating.* This is especially important on multiple projects, where some of the resources are fixed. This means that a high-priority project will get first call on resources. Consequently, low-priority projects will likely slip their schedules unless the resources are increased accordingly. You may recall Mary-Helen's problem with multiple projects. The priority on one project can affect another project, especially if it is suddenly changed, which brings us to the next point.

8. *The right to propose a project plan revision.* The Dynamic Project Plan can change. It has its own amending formula, in that it states the major milestones for decision reviews. The project may get severely bumped by other projects that have higher priority. If it is known that the project is definitely going to be very late, it behooves the project manager to propose a project plan revision, even before the next milestone. Too often, senior managers consider that the original targets are chiseled in stone and refuse to budge even though the circumstances have changed.

A summary of these eight rights is provided in Figure 10-1.

Other Rights That Apply Occasionally

The project manager should have *the right to decline a project.* This should be done only when the project manager feels that he or she could not succeed with the project. It is a right generally given in large organizations but not in smaller ones, where the number of project managers with special skills is very limited.

The right to use outside resources in place of internal resources is sometimes granted on projects with a high profile. If the internal

---

1. State what, not how
2. Assign task and get commitment
3. Allocate project budget
4. Communicate directly
5. Oversee work in progress
6. Nominate and veto team members
7. Obtain a project priority rating
8. Propose a plan revision

Figure 10-1. The eight basic rights of project managers.

resources are simply not available when required, and overtime or a short-term contract person cannot take care of it, it makes sense to spend the money on outside resources. It should not be necessary to increase the permanent staff in order to handle a temporary work increase.

Sometimes, the project manager has *the right to purchase materials directly* if the full-time Purchasing Department is not properly staffed to handle the project. The most controversial right pertains to the letting of contracts. In a competitive bidding process, the lowest bid gets the contract. If the project manager has knowledge that the lowest bidder will be unsatisfactory in quality or delivery, he or she should have the right to object. This is usually done by vetoing a supplier off the short list of approved suppliers and not having to give a reason.

TASK REPORTING IN DIFFERENT FORMS OF ORGANIZATION

Task Reporting in a Line Organization

As illustrated in Figure 10-2, for task reporting in a line organization, a person at the bottom of the line organization is assigned the coordinating responsibility for a number of people working in different departments on one project. No reorganization is involved. The title often given to this position is project leader, project officer, team leader, or project engineer. The reason for this is that the

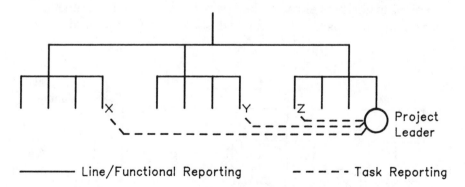

Figure 10-2. Task reporting in a line organization.

project manager is part of a specialty group and probably does a lot of the work himself or herself. The need to coordinate is delegated several levels down in this manner. It will work if the project manager is given some of the rights mentioned previously.

Task Reporting in a Matrix Organization

In Figure 10-3, the project management role has been elevated to the same level as a resource manager. Usually, this person is a full-time project manager and carries such a title. The specialized work is done in a number of departments. All or most of the project team members report to their project manager on a task-reporting basis. The tasked persons also report to their regular resource managers (also called functional managers). For this type of organization to work, the regular resource managers must agree to assign people to project tasks and be accountable for their work on the projects. It usually takes at least 100 people for a matrix organization to be efficient. In this case, the specialty departments are substantial and ad hoc teams are formed for each project.

Problems with Task Reporting

The problems with task reporting in either a line organization or a matrix organization are twofold:

1. A project manager or project leader does not have any direct or formal authority over the tasked persons. To work, task reporting depends on the separation of the "what" and the "how" and recog-

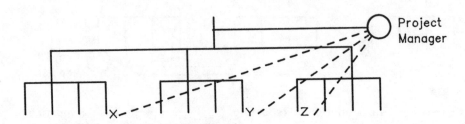

Figure 10-3. Task reporting in a matrix organization.

nition of the separate rights of project managers and resource managers.

2. The tasked person has more than one boss. For example, in Figures 10-2 and 10-3, person Y reports both to a project leader and to a resource manager. The resource manager has a right to get his work done on a priority basis. This frequently displaces the work promised to the project leader, and the tasked person is in the position of not being able to keep a personal commitment. This causes some mental stress and is one reason why a matrix organization is stressful initially. However, when the matrix is working properly, the tasked person and his or her manager will have a joint commitment to the project manager. Any change in the commitments would have to be reported and renegotiated.

There are two advantages to the matrix form of organization:

1. The specialties are grouped under one resource manager (functional manager), and the collective expertise is better than that of individuals working on their own.
2. Top management can have a direct path of communication to the project manager on all project matters. They can change priorities and get action at the working level much faster than if they had to go through layers of management. The matrix organization has been used extensively and successfully by large engineering consulting firms that have a number of specialized groups. A project is coordinated by a project manager on behalf of a client. Large aerospace, electronic, pharmaceutical and banking firms have also managed successfully with the matrix form of organization. However, it is not for everyone. We will look at least at one more alternative.

Full-Time Project Team

In the organization depicted in Figure 10-4, X, Y, and Z are assigned to a project manager for the duration of the project. Such a project may run over several years. If any of the people are unsatisfactory, the project manager has the same authority over them as any manager has over subordinates. Therefore, the project manager is fully accountable for being on time, being within the budget, and getting the right results. The full-time project team works well in medium or large size organizations, with hundreds or thousands of

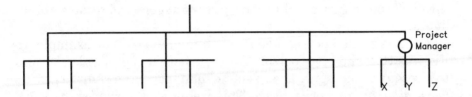

Figure 10-4. The full-time project team.

persons, and for medium or large projects. In large projects, there is no question about the efficiency of the team. For example, if an initial requirement for four specialists diminishes to two, this can be arranged. In a small project with a full-time team, you cannot pay for less than 100 percent of a person, even one who is only needed for half the time. The team approach is often used for one-of-a-kind projects when the time of completion is far more important than the cost.

THE PROJECT CHARTER

The project charter is an agreement between the project manager and the various jurisdictions that supply resources. Special authority is granted for the duration of the project. It is an extension of the project plan into the area of special authority.

The project charter is useful for such projects as moving an organization to a new location, installing a large-scale management information system, going to new technology, merging two companies, and a consortium project. If you are given such a project, you will need special rights or you will never succeed, despite goodwill and normal cooperation. For example, moving to a new location requires decisions on who gets what space and when. The charter should give the project manager the right to get these decisions or to make them.

THE TASK FORM

Figure 10-5 is a sample task form for the Goodwill Project, and Figure 10-6 is a sample task form for the Personnel Records Project.

ACTIVITY/TASK FORM

Project name GOODWILL **Pr. WBS no.** Round Two
Activity name Mail Letters Subtask **Its WBS no.** J.A.1
Predecessors Round One **Successors** Telephone customers

P: Objectives/Requirements Procure 2000 sheets of local branch letterhead

C: Budget/Cost target $100

T: Schedule/Time target; milestones Two weeks from requisition date, approximately Feb. 7.

APPROVALS:

Project Leader **Tasked Person** **Tasked Person's Superv.**
Harry (Buyer) (Purchasing Manager)

Figure 10-5. Activity/task form for the Goodwill Project.

ACTIVITY/TASK FORM

Project name _PERSONNEL RECORDS_   **Pr. WBS no.** _____
Activity name _Order Furniture & Await Delivery_   **Its WBS no.** _01_
Predecessors _MS2: Approved Design_   **Successors** _MS4: Delivered Hardware_

P: Objectives/Requirements _Procure special computer furniture as specified_

C: Budget/Cost target _$200 labor & $4000 equipment_

T: Schedule/Time target; milestones _3 weeks from approved requisition, approximately Mar. 1_
                                       MS: Vendor confirms order

APPROVALS:

Project Leader   **Tasked Person**   **Tasked Person's Superv.**
Jack Daniels   ------(Buyer)------   ----(Purchasing Manager)

Figure 10-6. Activity/task form for the Personnel Records Project.

ACTIVITY/TASK FORM

Project name _____ Pr. WBS no. _____
Activity name _____ Its WBS no. _____
Predecessors _____ Successors _____

P: Objectives/Requirements _____

C: Budget/Cost target _____

T: Schedule/Time target; milestones _____
_____

APPROVALS:

Project Leader _____   Tasked Person _____   Tasked Person's Superv. _____

Figure 10-7. Activity/Task form (owners of this book may copy this form for their own use).

THE PROJECT MANAGER'S SPECIAL AUTHORITY

The task form is an agreement between the project manager and the tasked person, along with that person's supervisor. It covers the time, cost, and results targets for a task. When all parties are in agreement, the form is signed, and it becomes a firm commitment.

A task form would not be required for the situation described in the Goodwill Project case. Harry is acting with adequate authority from the branch manager, Cal, and will get the work done in his office without difficulty. Would the task form be of value for the external work done by the Purchasing Department? It is obvious that this degree of formality would not be required. However, suppose that this Goodwill Project is to be extended to all branches across the country and Harry is to be a full-time project manager. Then he would be very dependent on the Purchasing Department for accomplishment of certain tasks. If Harry did not have prior agreement on the special authority needed, he could probably get it by discussing one of these task forms with the purchasing manager and the buyer involved. Assuming that they go for it, Harry would then actually get the special authority that he needs. If they don't go for it, he knows he's in trouble. Either way, the discussions would be useful on the multiplication of this project.

The example for the Personnel Records Project is right on target for the use of task forms. We can assume that Hilda's department is responsible for many projects and that they depend on the Purchasing Department to meet deadlines. Keep in mind that the Purchasing Department is set up for other kinds of duties, not to service the MIS department. Therefore, task form agreements should be tried.

QUESTIONS FOR DISCUSSION OR ASSIGNMENT

1. Suppose that a functional manager is appointed to be a project manager as well. All members of the project team are direct subordinates. What special authority or rights does this person need in addition to the usual authority of a manager over direct subordinates?

2. Examine the project manager's "Bill of Rights" in Figure 10-1 and the task form in Figure 10-6. Assume that the project manager initiates the form and gets it approved by the tasked person and

QUESTIONS FOR DISCUSSION OR ASSIGNMENT   199

by the tasked person's supervisor. Take each right in turn and discuss how much of the right has been gained by virtue of the agreement (about one paragraph each).

3. Using the blank activity task form of Figure 10-7, complete it for the original task in the Personnel Records Project which is called "Install furniture." It is to be done by John S. who is the furniture specialist who works for the manager of maintenance, David K. Obtain your data from Chapters 4 and 5.

4. Suppose that a project manager does not have the right to allocate the project budget to various tasks. Instead, each nonsubordinate department charges the project account with whatever it takes to do the task. The departments are not required to give estimates nor to work to a budget. What can the project manager put in the Dynamic Project Plan to reduce his or her accountability?

5. What are the differences and similarities between task reporting in a line organization and in a matrix organization? Which form of organization is the most suitable for a large organization that works only on projects?

6. Which form of organization is used in the Goodwill Project? Explain your answer.

7. Which form of organization is used in the Personnel Records Project? Explain your answer.

8. Would the full-time project team approach be suitable for either the Goodwill Project or the Personnel Records Project? Explain.

CHAPTER eleven

COMPUTER ASSISTANCE
do it right and save time

> **Key Idea**
>
> It pays to select project management software carefully to suit your special needs, and to plan its implementation.

In the computer age, we are constantly presented with success stories of computer usage. We are seldom told about the disasters of poor startups with new software. One wit has concluded: "To err is human, but to really foul up, one needs a computer."

Computers can shut down an airline, frustrate operators, and print a confusing overabundance of data. Many purchased project management software packages are sitting idle because of some problems in usage. The two cases in this chapter illustrate some of the pitfalls.

The full potential of computer assistance in project management can be realized by taking methodical steps in the selection and implementation of the software. These steps are amply demonstrated in the applications.

CASE 1:
THE NEAT DRAWINGS IMPRESSED THE MANAGEMENT

Mary-Helen was the insurance officer for the ABC Insurance Company. Since she first reported on her project workload to her manager, she had done well and was promoted to project leader. She had been encouraged to attend a course on project management. Now she managed nine projects.

For each of her nine projects, she made up individual schedules by hand. She explained them to her boss and he thought schedules were a good idea. In fact, he had had a graphic artist prepare an overhead visual of the schedule. Her boss had shown it to the executive committee, and they had been impressed.

After seeing the difference between what the graphic artist produced and what she had done by hand, Mary-Helen became reluctant to present her schedules at meetings. She had no graphic skills at all. She had a hard time drawing a straight line without a ruler. The corners of her boxes were seldom square. Her printing was readable, but she wasn't sure about dotting the letter i in a capitalized title. She knew, in general, what a good drawing should look like, because her husband was an engineer. He had his own drawing board and T-square and other paraphernalia for making nice drawings. She didn't know how to use them.

One of her friends in the actuarial department had some software for a spreadsheet. It included an interface with a graphics package that drew out neat bar charts. It also had an interface with a scheduling program, but they were not using it. Mary-Helen thought that a scheduling program might be of some use to her. What really clinched it was the neat schedule shown in the brochure describing the software. She set out to purchase the software program but was told that it had to be cleared with the Management Information Systems (MIS) Department. She talked to them and was told that the parent company had a project management program on their mainframe computer which she could use. She was given a demonstration, which turned her cold on the idea. It was much too complicated for her to use.

Mary-Helen was not one to be discouraged easily. She either had to learn how to draw or get a software package for scheduling. With a little understanding from her boss, they managed to purchase one through their library by classifying it as a manual. The software could be operated on their word-processing microcomputer. So all the problems were solved, and Mary-Helen printed her first schedule by computer. It looked like the schedule shown in Figure 11-1. Her boss was impressed. He used them in reports and presentations to his executives. Eventually, some of them found their way into presentations to clients.

In the course of time, because of her example and some encouragement from their manager, many of Mary-Helen's colleagues had also adopted project management techniques. Eventually, most of them were using the software package to produce their schedules. Those who had their own microcomputers had obtained licensed copies for their own use. The MIS Department was not altogether delighted, because the software did not have their approval, but was kind enough to look the other way. All the MIS Department wanted was to have control of the big computer programs which were used to run the company operations. They had found out from their

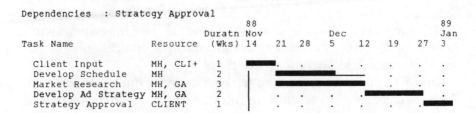

Figure 11-1. A neat schedule produced by a microcomputer program.

associates in other companies that MIS departments were losing the battle for controlling microcomputer software. It had ways of sneaking in and proliferating faster than MIS could standardize on the software.

Two years later, the project load on Mary-Helen's department had increased considerably. She was now a full-time project manager, and had several project leaders reporting to her. These people regularly reported their project workload to her on the form which she had first developed herself (Figure 1-1). With her software program, she entered the workload data into the spreadsheet portion and summed them up to find the total workload on her working unit. She soon saw that resource checking really involved the whole department or, for that matter, anyone working on projects.

Mary-Helen realized that it would really help her to have a software program which had a resource management feature. She had learned about this during her course in project management but hadn't seen the need for it until now. She also realized that for managing multiple projects, she needed reports on Free Float, so that late work by one person would not upset the schedule of another team member. None of the offered upgrades on her software had these features, because the vendors were catering to the market for the small, single project or to people who were already users of the vendor's spreadsheet program. She realized that another software package was necessary. However, the downside was that she and all the others would have to learn a new system. She could expect some resistance to adoption of any new software. If only her existing software package could be modified, she thought; but she found out that low-cost PC software cannot be changed. She concluded that it was good fortune she had found out about the software she was using, but it was a misfortune that she had not taken the time to assess future needs.

CASE 2:
HIGH GEAR WAS REALLY LOW GEAR

The Denver-based company that made biofeedback devices was now well into its use of computers. Wilf Baker knew that he had done the right thing. Larry had ironed out all the bugs of its introduction. Even the Engineering Department, which had been reluctant to join with them in the beginning, utilized it fully now. They used it for creating bills of materials and for their specifications.

Bill Boyd, the manager of engineering, was an advanced thinker. He was looking for additional ways for the computer to save them time. Their biggest problem at the moment was pushing through the engineering of a brand-new product line. It was now in the detailed engineering phase. Schedules were used to coordinate the work of Engineering and the other company departments. The project engineer in charge of the project was run off his feet. Bill decided that if the project engineer, Paul, would use the computer for his scheduling and updates, he would have more time to devote to other project work. Paul felt that he needed some help, and willingly agreed to start using the computer.

On the recommendation of one of Paul's friends, he purchased a well-known software package and started putting it into effect. Initially, he had some installation problems in matching it to the peripherals. Then he had to learn how to use the program. That took a couple of days more. He went back and forth between project and computer work and got some schedules out fairly soon. However, these were so inaccurate that he spent three days more on the computer to correct them.

Computers have an insidious way of commanding one's attention. Before long, Paul was neglecting his other project work in order to get the computer software straightened away. Not everyone was pleased, however. Because the software worked only in days, and the other departments worked in weeks, he had requested them to change their data from weeks to days. This only aggravated their frayed nerves, which were sandpapered sore by the rush of putting a project into production. Paul got a little rattled, too. It didn't take much to drive him back to the computer—at least computers didn't talk back. It seemed to some people that Paul got along better with the computer than he did with his fellow workers. It seemed to depersonalize him. He was not the same jovial, compromising person that he used to be.

Bill, the engineering manager, was beginning to have second thoughts about computerization. Far from helping Paul get more work done on his project, it had led to additional delays. Maybe they had rushed into it a bit too soon. Even Bill realized now that there were other project management software packages that may have suited them better than the one they were using. "Next time it will be different," thought Bill.

The Principles of Computer Assistance

There is one overall general principle that seems relevant to all cases of computer assistance: *Computer software will save time only if adopted carefully.*

The following subprinciples are self-evident.
1. Because off-the-shelf PC software cannot be changed by the user, you should first analyze your needs.
2. No software program suits all needs for all users. You must trade off simplicity for features.
3. Your needs and opportunities will change.

APPLICATION TO SMALL PROJECTS

Computer assistance is of no practical benefit to single small projects. If there are only 5 to 10 activities, which are mostly done by one person, it is faster to schedule by hand. Multiple small projects are another matter. Together, they add up to a medium or large project. They are good cases for computer assistance. Let us reconstruct the case of Mary-Helen and use the above principles.

When Mary-Helen realized her new need, she talked it over with her manager. He had heard of other disasters in software applications, so he suggested she first take a course on the use of computer assistance in project management. This she did. Afterwards, while applying what she learned, she realized that software could do many other things for her besides draw neat schedules. She got her boss's backing to put some time and effort into acquiring new software, and she listed this approved assignment as one of her projects.

First, with the backing of her boss, she did a survey of the other insurance officers who were potential users of the software. She even asked the MIS Department to respond as well. Thus, she networked with many people who had additional information on the topic.

This survey helped her narrow her selection down to two suggested software packages. After all, there were over 100 available, but her first step had narrowed the search to a final selecting effort that was feasible. One of these software packages was better than the other for diagrams. The other, however, reported Free Float in a convenient way, which the first one didn't do at all. Both of the programs had a subproject function. That is, if a subproject was updated, then the master project schedule was changed as well. It was interesting to note that the price difference from the first to the second was 1 to 4. (Vendor names or prices are not detailed in this book, because they change faster than one can produce new book editions.) Mary-Helen got demo disks from both of the vendors and saw to it that the other potential users had a look at what the programs would do. Nobody particularly wanted to change, but eventually they chose the first one, because it had good-looking logic diagrams and schedules, similar to those in Figure 11-2. Besides having a good graphics capability, it also was an easy-to-use program, and had an on-line tutorial. It required a minimum of change in their techniques when going from the present program to the new one.

Mary-Helen took up the new program with gusto and in a few weeks had results to show for it. However, she noticed that other department members were not following suit. They just didn't have the time to switch over, or they didn't perceive a need at the moment.

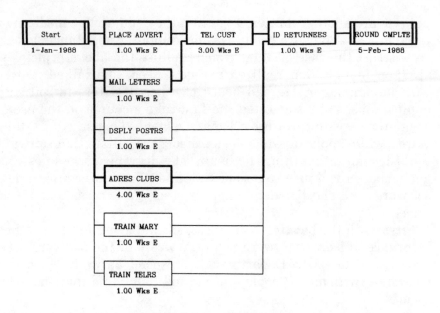

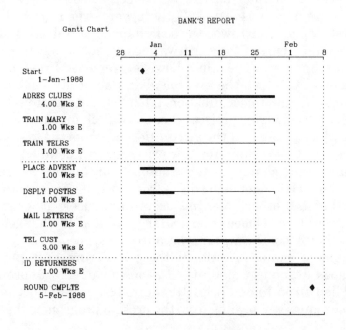

Figure 11-2. The graphics capability of software is a consideration.

Fortunately, her manager was sympathetic. He requested that Mary-Helen train a clerk to take whatever data the department members had prepared manually for the schedules, and to enter the data into the computer. The department members could defer learning how to use the new software, and then take over the work of data entry when they felt ready to do it. Eventually, the whole group swung over to use the new software.

The manager was pleased. They were finally moving into the computer age. There were two incidental benefits. One benefit was that his subordinates seemed to want to discuss schedules more frequently. That was good. As a second benefit, he was impressing his executives and client customers with the nice, neat schedules his department was producing.

Let us suppose that the transition was made successfully. What did it eventually cost? The software only cost about $400 for the licensed user and $100 for each of the other users. That's not much. However, we should include here the cost of the meetings and the startup time. This would not be less than two person-months. So, all in all, the cost of introducing the software was closer to $5000 than it was to $500. If you look at it this way, the cost of the software itself is not a big factor in the total cost of adopting it.

Back to our case. Later on, the facilities group for this large company wanted some software for one of their projects. They looked at Mary-Helen's choice and rejected it. They needed something for construction projects and so they ended up choosing completely different software. Not surprisingly, the MIS Department finally realized that it's hard to standardize on one program for all users.

APPLICATION TO A MEDIUM PROJECT

Let us reconstruct the case involving Bill Boyd, the manager of engineering for the Denver company. We will again use some of the principles of computer assistance.

Bill was well aware that the introduction of computers and new software could generate new problems. He had seen it happen with the business computer system the company had adopted. He was determined not to let it happen with his department. To start with, he telephoned some of his professional acquaintances. They worked in other companies of about the same size as his and also managed engineering departments. He found out the following facts:

1. There is no universal software that satisfies all users.
2. There is no project management software which integrates fully with other company software for general accounting. (In fact, at the time of writing, I know of one, but you must buy the computer and all its software packages for complete integration of your company. In addition, I have recently heard of a combined package for scheduling and accounting, but that is only partial integration.)
3. Many of the efforts to introduce project management software had withered on the vine.
4. Compelling people to use the project management software can lead to disaster.

Bill realized he needed some help. He purchased a copy of the annual *Survey of Project Management Software Packages* from the Project Management Institute (see Appendix B). In addition, he saw an advertisement for an evaluation, PM SOLUTIONS (see Appendix B). When Bill found out that the report's recommendations were based on objective tests, he bought it. Bill was smart enough to buy information on PM software instead of generating his own. (Rating reports are also published by *Software Digest;* see Appendix B.)

After a study of the documents he purchased, he decided to go along with the ones recommended in the report. He took their top recommendation plus one of the others which was next to the top. He had heard good things about it from his professional associates. He wondered why the second one was not at the top of the list. Later on, he realized that the report had emphasized load leveling for its top-of-the-line microcomputer software. Bill was not sure that he needed load leveling in his operation. Great for construction, no doubt, but maybe his operation wasn't ready for it yet. He ordered demo disks for both of the programs and prepared for the next step.

Bill looked for someone on his staff who was knowledgeable about projects. This person needed to have the time to go into this software selection and to implement it. One of his senior technicians was in a standby position on project work. The technician would also benefit from the new experience with computers. Thus, Victor was chosen to be the person who would pilot their department into project management software usage. Bill also set up an evaluation committee to which Victor would report when he had some evaluation data.

When Victor realized they were going to spend between $5,000 and $10,000 for one of these software packages, he asked for live demonstrations from the local representatives. This was better than seeing only the demo disks. It enabled him to ask specific questions relating to their needs. Also, he would probably get to know who else was using these software packages. Victor also added one other condition: A 30-day trial period if they chose to go with one. That was agreed to. (On top-of-the-line microcomputer software, there is enough profit for a respectable sales commission. This permits additional services such as demonstrations and restocking.) Victor also made sure that both software vendors provided free or low-cost technical assistance by telephone. (Some of the cheaper packages provide free telephone support, but the telephone is nearly always busy.) Victor checked these numbers out with some simulated problems, just to make sure he could get service when he needed it.

It was hard for the committee to make a choice. There were always tradeoffs. The first one had load leveling, which was good for optimizing the resource utilization. The second one did not have load leveling. However, it did have the feature of being able to get tailor-made schedule reports. It also had additional add-on programs for resource management and for materials management. The resource management software would effectively enable them to do load leveling with manual assistance, without having to encode all of the priority rules for automatic load leveling. The first program had the advantage of being able to enter the logic diagram by precedence entry on the screen. This was great for small projects but cumbersome for large projects. The second program required the preparation of arrow-node (activity-on-arrow) diagrams (see Appendix A). However, the vendor indicated that they would have a precedence entry update available within a year.

After looking at the demonstrations and playing around with the demo disks, the committee decided to go with the second software package. They brought it in on a 30-day trial basis. They stayed with it. Much to their delight, they found that the resource management and materials management add-on programs were worth getting into. It required some changeover from their present system, but it tied in with the project work. Figure 11-3 shows a schedule for which the symbols can be changed and also a resource histogram.

```
ELECTROMECHANICAL SYSTEM            Report Date: 11/20/88                          Page 1   Sec: 1
ADVANCED PROFESSIONAL DEVELOP.      Status Date: 07/07/88 Calc  88
Weekly Gantt - Early Start/Finish                              Jul   Aug   Sep   Oct   Nov   Dec
                                    Date    Dur  PC Resp. Aux-1 0 1 1 2 0 0 1 2 2 0 1 1 2 0 1 1 2 3 0 1 2 2 0 1
Snode Enode     Description         Control                    4 1 8 5 1 8 5 2 9 5 2 9 6 3 0 7 4 1 7 4 1 8 5 2
-----------------------------------------------------------------+-------+-------+-------+-------+-------+---
       1   20 DEVELOP PRODUCT PLAN           20   0 MK          $$$$$$$$$
      20   30 SET OBJECTIVES                 10   0 PM                 $$$$$
      20  110 ORDER LONG LEAD TIME           15   0 PU                 AAAAAAA+++++++++++++++++++++++++++++++++
      30   40 ALLOCATE WORK                  10   0 PM                      $$$$$
      30   80 DEVELOP SYSTEM AND SS SPECS    40   0 PM                      AAAAAAAAAAAAAAAAAA++++++++++++++++++
      40   50 DESIGN AND TEST SS1           160   0 L1                             $$$$$$$$$$$$$$$$$$$$$$$$$$$$$$$$$
      40   60 DESIGN AND TEST SS3           105   0 L3                             AAAAAAAAAAAAAAAAAAAAAAAAAAAAAA
      40   70 DESIGN AND TEST SS4            65   0 L4                             AAAAAAAAAAAAAAAAAAAAAAAAA+++++


06/01/88                       ***** Resource Allocation Graph *****
              2 PROJECT MANAGER    Capacity= 8    60.00 Per Hour   G&A= 50%
                                   .....From 06/01/88 To 11/24/89.....

                                                1 1 1 1 1 1 1 1 1 1 2
                  1 2 3 4 5 6 7 8 9 0 1 2 3 4 5 6 7 8 9 0
% of Capacity  0....0....0....0....0....0....0....0....0....0....0....0....0....0....0....0....0....0....0....0....0
               +++++++++++++++++++++++++++++++++++++++++++++++++++++++++++++++++++++++++++++++++++++++++++++++++++
      08/04/88 :*****************************************************.                                    (100.0%)
      08/05/88 :*****************************************************.                                    (100.0%)
      08/06/88 :*                                                     :                                    (  0.0%)
      08/07/88 :*                                                     :                                    (  0.0%)
      08/08/88 :****************************************************.                                     (100.0%)
      08/09/88 :****************************************************.                                     (100.0%)
      08/10/88 :****************************************************.                                     (100.0%)
      08/11/88 :****************************************************.                                     (100.0%)
      08/12/88 :****************************************************.                                     (100.0%)
      08/13/88 :*                                                     :                                    (  0.0%)
      08/14/88 :*                                                     :                                    (  0.0%)
      08/15/88 :****************************************************.                                     (100.0%)
      08/16/88 :****************************************************.                                     (100.0%)
      08/17/88 :****************************************************.                                     (100.0%)
      08/18/88 :*****************************************************:ZZZZZZZZZZZZZZZZZZZZZZZ             (150.0%)
      08/19/88 :*****************************************************:ZZZZZZZZZZZZZZZZZZZZZZZ             (150.0%)
      08/20/88 :*                                                     :                                    (  0.0%)
      08/21/88 :*                                                     :                                    (  0.0%)
      08/22/88 :*****************************************************:ZZZZZZZZZZZZZZZZZZZZZZZ             (150.0%)
      08/23/88 :*****************************************************:ZZZZZZZZZZZZZZZZZZZZZZZ             (150.0%)
      08/24/88 :*****************************************************:ZZZZZZZZZZZZZZZZZZZZZZZ             (150.0%)
      08/25/88 :*****************************************************:ZZZZZZZZZZZZZZZZZZZZZZZ             (150.0%)
      08/26/88 :*****************************************************:ZZZZZZZZZZZZZZZZZZZZZZZ             (150.0%)
      08/27/88 :*                                                     :                                    (  0.0%)
      08/28/88 :*                                                     :                                    (  0.0%)
      08/29/88 :*****************************************************:ZZZZZZZZZZZZZZZZZZZZZZZ             (150.0%)
      08/30/88 :*****************************************************:ZZZZZZZZZZZZZZZZZZZZZZZ             (150.0%)
      08/31/88 :*****************************************************:ZZZZZZZZZZZZZZZZZZZZZZZ             (150.0%)
      09/01/88 :***************************                          :                                    ( 50.0%)
      09/02/88 :***************************                          :                                    ( 50.0%)
```

Figure 11-3. A schedule and a resource management histogram from PMS-II.®

Bill Boyd, the engineering manager, reviewed the situation after six months. It had taken longer than he had expected. He was satisfied that they were smarter now than they were at the beginning. Nothing like this could have happened overnight anyway. They had missed using the software on the current project, but all was not lost. Victor had managed to capture the interest of the project engineer, Paul, who was anxious to use it on his next project. This almost guaranteed adoption by the organization, because Paul was an opinion leader.

Bill made plans to have it in use for 50 percent of his projects in another three months and on all projects within one year. After one year, he would inaugurate the materials management and resource management add-on programs. Victor was now available for other work. However, his supervisor understood that Victor would keep one-third of his time available to help people apply the new project management software. Success was on the horizon.

COMMON MISTAKES IN ADOPTING COMPUTER ASSISTANCE

1. They tried to do it too fast.
2. They tried to be cheap when they purchased the software.
3. They thought one program would suit all users and all applications.
4. They thought the acquisition of project management software would get them into project management. (It's a good start, but it's only ⅓ of what is needed for successful project management.)
5. They did not really learn how to use the program well.
6. They did not anticipate future needs.
7. They pushed too hard to get the system adopted by all.

EXPORT OR IMPORT OF PROJECT DATA TO AND FROM OTHER SOFTWARE

Wouldn't it be nice if you could switch to other software programs without entering your project data all over again? Yes, it would. This is a useful feature and you should look for some of the following functions.

Export of Data to Spreadsheet and Database Programs

Many PC-based project management (PM) packages have the ability to export (transfer) data to popular software packages, such as Lotus®, Symphony®, dBase®, and others. In practice, this means you can take project cost data, process it separately, and create new report formats, including colorful pie charts and histograms. However, only some of these PM packages can import raw data, and when they do, considerable setup is required. Moreover, the data may be transformed into appropriate integer or decimal values.

Some PM programs will allow you to create and export a file for use with other unnamed programs. However, using this facility is not straightforward. You would need to follow the manual carefully. Alternatively, you may get detailed help from the vendor's technical support staff.

Import of selected raw data from spreadsheets to PM software is now a practical feature which has been incorporated into quite a few PM software packages. For example, you could take a spreadsheet used to calculate payroll costs and transfer the summary columns to the cost data fields of your PM software.

Export to Mainframe Computers

Some sophisticated programs require mainframe computers. (When you read this, microcomputers may have reached the current mainframe capacity required for most PM software.) The owners of these mainframe programs have developed PC versions which are simpler to use. Individual project managers can work over their own projects on a PC. Then, their projects—and all others in the organization—can be exported into a file which is then uploaded into the full-scale mainframe PM software. There, all projects can be combined for master schedules, resource load leveling, and combined reports.

A few examples of this are PC versions provided for Premis®, Project 2®, Mister®, Artemis®, and Vision®. You can expect that all commercial mainframe PM software will have PC versions available.

There is another way to tie PC software to mainframe software. The vendor of the mainframe software may write a special subprogram for you. Then you will be able to convert your PM files from a

PC program into a form suitable for use with your mainframe program. For example, this is done for you if you purchase a Nichols® mainframe program. As another example, Microsoft® project files can be imported into the high-level program called Primavera.®

Export from a PC Program to a Selected Mainframe Upgrade

Because PC-based PM software tends to be user-friendly, and easy to use, it is much desired for small to medium projects. What if the project work grows enough to benefit from the sophistication of a mainframe program? This has not been overlooked, and I think there will be a trend to provide this feature. Ask about it. For example, Time Line provides project files that can be exported to use with two high-level programs, Ca-Tella Plan® and Artemis®.

COST DATA WITH SOFTWARE ASSISTANCE

Keeping track of budgets and actual costs is so easily done on a computer that most PM software for PCs is adequate for small to medium projects. Sums by subprojects and by departments are easily prepared.

Somewhere between a 10-task small project and a 1000-task construction project, the need for extra cost data fields increases so that only a few of the PM software packages for PCs are adequate for the latter. (A *data field* is the computer space required to hold a number, such as the cost. Imagine a page of cost data. Each number requires a data field.) A simple project can manage with two cost data fields per task, like budget and actual. At the next level one may want to record man-hours, hourly rate, manpower budget, overhead, and material expense. This would require ten cost data fields for budgets and actuals.

As projects get larger and more costly, one needs additional data fields for cost to date and for estimate at completion. If your small project is a subproject of a large project, you may be required to prepare and report the cost data in 10 to 20 data fields. The software requires a built-in mini-spreadsheet. At this level of software, graphs of cost versus time are also provided for cash flow reporting.

If your PM software has more data fields than you need, you should be able to ignore some of them or leave them blank. If not, you have a program which is more difficult to use than a simpler one. This is another reason why evaluation of the software on your own projects is a good idea before deciding to purchase it.

WHICH COMPUTER TO USE

If you work for a large organization, this has probably been resolved for you. Many organizations have standardized on PCs. By far the largest corporate use is the IBM PC, its clones and compatibles (including XTs and ATs). For these there is a wide choice of over 100 PM software programs.

A growing contender, at the time of writing, is the Apple computer series with its Macintosh®. They have an advantage when it comes to graphics because of the WYSIWYG system (what you see is what you get). The MacProject software for this is good for small to medium projects, but at the time of writing, it lacked reports on Free Float. Other vendors also have software to work on Macintosh computers.

One software program, Micro Planner®, has designed versions for both the Macintosh and the IBM PC. The project files may be transferred to either computer. This is useful for a project team using both kinds of computers.

The last word on computer adoption will never be spoken. Currently, Apple offers a computer to run on a DOS program, which allows it to run most software originally designed for the IBM PC.

A word about *compatibles*. They will run on software designed for the IBM PC and its clones, but occasionally there is a problem with some minor functions. The software vendor may be able to tell you if their program will run perfectly on your compatible, even if they don't provide technical support for your compatible.

Truly portable laptop computers can be a great boon to project managers. I had the first one on the market, the Radio Shack M100. It had a 4-line, 40-character screen, and 28K of memory. I still use it for word processing when away from my office computer. Its use helped me define what you will soon be able to do at a reasonable cost. (You can do most of it now at about twice the cost of an office computer.) You can be scanning and updating projects while traveling in an airplane or working at home. It is possible for you to have your favorite software with you, all project data, a personal time manager, a note pad, and a word processor. A hard disk or large, permanently powered RAM memory (also called a hard disk RAM) is what you currently would need. A floppy disk drive is not necessary if you go back and forth to one office which has a special interface to read your programs and data in and out of the laptop computer. I personally am looking for one with an integral hard-copy printer for letter-size sheets. (An early one to provide this was WANG.)

The modern project manager in the near future will have a laptop computer with an integral printer that in total weighs under 10 pounds. It will be capable of a three-foot fall without becoming inoperative. It will fit in a briefcase, with room to spare. It will have a high-definition screen, possibly in color. It will have provision to put the screen display onto a large-screen projector for use at meetings. Naturally, it will have a compact modem for sending data back to the office computer via telephone. I am optimistic about this. It should cost no more than an in-office desktop computer. Look for it. In addition there is software to operate your distant office computer from a laptop with a modem. This means that the laptop can access additional programs and data without having a hard disk of its own.

SELECTION OF PM SOFTWARE FOR A PC

There are seven criteria that I have developed in recent years for you to use in selecting your PM software. These criteria will help you make a wise choice for your own situation. It may seem like too much work for a purchase of $200 to $5000. Don't even think of it in those terms. As a business investment, it will cost you tens of thousands of dollars to get it operational with a project team. It will cost even more if you make a poor selection and end up replacing it with another.

Support for Your Brand of PC

Software promotional brochures can be misleading. One brochure, for example, has a section called "System Configuration Hardware

Requirements"; it names 23 specific computers. Another brochure has the statement: "All our software runs on standard, IBM compatible equipment." These are good guidelines, but is this enough? Do they have your kind of computer at their center for technical support? If not, you are at risk, because they can only give you good help over the telephone if they have an identical computer to the one you are using. Unfortunately for you, "compatible" only means what it says. There may be a function or so that will not work. Worse still, at some unusual point in a program, you may get locked out; all you can do is turn off the computer, lose your current data, and start over. If your computer is truly supported by the software vendor, you will get help with special problems. They'll even modify versions of a program to work on a supported computer. If your computer is not truly supported, you are the one who must solve the problem.

Loop Detection or Prevention

A loop in a network can give you an error in calculations, and you may not recognize it. A good software program will not let this happen, or at least will report the existence of a loop. Figure 11-4 is an explanation of a "loop." The times to do B and C are added repeatedly to the project completion time.

In an arrow-node (activity-on-arrow) diagram, a loop can be prevented by not allowing the end node of a task to have a smaller number than the start node.

In a precedence box-type diagram, a loop can be created which requires considerable analysis to find it. Although most will indi-

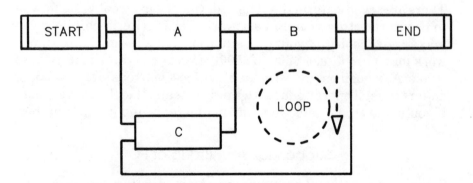

Figure 11-4. Good software will prevent or detect this loop.

cate where the loop is, some may produce only an error message—"I have a loop"—and leave it up to you to find it.

Open-End Detection

An open end is an activity not connected at one end. Some precedence software will not accept an activity without naming a predecessor and successor. Others will. See Figure 11-5 for an explanation of "open end."

Logic Network Printout

If you have a loop or an open end in the network you have entered, you may need to examine a printout of the logic diagram. This will enable you to find an error or omission in data entry. Without it you can examine your data entry again and again and never find the problem. We are blind to our own errors. Of course, a small network is more easily examined than a large one. If your networks are to have 25 or more activities, you will benefit from a logic diagram printout. Some PM software programs for PCs do not have it.

For Beginners and Small Projects

In this case you should look for a program without too many features. Extra features mean versatility, but there are many questions to be answered as you progress through the program. These confuse the novice.

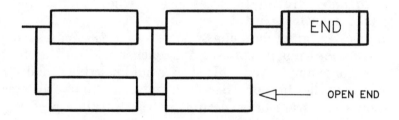

Figure 11-5. Good software will report on this open end.

A *menu-driven* program is almost universal in modern software. Commands do not need to be memorized.

A *help function* is essential for beginners. Wherever one is stuck in the program, a simple command will list and explain what can be done at that point. Good help functions are specific to the point you are at in the program. The next best is an indexed on-line text file which can be searched for specific help. The worst is a note which refers you to the manual. Beginners and infrequent users find manuals very complex. That is why a good help function is needed for them.

A *default* answer on every menu or question is great to have. If you're not sure what to do next, just press the return key and you will most likely get what you need.

A *check on magnitudes and characters* is useful. For example, you should not be able to enter February 31 or put the letter "o" in place of a zero in a field requiring only numbers.

For Advanced Users and Larger Projects

Free Float reports are important to projects involving more than one department. One needs to know the extra time available to finish a task before another department is scheduled to use the result to start the following task. Unfortunately, many fine programs report only the Total Float. It seems that on a small project, the Total Float and the Free Float are often the same. If occasionally they are different, one can determine the difference by examining the bar chart and annotating the differences on the chart.

The project file should be *easy to update*. A large project with over 100 activities will be time-consuming to update if you need to step through every task. One should be able to go directly to any single task and update it.

Forced dates are an asset, especially when adding multiple projects to a master schedule.

Windows are great for doing "what if" analyses. With them you can change one thing in a project, and concurrently see the effect on another. For example, you could stretch out an activity, and simultaneously see the effect on a bar chart and on a resource histogram.

Report choices are often desired by the full-time professional project manager. Some software programs have only predesigned reports.

Combining Multiple Projects

In theory, any PM software can be used for multiple projects by laboriously entering the project after project on to a master logic diagram. In good software for this purpose, each project is a stand-alone entity, but the resource base is shared by all projects. Each project can be easily entered into a master multiple project by replacing one of its activities with a whole project. (The added project becomes a subproject of the master.) As each single project is updated, the master schedule is also updated. This enables one to immediately see the effect of a shared resource. (See Figure 12-3 for an additional explanation.)

While quite a few PC software programs have the above subproject capability for scheduling, only a few will take overall shared resources into account when showing a resource histogram or when using automatic resource leveling.

Some Other Software Features

Among the features frequently offered in PM software for a PC are *resource histograms* and *automatic resource leveling*. While these are worthwhile features to have on medium to large projects, you can manage small projects without them. The reason for this is twofold: Firstly, you cannot assume that one specialist is as good as another. Secondly, small projects are frequently carried along with other routine work, which can be set aside during peak workloads on a project.

However, when multiple projects are considered, even small projects add up to the workload and complexity of medium to large projects. For this reason, resource histograms and automatic resource leveling is covered in detail in the next chapter.

Figure 11-6 is a summary of the above criteria for selecting PC software for project management.

AN EXAMPLE OF A MEDIUM PROJECT

The Personnel Records Project has been entered into two PM software programs for PCs. These were Harvard Project Manager, version 2.01, and Time Line®, version 3.0. See Figures 11-7 and 11-8.

PC SOFTWARE CRITERIA IN ORDER OF IMPORTANCE

1. **Supported** for your brand of PC
2. **Loop** detection or prevention
3. **Open-end** detection
4. Logic **network** printout
5. For beginners & **small** projects:
   Menus; Help; Defaults; Checks magnitudes and characters; Prompts
6. For advanced & **larger** projects:
   Reports FF; Easy to update; Report choices; Forced dates; Resource histograms
7. For **multiple** projects: Can combine networks & data; Sums resources over all
8. Automatic resource leveling

Figure 11-6. PC software criteria in order of importance.

MULTIUSER PROGRAMS

Suppose you are the project manager for a medium project and suppose also that five separate departments use the same kind of PC and software. Then the subschedules and sub-budgets can each be updated on a PC and sent in the form of disks to you, the project manager. You can then read them into a PC and update the master schedule.

Wouldn't it be nice if each department and yourself were all linked on a computer network? Then, at the instant anyone updated their data, you would have it available to you on your own computer.

Organizations with many PC users are working toward *multiuser systems*. This requires that the PM software be written to use the multiuser operating system that links these PCs together. The PM software may be written to use UNIX and VMS, or alterna-

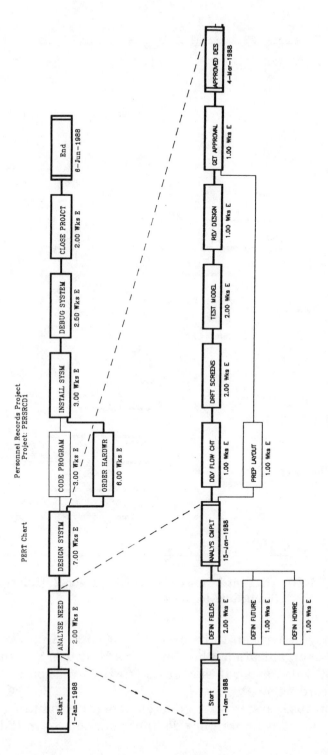

Figure 11-7a. Harvard Project Manager, version 2.01, levels 2 and 3 logic diagrams.

224 COMPUTER ASSISTANCE

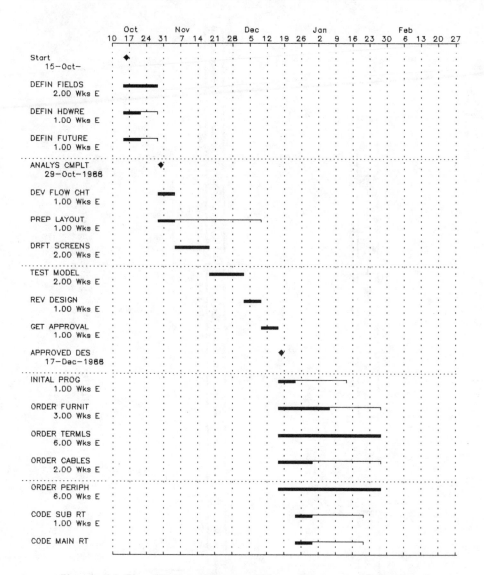

Figure 11-7b. Harvard Project Manager, version 2.01, level 3 schedule for part of a project.

tively, it may be written to be used with a Local Area Network (LAN). If your organization is heading into a Multiuser System, ask your PM software vendor if they have, or will have their software changed accordingly.

While multiuser systems are great for general accounting, operations and word processors, they do limit your choices in PM soft-

MULTIUSER PROGRAMS 225

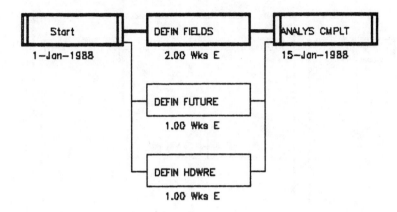

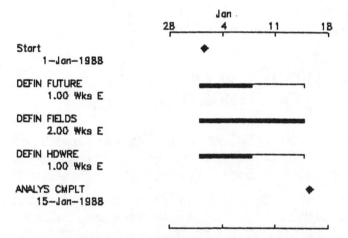

Figure 11-7c. Harvard Project Manager, version 2.01, PERT and Gantt charts for a subproject.

ware. One of the advantages of the PC is the autonomy that the users have in selecting software that suits their personal needs, rather than the needs of a previously installed system. So, even if your choice of software does not embrace a Multiuser System, there is still the advantage of freedom of choice. This includes the choice to drop a software program and go to another which has even better features for your personal usage.

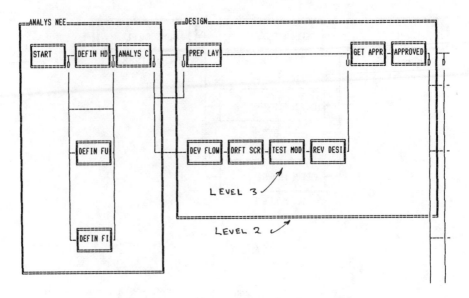

Figure 11-8a. Time Line® version 3.0, levels 2 and 3 logic diagram.

QUESTIONS FOR ASSIGNMENT OR DISCUSSION

1. In this chapter, read over Case 1 and Application to Small Projects. In about one or two paragraphs, summarize the problems Mary-Helen got into and how she could have done better.
2. In this chapter, read over Case 2 and Application to a Medium Project. In about three or four paragraphs, summarize the problems Bill Boyd got into and how he could have done better.
3. This is a group project. Make your own case history of an actual introduction of PM software to an organization. This might be in the memory of one of the group, or you may take the time to collect information on a real happening like this at your school, in government, in business, or in industry. Examine your case history for examples of the *Common Mistakes in Adopting Computer Assistance,* as outlined in this chapter. Show to what extent they followed *The Principles of Computer Assistance* outlined in this chapter.
4. Take a small project that you are working on, produce logic diagrams, Gantt charts, budgets, and resource histograms by

QUESTIONS FOR ASSIGNMENT OR DISCUSSION 227

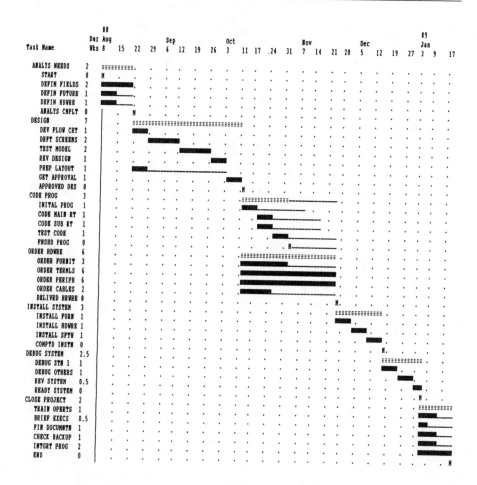

Figure 11-8b. Time Line® version 3.0, levels 2 and 3 schedule.

using available PM software for a PC. This is to demonstrate your mastery of a software program.

5. Take a medium project, do question 4, but also add similar reports for subprojects or subreports for other departments doing parts of the project. Your reports will cover levels 2 and 3, such as the reports shown in Figures 11-7 and 11-8.

CHAPTER
twelve

MULTIPLE PROJECTS
look at the load on the resources

> **Key Idea**
>
> Projects become interdependent when they share resources.

Basic project management starts by assuming that the people and other resources will be there when they are required. This is seldom true, however, when an organization has multiple projects. Rather than increasing or decreasing the people on staff to match project needs, the organization keeps an average level of staff. Consequently, the staff will be overloaded some of the time, and if staffing is not managed well, there will also be wasteful slack periods. The key to managing multiple projects is to adjust the schedules to suit the available resources. This calls for resource and schedule planning.

When resources are not available to serve two projects at once, one project must get priority over the other. A common problem with priority setting is to let urgency take over and not to consider the long-term payoff of the individual projects.

In the following cases, you will learn how projects affect one another. Management and working levels must address this interaction; they do this by Load Forecasting.

CASE 1:
THE MERGER CREATES A BOTTLENECK

Mary-Helen had her nine projects in order, and things were going relatively smoothly. That was just before her organization went through the convulsion of a merger with another insurance firm. Some projects were put on hold; new ones were created; and many insurance products needed altering. Headquarters promoted her manager, Bill, to executive vice-president. Good fortune also befell Mary-Helen; they promoted her to Bill's job. Now she was the manager. In turn, she reported to a new boss who was acquired through the merger. His name was Jeff, and he was anxious to make a good impression on his management.

CASE 1: THE MERGER CREATES A BOTTLENECK

Mary-Helen now had responsibility for more than 50 projects, which she managed through four project leaders. She made sure that the project leaders presented her with workload charts. She adjusted deadlines on projects to suit the availability of her subordinates.

As priorities were changing rapidly, Mary-Helen could see the value of computerizing the schedule. To this end, she had appointed a young man who had recently graduated from business school. He had the necessary computer skills. It was an exciting time in Mary-Helen's life. She showed her confidence by a spring in her walk and the authoritative way she made decisions.

The storm of the merger of the two organizations gradually subsided. Jeff found time to have a good look at the portfolio of projects that Mary was managing. He commented, "You sure have your work organized. I wish the other departments were doing this well. The merger has brought on a lot of new obligations. I see a lot of work in merging our policies and creating new ones. Because we are going to be stronger, our competition is giving us a hard time. They are quite aggressive in their business approach. We have to get on the market with some new products as fast as we can. We should advance five of your projects by six months so that we can achieve a good market position. Can you do it?"

Mary-Helen paused for a moment while she collected her thoughts. "Jeff is quite different from Bill," she thought. "Bill would want to talk this over, but I think Jeff wants to get his way without too much discussion." She looked Jeff in the face and said, "Sure, it can be done, but . . ." She paused a moment when she noticed a flick of anger in Jeff's eyes and then continued, "but it will affect some other projects, Jeff. Can I have a day to look at our workload to see what I can do?"

"Well, I guess so. I don't think we have any choice in the matter. We are going to be number one in this business, and this is what it takes. See me tomorrow at ten." After Mary-Helen left his office, Jeff thought, "Mary-Helen seems to know where it's at. She comes highly recommended. Normally, I don't take any nonsense from subordinates, but I'll hold off until tomorrow's meeting."

After she got back to her office, Mary-Helen had some second thoughts, too. "The new boss is a bit pushy. I wonder if he ever had a woman manager before? Hey, wait a minute! Maybe I'm getting touchy on this subject. He might be that way with everyone. I'll find out soon enough." She got out the loading charts produced by her project leaders and worked over them briefly. She then called an emergency meeting of the project leaders. At this meeting, they worked out an advanced schedule for delivery of the five important projects. To the best of their judgment, they decided which of the other projects could be deferred.

The meeting at 10:00 the next day with Jeff went smoothly. It pleased him to see that the schedules of the five key projects could be advanced. He expressed some regret, however, that the other projects would be delayed. He wondered why they couldn't make this up with overtime. Mary-Helen stated that they usually worked plenty of overtime just taking care of problems. She thought it wise not to schedule overtime for their projects, because then they wouldn't have that reserve overtime for emergencies. However, she could move up the dates on the delayed projects if she had more help.

"No way," said Jeff, "The company has a freeze on all hiring. As a matter of fact, one of the advantages they see in a merger is to let people go, so although we might get a few good people from my side of the new company, I think our overall staff size will be decreased. They want to run lean. Besides, we should be trimming our overall manpower as we get more into the use of computers. That's one thing the new management will back us up on. Try to use computers instead of people."

"I am glad you mentioned it," said Mary-Helen. "In fact, we have been getting into computers. I would like to have at least one more computer station. Then, I'd have one person use it full-time for helping us get into computers. That would allow the project leaders to have ready access to a computer when planning their programs."

In the next few months, things went faster, but relatively without incident. Mary-Helen's team worked hard on the urgent projects, and most of them were ready for the advertising phase. The Advertising and Publications Department, managed by Chet, had been very compliant and had agreed to advanced dates on every project. They prepared the copy and artwork for promotions of new and existing products. Chet's unwritten rule for getting ahead was to agree to do everything that his management asked him to do. He was very compliant. So it was just business as usual when he agreed to advance the dates for the five key projects that Mary-Helen was handling.

After she missed two completion dates because of delays in the advertising, Mary-Helen realized that she had found a bottleneck. It was true that the Advertising and Publications Department was working hard on their projects. If Mary-Helen wanted one task advanced over the others, Chet was willing to do it. She had heard by the grapevine, however, that this frequent changing of priorities was driving his subordinates crazy. They would just get started on one project, and then they would have to drop it and start on another. This wasted time. They were in a muddle and getting nowhere. Mary-Helen knew that there was an overload problem. She tried mentioning to Chet how she had worked out the load on her key people. It showed her in advance where there could be a potential overload. Chet was not the sort to listen or to ask for advice. He was independent. He tried to solve his problems by working harder, but the bottleneck remained. Mary-Helen began to realize that her department alone could not solve the multiple project overload problems.

CASE 2: THE PAST PROJECTS WOULDN'T SETTLE DOWN

The Personnel Records Project had finished the installation phase. The final phases of the "Debug system" and "Close project" activities were George's assignments. He was also the programmer who designed the system. George had estimated that he could do it in three and a half weeks. This was what the schedule provided.

Jack Daniels was beginning to relax on this project. He seemed to be in the homestretch now, and things were running smoothly. Jack looked forward to having time to get on to his other projects. As he was sorting through his telephone messages, he noticed an "urgent" one from the personnel manager. "Oh oh," thought Jack, "I'll bet this isn't just a social call."

Sure enough, the news was not good. "When is the system going to be up and going?" asked a rather tense personnel manager. "Your man, George, is never around when we want him. Station 1 is debugged, but the others are not ready. Our operators were standing by last week for training, but George showed up for only two hours during the whole week. They tell me that when they leave messages for George, he doesn't bother to return them. Look, Jack, it was bad enough that we waited an extra six weeks for the furniture. Now we are being held up again."

Jack called George into his office: "You allowed three and a half weeks to do these tasks, and four weeks have gone by and they're still not done. Which reminds me, I haven't had a report lately with your forecasted completion on it. When do you plan to finish up the project?"

There was annoyance in George's voice as he replied, "I am doing the best I can. I can't help it if the Payroll Department ran into a bug in the software we did for them. If I hadn't taken time out to do that, the payroll would have been late. I no sooner fixed the one bug when I created another. I even worked evenings testing the system to make sure there were no more problems."

"Okay, George, I can see how that took priority on your time. Did you tell the personnel manager about it? He said that you didn't even return calls. I know how it is when you get caught up in a challenging problem. You tend to forget everything else. Still, from management's point of view, we must keep the other managers informed. I'm not blaming you for what you did, but we should have been informed. Would you take a few minutes and rework the schedule? Tell me when you think you will finish. By the way, if you need some help, I may be able to release a programmer to help you. Better still, let's take a look at the schedules together right now. Then I can report back to the personnel manager. Let me handle him for now, but in the future, tell him what's going on. I'm sure he didn't want the Payroll Department to be shut down, either."

At the end of the day, when the storm had subsided, Jack reflected on what had happened. George had said that he could do the work in three and a half weeks, and that seemed possible. However, he had not allowed for maintenance calls on projects that he had already finished. In other words, he probably only had about 20 hours a week to devote to the Personnel Records Project. He spent the rest of the time on callbacks to projects that wouldn't settle down. Also, there was some administrative time. Jack would make sure in the future that all of his subordinates considered their ongoing work as well as new project work. Besides, the resulting reports would give him a better idea on what the administrative load was really like.

DISCUSSION

You have seen two situations that affected project schedules. In the Personnel Records Project, the time needed for the regular, ongoing work was not allowed for in the project time estimate. It is not uncommon for people to assume that they could work full time on a project. They base their estimate on the hours of work needed to do the project, rather than on the elapsed time to do it. In other words, if George had allowed three and a half weeks of work at 50 percent load, the elapsed time would have been seven weeks. An alternative would have been to have someone assist him with the work, so that, together, they could get it done in three and a half weeks.

The other situation—the problem with the Advertising and Publications Department—shows how one project affects another. When there's an overload, there can be too many number-one priorities. Not all the work can get done. It's too late then to do much about it. One needs to forecast the load on a department in advance. Then one can take offsetting actions.

Although load forecasting is easy to do, very few department managers are doing it. Attendees at my seminars have discovered how easy it is to do. They can even train a clerk to do it for them. An ounce of resource analysis is worth a pound of cure.

A Principle for Multiple Projects

Other projects and other work affect the schedule of a project. To minimize this impact, plan the workload in advance.

APPLICATION TO A MULTIPLE-PROJECT LOAD

Suppose that Chet, the manager of advertising and publications for the insurance company, had listened to Mary-Helen. They could have developed a forecasted department load like that shown in Figure 12-1.

| PROJECT | HOURS PER WEEK REQUIRED ||||||||||
| | WEEK NUMBER ||||||||||
	1	2	3	4	5	6	7	8	9	10
Project A	20	40	60	60	20	20				
Project B		20	60	80	80	40	20			
Project C		10	50	50	50	40	10			
Project D		80	80	80	50	50	40	20		
Project E			60	60	60	40	40	40	20	
TOTAL	20	150	310	330	260	190	110	60	20	

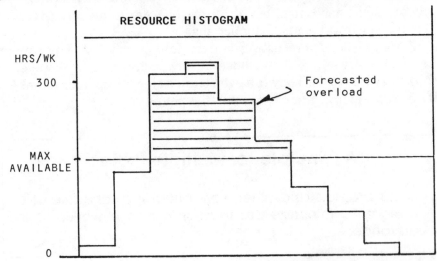

Figure 12-1. Forecasted resource load.

RESOURCE AVAILABILITY AFFECTS THE SCHEDULE

For most organizations doing multiple projects, limits are put on people and equipment resources. Thus, one project can affect another. The alternative is to adjust the resources to suit the workload. This is usually the practice of consulting firms. For example, an advertising agency will usually have free-lance workers available to take the overload work. Many free-lancers work out of their homes and don't require a steady job. In fact, society is changing so much that there are many people who now prefer this lifestyle. Engineering and software consultants also adjust their resources to suit the load. They do this by planning to have additional people on hand when required. In addition, they contract out overload work to other consultants. Thus, they are able to respond to customers who want their schedules changed.

In most organizations, changes in the size of the staff are defined by long-term needs. The staff size should be such that they are overloaded some of the time and underloaded the rest of the time. In other words, they can get the work done, on the average, without being overstaffed. Also, there are often restrictions on the amount of paid overtime that can be worked by staff people. This restriction makes it difficult for resource managers to respond to rapid changes in priorities.

If a department head plans resource needs in advancce, he or she will be able to get authorization for overtime or for a temporary staff increase. This can be done in time to save a project schedule. Because resource planning was done, there will be credible data to show that the department cannot do all of its projects at the same time.

COMPETITION BETWEEN PROJECT LEADERS

Each project leader gets recognition for having brought a project in on schedule. When resources are shared, however, there is a great potential for conflict over resources. The project leader who can get the resources can make a better showing, so project leaders become adept at using persuasion, favor-for-favor, sweet talk, or coercion.

On the one hand, the attention given to individual projects by project leaders is a good thing. The projects do better than if they were managed by due process. The project leader's attention ensures that there is no wasted time. On the other hand, with limited resources, there are often winners and losers. Push does come to shove, and the more aggressive project leaders seem to have the edge. Sometimes, high-profile projects are given to aggressive project leaders for just this reason. In the long run, however, a project's success should not depend on the personality of the project leader assigned. It should depend on the worth of the project.

To minimize unfriendly competition, one needs an early warning system of detecting a resource overload. Then management can adjudicate by assigning priorities to projects during the overload.

ANALYZING YOUR OWN WORKLOAD

The project leader is often a scarce resource. When there are multiple projects, the workload can peak and be more than the project leader can handle. (Refer to Chapter 1 for the case of Mary-Helen and the insurance company. With only five projects, she was overloaded for a two-month period, as shown in Figure 1-1.) It is the advance knowledge of this work overload that is of great benefit. One can then take offsetting actions. If not, one could be well into the overload and failing to deliver on projects before realizing the problem. Then it is too late.

The project leader must be organized both on project work and on other work assignments. (Chapter 13 covers this more extensively.) I have found that project leaders on multiple projects need to have training in time management in order to solve the total problem. This is because they are pressured from all directions and need to plan out their work instead of responding to the pressure of the day. When you put project management and effective time management together, you have the material I use in my combined seminar, "Managing Multiple Projects Under Pressure." Truly, this describes the typical work situation.

PRIORITIES WITHIN A PROJECT

Once you have a logic diagram for a project, you can determine the priorities on your time for the project. Obviously, you must do the predecessors before starting a new activity. You have some options with parallel activities. However, they, in turn, have priority on your time over something that follows them. So, by and large, the logical sequence establishes the priorities on your time.

PRIORITIES AMONG PROJECTS

When you have enough resources to handle all projects, there is no need for setting priorities among projects. When there is a scarce resource, however, priorities on its use must be established. The scarce resource may be you, a unique skill that is required, equipment, or a facility. It follows, then, that if you can increase your resources to handle the workload, you do not need to set priorities among projects. If you can't increase the resources, priorities are a must.

There are two dimensions of priority on your time. One is the *payoff*, which might include return on investment, reputation, social value, praise from your boss, and so forth. The other dimension of priority on your time is *urgency*. This is related to keeping promises, avoiding penalties, an executive directive, a crash program, or meeting deadlines established by outside circumstances.

The payoff dimensions of priority are usually long-term in nature. Therefore, top management should set them when initiating or reviewing projects. Many project leaders work in organizations in which the long-term priorities based on payoffs have not been set by top management. Some of them submit their own drafts of long-term priorities and then discuss them with their manager. Others find it pointless to initiate such a discussion. Instead, they hand in a written document of the long-term priorities as they see them, and they state that they will work on that basis unless informed otherwise.

Here is one important fact about the situation: If the long-term priorities are not set by the top management, they will be set at the lower levels. This is usually done by resource managers, because they must decide on the allocation of their resources. They solve the problem the best way they can. However, this may not be consistent with what's really important at the executive level. They can only guess.

In the absence of long-term priority setting by top management, resource managers can appear to be petty tyrants. They are forced to decide on the allocation of their resources. They work on the projects according to how they are treated by the project leaders, according to past relationships, according to blood relationships, or according to whatever rules they choose to set. Top management must recognize that if they do not set priorities among projects, resource managers will do it in ways that may not be the best.

Urgency is the dimension of priority that can kill the planning that goes into meeting payoff priorities. A valued customer can upset a whole schedule with one request to a top executive. That customer's project can become number one and push others off the schedule. Later, the delayed projects become number ones. Urgency seems to take over every time.

Another urgency situation is when a project has run into trouble and is seriously behind schedule. Nothing has happened to the long-term value of the project, but promises must be kept. Urgency takes over again.

Some projects have a high profit-making potential if they are put on the market early. If they are late, there is a subsequent loss of profit. In such cases, the payoff is related to urgency, and it is easy to make a decision. On the other hand, beware of giving in to urgency when a delay of a few weeks would not affect the long-term payoff.

The way to respond to urgency is to assess the impact on long-term payoffs before responding. Management has the right to know (and the obligation to ask) the overall effect of a change of schedule when something suddenly becomes urgent. A comprehensive schedule of all projects, and an easy means of revision, make it possible to assess the changes in a hurry.

AN APPLICATION OF PROJECT PRIORITIES

Let's take the projects on Mary-Helen's list, as shown in Figure 12-2, and establish payoffs and urgencies according to the foregoing guidelines. In the figure, I have used X's for payoff. The more X's a project has, the more the perceived payoff. I have used +'s for urgency. The more +'s there are, the greater the urgency.

PROJECT	PAYOFF	URGENCY
MILLER PROJECT. This is an update of an existing product. The improvements will make it more profitable. The incremental payoff is not great. The urgency is minimal because there is an existing product.	X	0
JOINT PROJECT. This is a joint program with another insurance company to make adjustments to a policy as required by law. The legislation takes effect in 2 months, so it is urgent. There is no increased payoff for doing it, but deletion of it from the product line would cost some loss, so there is some payoff.	X	+++
HIGH PROFILE PROJECT #1. This is an exploratory type project which is being pushed by one of the executives. It has a high profile, but the payoff is not known. It has been promised in 3 months and the boss thinks it's important to keep the good will of this executive. Therefore, it is regarded as having a modest payoff to the department. It also has some urgency because executives won't wait forever.	X	+
HIGH PROFILE PROJECT #2. This is to copy a competitor's product and it will be profitable. Therefore, the payoff is good. Although it has a high profile with the executive management, there is no deadline. However, the longer it takes, the less the long-term profit.	XX	+
TEACHER'S PENSION PROJECT. This is a very profitable product. However, it is not due for 6 months, so at this point, it is only a little urgent as late introduction will reduce the profit.	XXXX	+

Figure 12-2. Mary-Helen's projects and their priorities.

RAPIDLY CHANGING PRIORITIES

At my seminars, I frequently ask: "Of those handling multiple projects, how many have the long-term priorities set by top management?" About one-third respond positively. For another third, it doesn't matter. The remainder describe their situations as "a madhouse."

Even when top management sets long-term priorities for projects in an orderly fashion, rapid changes of priorities can reduce the schedule to a shambles. Read over the following situation and see if it resembles yours.

A chief executive officer (CEO) gets a call from a friend. "Hi there, Charlie. This is Al, here. How are you doing, you old son-of-a-gun? I haven't seen you down at the club lately. Is everything okay with you and Mary, and the kids?"

"Al, this is a surprise. It's good to hear from you." The conversation goes on in this friendly vein. You see, we have a buddy-buddy network here. It helps grease the wheels of commerce.

Eventually, they get down to the purpose of the call. "Look, Charlie, I've got a little problem. I wonder if you can help me. I've been trying to get our order pushed ahead by two weeks, but your people tell me it doesn't have enough priority for that. This is important to me, Charlie, so do you think you can do something about it?"

"Okay, Al, I'll look into it and let you know what we can do."

So the CEO goes to his vice-president. He finds out that Al's project has a 10 priority rating; there are nine projects ahead of his. He says, "Would you look into moving number ten up to number-one priority?"

The VP goes to the manager of operations and says, "The CEO wants us to do something about moving number ten up to number one."

The manager of operations, in turn, goes to the resource manager and says, "Will you do something about moving number ten up to number one? The CEO wants it."

The resource manager, in turn, goes to the project leader and says, "Drop everything and do number ten."

A few days later, the CEO gets a congratulatory message from Al and thinks that everything is okay. Two weeks later, there is much consternation when Charlie finds that the original number-one priority has been delayed by a couple of weeks. A key customer is very much disturbed. The explanation comes back like this: "We thought that number ten was the most important project, so we moved it up to number-one priority. Naturally, it displaced a few others. It's what you wanted, isn't it?"

The CEO is annoyed and comes back with, "What I wanted? What I seemed to remember was asking you to *look into* moving number ten up to number one. I expected you to report back to me."

You can see here that the CEO asked the right question, but the situation was influenced by the first rule of management: Whatever interests the boss fascinates the hell out of me. After four levels of fascination, a wish becomes a command. This is a real problem for executives, and they know it.

How should subordinates respond? Clearly, they should report back the consequences of an action to change priorities before upsetting the previously arranged schedule. Who is to do this? When you get right down to it, the person at the working level is more aware of the impact on other projects than a senior person would be. Therefore, the project leader should respond something like: "I'm ready to move number ten up to number-one priority and get it out two weeks earlier, but it does impact the other projects. It looks like number one would be delayed about two weeks." This message would go back up to the CEO. Because of the many levels of management and because people are away frequently, it may take a week to get the answer. One week is too long. The CEO is likely to get frustrated.

It's not surprising, then, that a CEO may frequently revert to something that always works. He may say: "Right now, this number-ten project is the most important, and I want it out two weeks earlier." If the subordinates jump into action, the CEO's behavior is reinforced. He is likely to do it again. In fact, he'll *have to* do it again and again. Changing priorities suddenly will cause unwanted consequences. Soon he will come back and say, "Drop everything, and do number one," and then, a day or so later, "Drop everything and do number three."

It might be reasonable to operate this way in a one-man-run organization, such as a local automotive service shop. When customers come in, they get some attention. When they leave, someone else gets attention. At the end of the day, four or five jobs can somehow get done. Such is not the case in a large organization. Changing priorities rapidly can cause chaos. It also causes inefficiency, because starting and stopping on projects always induces some wasted time.

Let's summarize it this way. In a small organization, with only one or two levels of management and not many projects, it is possible to change priorities on a daily basis and get by. There is likely to be some inefficiency, but I'm sure you have seen it working. A large organization, with three to five levels of management, has many people to coordinate, so the changing of priorities must be done in a more methodical manner. Granted, in many cases, it must be done very quickly, too. Some organizations must be very responsive to customer demands. How is it to be done? There is an answer: There is a very fast and efficient tool that will help us; it's called a computer.

A COMPUTER WILL HELP

First, I will describe the ideal situation, and you can use it as a model. You can gradually improve an organization that has too many changing priorities and multiple crises. It can become an organization that changes priorities rapidly and is still efficient. Suppose that there is a master scheduler. This person has a good software program and is using a microcomputer. (A mini or mainframe is also okay.) All projects, large and small, are on the computer. It has the schedules, budgets, and resource requirements. It also has a list of all required skills and their availability as resources. It can also track other limited resources, such as facilities and machinery.

There are several ways in which this can work.

1. *All projects are first assigned priority numbers, based on a combination of payoff and urgency.* Each project, in turn, is allocated resources by the computer (or scheduler) from the resource base, starting with the highest priority and working toward the lowest. When a resource is used up, the next project is scheduled according to the next availability of that scarce resource. It will naturally be later. Thus, projects with lower priorities simply get done later. When the schedule is prepared, the executives can look at it and make some adjustments. They may change priorities on some projects to see what happens. Or they may temporarily increase the resource base in some of the departments that are short; this might be done by authorizing overtime or short-term assistance. After some negotiations between the resource managers and the priority-setting executives, a workable schedule will be realized. Actually, this method could be done manually in about two days for 50 small projects. However, a computer can solve it in as little as two minutes, although some software programs may require an hour.

2. *All projects are linked together into one master project.* The master project represents the total work of the organization. The

resources needed for all projects are summed up by the computer program. Histograms are plotted out to show the overloads or underloads for all projects taken together. Where there is an overload, the matter of priority must be settled, or else the resource availability must be increased.

3. *Load leveling is done by a computer program (also called automatic resource leveling).* This requires more sophisticated software. It also requires that the scheduler who enters the data has priority numbers assigned to the projects. There must be a very good database, additional criteria regarding earliest starts and latest finishes, minimum float, and a few other criteria that the computer will ask about. Given the data and criteria decisions, the computer can produce schedules that use only the available resources. The projects or tasks with the lowest priorities are generally scheduled for the latest completion.

Strictly speaking, a computer will examine the resources at a detailed task level. If a number of tasks are to start at the same time and there are not enough resources, the program may first try to do some tasks later without exceeding the total float. If there is still a conflict over resource availability, the program will apply the project priority number. Thus, high priority projects get first call on resources and low priority projects get delayed.

These load leveling programs are used on very large projects for which hundreds of skilled tradesmen must be employed. Basically, they produce an outline of a schedule that must be examined for feasibility by the resource managers and then adjusted and implemented. Originally, load leveling required a mini or mainframe computer, but there are now programs that will do it on a microcomputer. Keep in mind that to do this, all projects must share a common resource base. Some programs can do load leveling within one project and its resource base but cannot do it across all projects. If you plan to do resource/load leveling on multiple projects, a load leveling feature by itself may not be enough. It must be capable of doing multiple projects with a shared resource base.

WHICH METHOD TO USE

The first and second of the foregoing methods are the easiest to get into because they can start with a manual system, which is also a backup if the computer crashes. A fairly simple computer program can be used. If there are 50 people working on projects, it would be reasonable to have one full-time scheduler. This person would do the analysis and produce suggested schedules and lists of resource requirements. Naturally, the scheduler will do faster work if a proper computer program is used.

The second method is a step up from the first. It can be introduced when people understand the techniques and when suitable, good software has been found. Regrettably, any software produced today for microcomputers has some shortcomings in terms of somebody's needs. The software may have most of the features you want but not load leveling. You will need to make tradeoffs when choosing one microcomputer software program over another.

The third method, using load leveling software, has the advantage that updates can be done almost instantaneously—not only by the scheduler, but by any project manager. Even an executive can have a terminal in his or her office. Because this sophisticated method is possible, I foresee that most people will end up doing it this way. However, this is not something that will happen overnight. If you are going to go in this direction because of rapidly changing priorities, you should phase it in gradually.

SYSTEMATIC CHANGING OF PRIORITIES

Suppose that we have instituted one of the foregoing systems. The CEO gets a call from Al, a long-time friend, who says that if his order is completed two weeks ahead of schedule, he can give a lot more business to the company. Now it makes sense to give a higher priority to Al's order. Still, the CEO needs to assess the consequences. He can do this rapidly by having the scheduler run through some changes a few times. In effect, the scheduler has a model of the workload of the organization. This model can simulate the future, given a change in priorities. The CEO might try changing number ten to number one, and if that doesn't work, changing it to number six. If that doesn't work, he will know which resources need to be increased in order to handle it. Then he can simply order the scheduler to issue the new schedules on his authority. The resource managers would have 24 hours either to respond or to show why it wouldn't work. This latter safeguard is necessary, because not all resources are interchangeable or easily increased. By and large, the changing of priorities would be orderly and systematic. Most of the new schedules would be correct. The advantage to the executives, of course, is that they can respond to changing customer needs very fast. The advantage to the total organization is much less disruption to ongoing work and much more efficient use of staff time.

ALL DEPARTMENTS NEED TO GET ORGANIZED

If resource managers are going to be able to respond sensibly to the changing of priorities, they must do their bit first. In fact, they are key players in the game. Resource managers need to keep track of their resources and they need to schedule the workload. They also need to forecast their workload and avoid overloads and underloads. It is true that this adds a bit of management work, but it's mainly at the planning end. What planning saves in the project manager's execution time is probably 10 times that spent in planning. In a multiple-project environment with fixed resources, one must have a planned workload. Without it, the work quickly degenerates into a shambles. One crisis creates another, until we get into what is called "crisis management."

SOFTWARE WITH MULTIPROJECT CAPABILITY

Many vendors of project management software for PCs will claim that their programs have multiproject capability. However, it may not be the type that I have described. Some of the programs require that you build the master network (logic diagram) by entering all the logic diagrams manually into one master network. This is not easy, because 50 small projects easily add up to one large project, which is hard to enter and process. Furthermore, each of the small projects is changing its start and finish dates. These changes must

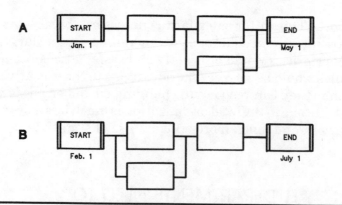

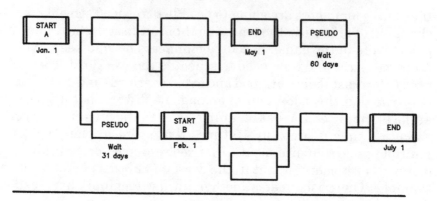

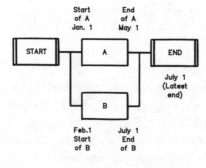

Figure 12-3. True multiproject capability of software.

- Build independent projects and *link* them together to form a superproject.

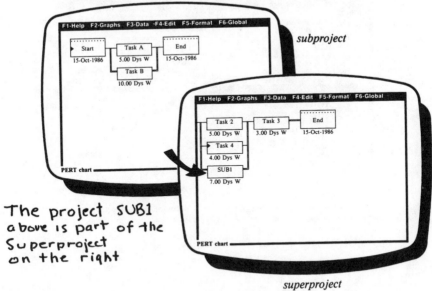

Figure 12-4. The multiproject capability of Harvard Total Project Manager II, version 2.01.

be reflected in the master network, which has temporary lag times built into it.

Software with true multiproject capability can link together all of the small projects. One superproject or master project covers all of the work. From this, we can derive a master schedule and budget. At the same time, all of the small project resource requirements must be added together. The resources for the master schedule must cover all of the projects. Furthermore, a good software program will allow the small projects to be run individually and changed by the project leaders in charge. When changes are made, the project leaders have the option of including them in the master schedule. In this way, the master schedule is kept up to date without additional work. This may be done on one shared computer, or on a Local Area Network (LAN) of computers tied together. Look for PM software that has a specific version for a LAN.

Figure 12-3 illustrates what is meant by true multiproject capability. Suppose that you have independent projects A and B. They are to be added together in a master project, even though they are

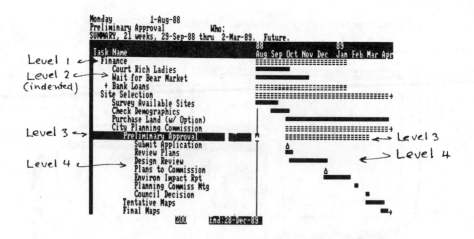

The Gantt Chart task outline structure allows you to organize your project starting with broad topics and then adding specific details.

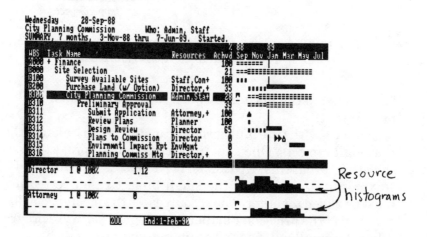

Resource Histograms are bar charts that graphically depict resource workloads.

Figure 12-5. The multiproject capability of Time Line®, version 3.0.
Copyright Symantec Corporation, 10201 Torre Avenue Cupertino, CA 95014, (408) 253-9600. Time Line is a registered trademark of Symantec Corporation.

independent of each other. Projects A and B can be added together only if we insert pseudoactivities to cover the lead or lag time differences in the starts and in the finishes. Thus, if project A starts sooner than project B, a lag time activity should be inserted. It can be called "Wait x days for the start of B." Likewise, the two projects may not end together, and there may be lead or lag time at the end. This is necessary so that all the networks can be tied together.

Fortunately, most modern software allows us simply to enter the start and finish dates of independent projects and combine them into a master project. The software takes care of adding the leads and lags. I have used the term *master project* for a combination of projects. Various software vendors use different terms; the following is a partial list:

Higher Level	*Lower Level*
Hammock	Activity
Summary	Detail
Superproject	Project
Project	Subproject
Net	Subnet

The example of multiproject capabilities shown in Figure 12-4 comes from Harvard Total Project Manager II®, version 2.01. (In 1988 it was renamed Harvard Project Manager®.) The example in Figure 12-5 is from a program called Time Line®. The upper Gantt chart in Figure 12-5 shows how summary and detail tasks are shown on one schedule. The lower part of the figure shows how resource histograms can be displayed below the Gantt chart.

In Figure 12-6 I have simulated the combining of three projects —A, B, and C—by making duplicates of the Personnel Records Project level 3 schedules and having them staggered by one month in starting dates. The load leveling has been done by Harvard Total Project Manager II®, version 2.01.

SUMMARY

As you have seen, the main problem with multiple projects is that they can affect each other when there are fixed, shared resources.

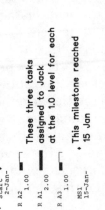
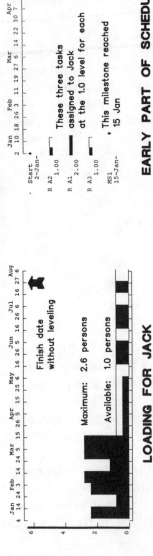
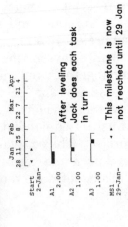

Figure 12-6. Load leveling for Personnel Records Projects.

Fortunately, by looking at resource loadings, we can predict overloads or adjust the resources to fit the project schedules.

When we have multiple projects on tight schedules and limited resources, we must also have priority setting. This is best done by senior management. It's also up to senior management to see that the frequent changing of priorities does not make a shambles of the orderly setting of long-term priorities. This is done by having a master schedule of the workload of the organization. With the help of computers, this can be done easily.

If you are a project leader and not a CEO also, you should advise your manager of the impact of changing priorities on the other projects that you manage. That is the least you can do. At the same time, you could generate some interest in multiple-project management by working on the impact of resources on the projects that you are managing yourself. When you have it working well and put it on a computer, you can demonstrate the advantages to other people. Ultimately, if the situation is one of frequently changing priorities, all projects in the organization must be in the computer database.

QUESTIONS FOR ASSIGNMENT OR DISCUSSION

1. What two reasons are given in this chapter for one project affecting another?
2. In the example given for the application to multiple projects, Chet, manager of the Advertising and Publications Department, was the only bottleneck at the time. If he has only 10 subordinates, is it necessary for him to have a full-blown project management resource analysis program? Could he do it manually? Would a spreadsheet program, such as Lotus, be of assistance in this kind of analysis?
3. Because multiple projects affect each other, we may need to have long-term priorities established. What are the conditions under which these priorities must be established, and what are the conditions under which they are not needed?
4. Simulate a multiple-project load analysis by using a project management software program that is available to you. Imag-

ine that the Personnel Records Project is going to be repeated five times, with a month of delay in the start of each project. Show the combined load on the programmers for the duration of the five projects.

5. This may be an individual or a group assignment. Take about five projects from an organization of a member of your group, or other projects that are available to you as an investigator. They should share at least one scarce resource. Combine them into a superproject manually or by computer, and show the load on the scarce resource. Set the resource availability so that it is overloaded, and show how you would reschedule the projects in order to keep the resource base constant.

6. Write an essay of about 2000 words on the differences between managing single projects and managing multiple projects. Do your own research.

CHAPTER thirteen

MANAGING TIME
for the busy project manager

Key Idea

Organize your use of time so that you will succeed with your projects.

Project managers frequently find themselves harassed by demands on their time. The management of projects involves the identification and correction of many real and potential problems. More projects mean more problems.

Because the project manager cannot be everywhere at once, only one problem at a time gets attention. The ignored ones get worse. This causes more interruptions, which, in turn, cause inefficiencies in the use of time to solve problems correctly. Incompletely solved problems surface again and require urgent attention. The project manager feels like the horseman who is riding off in all directions.

Besides their project work, other special assignments and administrative work are loaded onto the project managers. There is great potential for creating time-harassed individuals who are not very effective.

The following cases illustrate how easily a project manager can get tied up in knots. Following the cases, you will learn some practical ways to keep yourself well organized on projects.

CASE 1: HARRY DID THE PROJECT BUT NEGLECTED OPERATIONS

Harry knew how to run a bank. He had been an assistant manager in several banks for the past nine years, and he was hoping to become the general manager of his own bank. Harry's job was so routine that he did not need to plan it. When the bank's Goodwill Project came along, it added some zest to his work. Besides being interesting work, Harry realized that he could make his mark in the

CASE 1: HARRY DID THE PROJECT

company by being successful with this project. It might speed up his promotion.

Harry worked on the project with enthusiasm. He held a review meeting on it nearly every day. He drafted the letter that was to go to customers and revised it many times. He wrote his own advertising copy for the newspaper. He spent considerable time on the telephone seeking out speaking engagements. All of these project tasks were interesting to do.

Harry didn't realize, however, that a project has a way of taking over from routine operations. Project work has variety, but operations involve mostly repeated work. Inch by inch and day by day, the project took Harry's attention away from operations. Performance reviews and salary reviews could be deferred. Operational reports could be lightly scanned, and minor deviations did not need his immediate attention. Many things could be deferred. The bank facilities needed some improvements, such as adding guiderails for lining up, but that could wait. If the books didn't balance at the end of the day, they would probably find a difference in the next day's balance. Whereas Harry had previously insisted that the bank's daily records balance to within one dollar, he readily convinced himself that ten dollars was close enough.

One of the tellers asked to see him about a personal problem, but he kept putting it off. When she finally did get to see him, he took so many telephone calls about the project that she really didn't have a chance to get to the point. What she had wanted to know was whether or not she could get an additional six months of maternity leave if she decided to have a baby in the near future. It was a reasonable request, but she had to defer it to some future time. Meanwhile, she mentioned it to her mother and got a sympathetic hearing. Her mother was delighted with the prospect of having a grandchild and offered to do the baby-sitting if her daughter would move to the city where her mother lived. Coincidentally, the teller's husband also thought that it would be a good idea to move to the big city. So they made their plans. The teller lined up a job at another bank in the big city and left Harry's bank with a minimum of notice.

Other events happened, and Harry didn't know why or how they were caused. Little by little, the operations began to slip. Customers had to wait longer for loan reviews. Special transactions were sometimes delayed because Harry was out of the office on project work.

Fortunately, Cal, the general manager, was an astute observer. He liked the way Harry had jumped into the project and worked on it with enthusiasm. He had seen this happen before. Project work is exciting compared to routine operations, and it has a way of taking over. He took the time to explain this to Harry. It really opened Harry's eyes. He realized that operations was job number one; thereafter, he managed his time more effectively.

CASE 2:
JACK IN THE PRESSURE COOKER

As Jack turned his car into the employee parking lot, he gave one more sigh of disgust. The only parking places were the risky ones at the ends of the rows. He should have come earlier. He had tried, but the roads were crowded with other drivers in a hurry, and he was not able to arrive early. Now, as he walked into his office, he wondered if he had locked the back door of the car. There had been some car break-ins recently, and he remembered that some of his recreational gear was still on the back seat. Then he thought about the urgent things that he wanted to do when he got to the office, and he kept going.

As he entered his work-strewn office, he saw a big note on his desk. One of his programmers wanted to see him as soon as he arrived. Before he could tend to this, the telephone rang, and he had to commit himself to a meeting that would start in an hour. While driving to work, he had resolved to start first on the schedule revisions for the Personnel Records Project. He got out the schedule and spread it on his desk. Just then, he remembered the note from the programmer and gave him a call. The programmer, George, had been up late trying to get a bug out of the new software for inventory control. Operators had posted new inventory to the wrong account numbers, and they needed some counterchecks to prevent this from happening again. In the meantime, the Sales Department had promised delivery of

CASE 2: JACK IN THE PRESSURE COOKER

nonexistent inventory. George was busy fixing up the software, but he couldn't correct the records without some clerical assistance. He needed a clerk. He had spent several days going over the paperwork and checking it against past entries. In response, Jack got busy on the phone and tried to get a clerk released from the data processing pool. He went down to see the data processing manager in person and settled the matter.

When he got back to his office, he had only five minutes to prepare for the meeting. However, sitting on his desk was a message to call his manager at once. He called and got a busy signal, so he decided it was best to go over and wait outside the manager's office. He saw her, but this made him a bit late for the other meeting. Jack was totally unprepared for the meeting, but at least he had an alibi that the others would understand. The meeting turned out to be a waste of time. The two people who were involved could have settled it without a meeting. It was just another ad hoc meeting that was generated by a project problem. Jack had attended because he expected people from other departments to come to his special project problem meetings in return.

Just before lunch, Jack got back to his office and settled down to look over the project schedule. The personnel manager had already reminded Jack once this morning that he had promised to work out something on the furniture delay. His lunch time was nearly up when Jack had a handle on the answer. He got coffee and a sandwich from one of the vending machines, appeasing his hunger while he scanned the incoming mail.

At the end of the day, Jack was exhausted. He had been in a fire-fighting mode all day. With five projects nearing completion, he was a busy man. While he was busy solving problems on one project, the other projects were developing their own problems. He had not gotten around to do any planning for the new project, as he had intended. He threw the planning documents into his briefcase and took them home. What he really needed was some rest and relaxation.

Jack's day was similar to that of many busy project managers. It's an exciting life when one is succeeding; otherwise, it is better described as frenetic. Jack's day was fractured by many interruptions, wasted time at meetings, and an inability to give attention to items with long-term payoff. He was busy all day, but he did not feel that he had done the right things.

> ### Principles of Time Management for Project Managers
>
> 1. Priorities on your time should balance long-term pay-offs and short-term urgencies.
> 2. Interruptions must be controlled and minimized.
> 3. Time spent at meetings must be minimized.

APPLICATION TO A PART-TIME PROJECT MANAGER

At the bank, Harry finally got himself organized so that project work and operations were in the proper balance. For him, operations were top priority, and the project was number two. As long as Harry responded to whatever was urgent, his time might be dominated either by the project or by operations, depending on current circumstances. The long-term planning and deferrable items would be neglected. This is known as "the tyranny of the urgent."

Harry decided to plan his day so that he spent an appropriate amount of time on each kind of work. Since most of his workdays were pretty much alike, he made out a daily timetable of his activities (see Figure 13-1). This guideline governed him for the current month.

TIME OF DAY	GENERAL ACTIVITY
9–10	Scan reports and start actions.
10–12	Open. (Appointments, in-basket, project work, current urgencies)
12–1	Lunch, with rest and recreation.
1–2	Return calls and follow up on actions started in morning.
2–3	Follow up on project work. (Quiet time)
3–4	Open. (Return calls, proof letters)
4–5	Assist in balancing daily records and vault storage.

Figure 13-1. Harry's daily timetable.

APPLICATION TO A PART-TIME PROJECT MANAGER

Basically, Harry planned his day so that he spent a reasonable amount of time on both project work and operations. There was plenty of open time for him to look after current urgencies. When they didn't happen, he could devote his open time to elements of work with a long-term payoff, such as performance reviews with his tellers.

Harry also found it necessary to control his work on a daily basis. He made up task lists, such as the one shown in Figure 13-2.

Thus, Harry first planned out his regular allocation of time in a general way. Then he made up task lists of current things he needed to initiate or follow up on. Harry looked at these task lists several times during the day and worked on those items during the time he held open for general work. As the day progressed, items might be added to the list that would prompt him to act accordingly.

As explained in the previous chapter, the X's on the task lists represented the long-term values of the tasks, such as monetary gain, social points, or general business gain. The +'s indicated the degree of urgency. Some items, such as the salary review for tellers, were deferrable until they were overdue. Then they would become increasingly urgent, and +'s would be added. Other items that had deadlines, such as telephoning the newspaper about the advertising, had significant current urgency. The current urgency of a task was shown by the number of +'s, whether the task was project work or operations. However, it got more X's if it supported operations than if it supported the project. That was Harry's application of long-term payoff to the priority dimension. By giving priority on his time to the items with the most +'s and X's, Harry was able to control his work on tasks in a way that balanced urgency and long-term payoff. Using this priority rule, as soon as he had some

PRIORITY		TASK
Urgency	Payoff	
+ +	XX	Performance review of HJ
	X	Salary review for tellers
+ +	X	Telephone about advertising
	XX	Plan Project
+ +	XX	Wedding anniversary gift
		Etc.

Figure 13-2.   Harry's task list.

discretionary time, he would first do something on the performance review and anniversary gift.

APPLICATION TO A FULL-TIME PROJECT MANAGER WITH MULTIPLE PROJECTS

As you have seen in Case 2, Jack Daniels was pushed and pulled by his multiple projects until he no longer had control of the situation. This is not unusual. People who are good supervisors and also manage one or two projects can probably get by with minimal time organization, as Harry learned to do in the preceding example. However, if they have 5 to 20 projects, many of which are being completed at the same time, their time can be fragmented into responding to so many demands that they become inefficient.

Jack had a good friend who had a similar job in another company. One night, after a candlelight dinner with gypsy musicians, she got to talking about their relationship. Jack had canceled dates three times in the last month and was frequently very late. She wondered if Jack could really fulfill his wish to be a family man. You see, they had plans for marrying and raising a family. This little conversation disturbed Jack, and he didn't say much for the rest of the evening. Over the next few days, he thought about it more and more. Jack wondered why his friend didn't understand his time management problems. He just had so much to do. He knew that her job was equally difficult, but she seemed to have time for herself. Swallowing his pride, he brought up the subject soon thereafter. He asked how she managed her time. Fortunately for Jack, she had been in the same situation and had attended a time management course designed especially for busy project people. She passed on to Jack what she had learned in the course.

First of all, he needed some way to schedule his time. She had found that a detailed weekly or monthly schedule was impossible to keep in a multiple-project environment, so she suggested that Jack schedule no more than one day at a time. Jack took her advice. An example of one of his daily schedules is shown in Figure 13-3.

You can see that Jack tried to organize his day to include some quiet thinking time and some time when others could see him. The rest of the day included only a few prior commitments, such as

APPLICATION TO A FULL-TIME PROJECT MANAGER

TIME	KIND OF ACTIVITY
8:30–9:30	Appointment with self (quiet time)
9:30–10	Review meeting on Personnel Records Project
10–3	Open
3–4	Weekly review meeting with the manager
4–4:30	Available time

Figure 13-3. One of Jack's daily schedules.

meetings. Most of the time was open. During this open time, he did additional thinking, coordinating, and working on his task list. Except for very short items, he put everything on a task list and rated them for priority on his time. Figure 13-4 shows one of his *priorities cards* (task list). It was on a 3 × 5 card that he carried in his shirt pocket.

Notice that the first task—preparing a plan—has three X's. This means that the task has high long-term value (payoff). Any project plan has high payoff, but one project may rate somewhat higher than another if there are two plans competing for Jack's time. However, as there are no +'s on this task, it's still not close to a deadline. As the deadline approaches, Jack would add some +'s, and

PRIORITY		THINGS TO DO
	xxx	- Dynamic Project Plan for new project
	x	- Order laptop computer
+ + +	x	- Revise schedule on Personnel Records Project
	x	- Salary review for George
		- Etc.
		- Etc.
	xx	- Draft proposal for standardizing data processing
		Telephone Calls to Make
+ +		- Buyer re: furniture date
	x	- Personnel manager to explain delay
+ + +	x	- Dental appointment for abscessed tooth
		Things to Buy or Pick Up
x		- Bicycle
+ +		- Gas for outboard motor

Figure 13-4. One of Jack's priorities cards (task list).

the plan would get more of his attention. The rule for priority on your time is to do, first, the task with the most marks—that is, the greatest sum of X's and +'s.

The next item on Jack's list is to order a laptop computer. He has placed some long-term value on this task, but since he has other portable computers to use, and there is no deadline, it has only one X.

The next item has three +'s and an X, indicating that this revision of a schedule is now urgent and must compete for his attention with the first task on the list, which has three X's. Both tasks will probably get done.

Notice that the next item has no urgency marks and relatively low payoff in terms of Jack's job. The salary review for George is deferrable, up to a point. It might be deferred up to six months, as long as Jack is able to make it up in corrresponding salary benefits. What could change this priority on Jack's time would be the knowledge that George is disgruntled and looking for another job.

One thing wrong with Jack's list is that he has nothing on it of a personal dimension. This priority list is going to be so powerful that it will make him into a workaholic. The way to prevent this is to add something on his personal life. Let's do it for him. Under "Telephone Calls to Make," add a line:

+   XX   Get tickets to theater

and under "Things to Buy or Pick Up," put:

    XX   Look at engagement rings

and under "Things to Do," add:

    X   Copy disk of computer games for nephew

Now we have done something to balance Jack's lifestyle. Good luck with your relationship, Jack. You and your girlfriend make a good team.

PRIORITY ON YOUR TIME HAS TWO DIMENSIONS

Many people are ruled by the tyranny of urgency. They give priority on their time to the task that appears to be needed soonest. Unfortunately, urgency is often defined by *other people's* terms. Here are some examples:

1. Someone comes to your office with a document to show you and gets 100 percent of your attention.
2. The phone rings and you answer it. (Someone has you on a prospect list for a new car.)
3. Your manager says, "Come into my office for a moment."
4. You suddenly remember the data that your boss requested by noon.

At the end of the day, you find that you have been busy responding to many urgent things, and quite a few of them were trivial. What you did not do was prepare your project plan—the item that had real potential for payoff.

If your day is not very busy, responding to urgency is not wasting your time. You will still have time to do the things that are not urgent but which have long-term value. On the other hand, if you are so busy with urgent things that you are putting off the things of high value but no urgency, then you are deep in the time trap. To get yourself out of the time trap, you need to have some way of responding to both urgency and long-term payoff.

When an item is urgent only to someone else, it should have low priority on your time. An example of this is a telephone interruption by someone who wants to sell you a new car when you are not looking for one. If an item is urgent and there is also payoff—such as getting out a new schedule to correct some problems—then it should get priority on your time. If an item is urgent and you don't know the long-term payoff—such as someone bringing a document to show you in your office—evaluate it first before giving the item more of your valuable time.

To help you control your use of time you should make up a priorities list. (This is the same as a task list; if it is listed on a card,

I call it a priorities card.) Put on it reminders of tasks that you want to do and requests that have been made on your time. Some other things may come up that require immediate attention, and they won't get on your list. However, by using such a list, you will form the habit of evaluating a new request before acting.

As shown in the previous examples, I have found it convenient for busy people to divide their priorities list into three categories: a "To Do" list for things to do in the office, a "Telephone" list for calls that can be made in or out of the office, and a "Buy and Pick Up" list for things to do when near a shopping plaza. Then each item should have a priority rating. Again, the higher the long-term payoff, the more X's; and the more the current urgency, the more +'s. You give priority on your time to the item with the greatest number of marks, whether they be X's or +'s. Although urgency and long-term payoff are independent of each other, you have only one kind of time to give to them, so just add the X's and the +'s. If you find you are giving too much time to urgency and not enough to long-term payoff, you will simply use fewer +'s in the future. It doesn't take long to strike a good balance.

Besides a priorities list, you also need a list of appointments. If you have only a few, they can be put on your priorities list. Most likely, however, you will also be committed to some appointments days and weeks in advance. For this you should have a diary-type record, perhaps in a little book that you carry around with you. You might be able to combine your priorities list and your diary into one book. (Examples of such devices will be described later.)

WHAT IS LONG-TERM PAYOFF?

In my seminars on effective time management, I find that people seldom have any difficulty indicating what's important in their jobs. If they have job descriptions, it is clear where they get their points. Most people also have a good idea of what's good for their organization, and they can assess the long-term payoff of a task that is relevant to their particular jobs. An organization has objectives that provide the guidelines for determining long-term payoff. (Some authors use the word *goal* instead of the word *objective*. I use the words interchangeably.)

Long-term payoff on the personal side usually requires some private thought. I frequently find that young people who have mastered an education seem to be at loose ends with regard to what they plan to achieve during the rest of their life. Mind you, I'm not knocking this. Some of my very best friends have done extremely well in life without setting difficult objectives for themselves. On the other hand, many people have expressed regret at having drifted through life for 10 to 20 years without a sense of direction. Only human beings can set goals and achieve things; it's a thinking person's sport. Because goal setting is important to people in managing their time, I gave it considerable coverage in my book *Mastery and Management of Time* (Prentice-Hall, 1978). If you do set objectives (goals) for yourself, you should consider the following categories:

1. *Work objectives.* If you have a manager, it would be a good idea to discuss these objectives together.
2. *Career objectives.* What do you wish to achieve in the career part of your life?
3. *Personal objectives.* What do you personally want to achieve (for example, play the piano, win the local chess championship, or write a worthwhile poem)?
4. *Social objectives.* Do you have any goals for family size and timing? How important is your social conscience? Do you want to aid charities or reform society?
5. *Spiritual objectives.* These pertain mainly to how people should live together and how they should behave toward one another. This is your view of morality, even if you don't abide by it yourself.

Note: Your relationships with "significant others" should be included in the foregoing objectives, probably under personal and social objectives.

Objective setting (or goal setting) is not something you need to do every day, or every week, or even every month. Once you have set your goals, they tend to stabilize for a number of years until your lifestyle changes. A change of job, marriage, a death in the family, separation from valued friends, and so forth, can cause you to review your objectives.

There are three important factors in achieving objectives:

1. Items that help you achieve your objectives must appear on your priorities list so that you can take positive steps to achieve them. Otherwise, objective setting will tend to become a futile exercise (unless fate is kind).
2. Knowing your objectives will enable you to take advantage of opportunities that come your way. As one philosopher has said, "No fair wind blows for a ship without a port of destination." When you know where you want to go, you will recognize opportunities that favor your getting there. That is one beauty of setting objectives.
3. Don't set impossible objectives, and don't set too many. From a practical point of view, you have only one life to live. Some objectives require tradeoffs with one another. To handle this, you should rank your objectives in order of importance to you.

INTERRUPTIONS WASTE YOUR TIME

When you are interrupted, your trend of thought is disturbed. When you get back to your work, you first need to figure out where you were. The time for this review is wasted time. The longer the interruption, the more time is lost in getting back to the point where you left off. This time is lost to you forever. Therefore it behooves you to minimize the number of interruptions.

Project work requires some quiet time to get something of value done. Most project work has threshold values that require several hours of quiet time. If you are interrupted before the threshold value is completed, your time is mostly wasted. When you get back to it, you have to start at the beginning.

There are three rules for dealing with the problem of interruptions:

1. Minimize the number of interruptions.
2. Minimize the length of each interruption.
3. Minimize the stress of each interruption.

If you minimize the number and length of interruptions by the following techniques, you will naturally have less stress.

COPING WITH INTERRUPTIONS

The following are some validated ways of coping with interruptions. These are techniques that I present in my seminars on effective time management.

1. *Face away from moving traffic.* The principle behind this is that your peripheral vision is about 135 degrees, and it is sensitive to motion. You can scan a page with a 1 degree beam of vision, but if someone moves in your peripheral vision, you are programmed to pay attention. You will most likely look up. In our culture, if the other person is looking at you, that will start a conversation. So, not only are you interrupted by the motion, but it leads to a prolonged interruption. Reorient your desk, move file cabinets, close doors, or turn your body so that your peripheral vision is protected while you are working at your desk.

2. *Stand up when someone comes to see you at your workplace.* You will give the caller 100 percent of your attention, but stand-up meetings are more likely to be short and businesslike.

3. *Keep repeating, "What can I do for you?" during a business interruption.* This will help the caller get down to business. (If there is no business, and it is only a social call, this will keep the interruption short.)

4. *Show the caller exactly what you are busy with, and mention the deadline.* Most social callers will volunteer to withdraw when you have deadlines to meet, because they have faced similar situations.

5. *Draw the caller into some of the work at hand.* The caller may only need a change in his or her thought pattern. Working with you on a problem may be just as refreshing as chit-chatting.

6. *Keep file folders for frequent callers.* In them you put business items that are deferrable. When these visitors call on you, you can take the items up. You thereby minimize the number of interruptions for yourself and for them. You should at least have a folder with your manager's name on it, as well as folders for subordinates and project team members.

7. *Examine your own behavior.* Why do you allow people to interrupt you time and time again? Psychologically speaking, no one continues a behavior without some form of reward. What are you getting out of the interruptions? Would you rather socialize than

work? Is it important to gain social points with your callers in order for you to get your other work done? Are you afraid of losing some social points? If you don't give your time, will there be some form of retribution?

It's not easy to examine yourself as a cause of interruptions. No doubt, a substantial part of the blame lies with other people. Some interruptions are inherent in the nature of multiple-project work. If you have done all of the other things discussed here, and interruptions are still a problem for you, it's time to look at yourself. Why are you shooting yourself in the foot? At least 1 in 10 people unwittingly contributes to the number and length of the interruptions he or she suffers.

QUIET TIME AND AVAILABLE TIME

Wouldn't it be nice to have some quiet time every day? It's up to you. Interruptions involve other people in your organization, and as a group, you all have something to gain by organizing quiet time and available time.

This is how it works. First, decide when quiet time would be possible in your job, taking into account your need to be available to other people and your own biorhythm. Suppose that you decide that your quiet time should be from 9:00 to 11:00 every morning. Then you must set out to get agreements from others to make this possible. Seek out another person with whom you have many dealings—a colleague or a subordinate—and set up an agreement. If you are a manager, you might work this out with all of your subordinates together. Get an agreement on what would be the best time not to disturb each other unless it is an emergency. Agree to enforce the agreement for a minimum of three weeks. If you don't enforce it, you will go back to your old habits and the whole idea will fall apart very quickly.

To succeed fully with "quiet time," you need a co-commitment for "available time." If people put off seeing you during your quiet time, but you are not available at other times, they may revert to interrupting you when the thought first occurs. They will treat the interruption as an emergency. Practically speaking, the half-hour before lunch and the half-hour before quitting time are often suitable for available times. You guarantee to be available at those times to those people who have made commitments to give you your scheduled quiet time.

The time between quiet time and available time is a free-for-all, but it will be much better because of the agreements. If you don't know when another person will be available, the tendency is to interrupt as soon as you perceive the need. If there are co-commitments, you will have to consider whether it is an emergency or whether it can be deferred.

Establishing quiet time and available time is a good idea for people who must work together. It will allow them to get more work done and have less frustration in doing it. This is one element of time management that people can do for each other.

MEETINGS THAT WASTE TIME

About one-third of the people who come to my time management seminars complain that they must go to meetings that are a complete waste of their time. The remainder admit that much of the time at meetings is wasted—for them, that is. This is particularly true of specialists and professionals. Most projects involve the coordination of a number of specialties. When a project is discussed, it usually requires only one or two of these specialists at a time. The other specialists cannot contribute, so their time is wasted. Hence, project work leads to inefficient utilization of one's time at a meeting.

There are often problems that need to be looked at because of the project management reporting system. This calls for meetings. However, you should not try to solve a problem at a meeting if it would take more than a few minutes. A meeting to discuss a problem should clarify the problem and assign it to someone for action; then the meeting is over. A stand-up meeting is just fine for this.

Periodic meetings for project status reviews are useful if they are not held too frequently. Early in a project, once a month might be enough; later, once-a-week meetings—and occasionally, once-a-day meetings might be required. There are only four items for the agenda of a periodic project status meeting:

1. New happenings on the project that the team should know about.

2. Tasks that have recently been completed.
3. Tasks that need to be started.
4. Identification of problems and assignment for action—by whom and by when.

The periodic meeting is not convened to solve problems, only to identify them. It can be over in 15 minutes to half an hour. If the project work is heavy, try stand-up meetings of not more than 15 minutes. Write the minutes on the writing foil over the platter of an overhead projector, and have copies made for the participants to take away with them. Alternatively, have 3 × 5 cards for people to make notes about items they have been assigned for action. The cards could be colored so that they will stand out on a desk littered with papers.

The number of attendees at meetings should be minimized. Classify attendees as "should attend" and "may attend." Put courtesy invitations in the "may attend" category, and spare these people the agony of wasting their time. After you tidy up your own meetings, you can ask other people to classify you on their attendees list as "should attend" or "may attend."

Time-shared meetings are very appropriate for project work. Four or five disciplines or specialties may be required to cover all aspects of a project, but only one is needed at a time. Each important agenda item should have a start and finish time and the initials of the people needed for it. They need attend only this portion of the meeting. It makes a lot of sense. You can organize your meetings better if you use the Time Mastery Form for Agenda and Instant Minutes that I have developed. (This is shown in Figure 13-5. Owners of this book are free to make copies for their own use.)

WORKLOAD ANALYSIS

In Chapters 1, 11, and 12, I gave examples of the total workload in hours per week for project managers. You can also transform these totals to histograms, which show at a glance the degree of overload or underload. Besides your project workload, you should also include other assignments and administrative work. Then your totals can be compared realistically to your scheduled work week.

WORKLOAD ANALYSIS 273

| TITLE OF MEETING _____ CALLED BY _____ TEL _____ |

PURPOSES/OBJECTIVES

DAY, DATE, TIME & PLACE _____

SHOULD ATTEND	DID	MAY ATTEND	DID

AGENDA (Leave space between items for INSTANT MINUTES)			BEFORE MEETING	ACTION AFTER MEETING	
ITEM NO. & PRIORITY	HEADING/MATTERS TO BE DISCUSSED	TIME ALLO-CATED	PERSON RESPONSIBLE	BY WHOM	BY WHEN

Figure 13-5. Time Mastery Form for Agenda and Instant Minutes.

The main advantage of workload analysis is the prediction of serious overloads. You don't need to be very accurate to predict a serious overload. When you are faced with a serious overload, you and your manager can talk priorities, shift the load, or get additional help. You will all be better off. Your workload analysis should be reviewed on some regular basis—say, weekly or monthly. You should also review it when the schedule is changed on some major project. You may have your workload fairly leveled out, but then the schedule may be changed on some key projects so that the completion dates all pile up together. Your workload analysis would be tracking this and would give you an early warning signal.

A 3 × 5 CARD ORGANIZER FOR TRACKING PROJECTS

Wouldn't it be nice to have all of your project tasks on cards in front of you at one time? Then you could review them at will, work on some, change some, or update their status. Add to this the portability of a three-ring binder—and you have a product called Scan/Plan®.

I have found it convenient to organize a small project by writing the tasks on 3 × 5 cards. I can lay the cards out on my desk and decide which one to work on next, add action notes to my current priority card, and put the cards away until later. This is what an organizer is for, especially when one has more than seven cards. I could staple the cards together or put them in a recipe box, or I can put them in an organizer. With the Scan/Plan Creative Organizer®, I can keep 31 cards in view on one letter-size page, write on either side of the 3 × 5 cards, add cards, or take out completed cards. Figure 13-6 shows some of the Scan/Plan organizers for storing cards in three-ring binders, in a pocket packet, or in a file drawer. The Creative Organizer is also available for 5 × 8 cards.

If you were using Scan/Plan to plan a small project, you would first take a pink card and put the project title on the lower quarter-inch, with the due date following the title. Then you would add more project data to the card, such as its objectives, key contacts, and telephone numbers.

Then you would take a pack of white 3 × 5 cards and put a project task title and its due date on the bottom edge of each card. (For a medium project you might need to develop a logic diagram and schedule in order to have due dates.) Then you would insert the cards in a Scan/Plan organizer, such as that shown in Figure 13-7.

The next day, you open your Scan/Plan three-ring binder at this project and decide to do some work on it. You take some small,

A 3 × 5 CARD ORGANIZER FOR TRACKING PROJECTS 275

Figure 13-6. The Scan/Plan Creative Organizers. Permission granted by Scan/Plan, Inc., P.O. Box 1662, Santa Monica, CA 90406.

color-coded stickers (in colors assigned for each team member) and attach them to the lower right corners of the task cards to be assigned to the appropriate people and write the due dates on them. Then you meet with the team members and get commitments for completing the tasks. If a due date is changed, you can simply peel off the sticker and put a new one on.

A week or so later, when you have a meeting with a team member to follow up on the progress of assigned tasks, you make notes on the ample space remaining on the cards.

When you leave on a plane trip, you take your Scan/Plan three-ring binder with you and review progress on projects. You add notes or new cards where warranted.

When a project is completed, you take the whole unit out of the binder and put a rail guide in the slot provided. You can then put it in a file drawer for future reference.

So what do we have here? We have a very nice way to plan and monitor a number of small projects! On a one-page organizer, we can

Figure 13-7. A Scan/Plan organizer for a small project.

have the equivalent of 31 indexed sheets. They can be changed at will and put in any order. We can flag the key ones with color-coded peel-off stickers. We can combine the project organizer with another 31-card organizer that has a card for every working day in the month. All this goes in one three-ring binder. If we get used to its convenience, the system can be expanded to other uses. We can expand to one binder for each project, complete with 3 × 5 organizers for each subsystem, and have room for data sheets and correspondence relating to the project. When the project is over, the binder converts to a hanging file archive, which can be readily accessed for records. In fact, the beauty of the Creative Organizer is that you can create a system to suit your needs. (For source details on the Scan/Plan Creative Organizer, see Appendix B.)

A MEMO BOOK AND SOFTWARE COMBINATION FOR MANAGING YOUR TIME

I have examined many notebook systems for time management but I have found very few that would be suitable for project work. The Day-Timer series made by Day-Timers, Inc., is the most commonly used system by people who attend my seminars; at one time I used it myself. If you go into a regular office, it will be of great help to you. However, Day-Timer seems to be designed primarily for operational managers, executive-level managers, and those who have only a few small projects to handle. Day-Timer now has project worksheets available to insert into your Day-Timer notebook.

I have looked at more than a dozen time-planning systems. If you could total up all the supervisors and managers who could use them, it's a very big market. And that's where most of the systems are aimed.

I have found one time-planning system that is very adaptable to project work, and it has a corresponding software package. The project manager of the future will probably be using a laptop computer, and this particular system is adaptable for that. Time/Design® was originally developed in Europe and is now heavily promoted in the United States, as well. What I like about it is the full integration of large task lists and a diary. You can fold out a sheet of your tasks and enter them into the calendar portion for the time you wish to do them. There is one page for every day. If the tasks are not done when planned, you still have them on your task list and can carry them forward. When a task has been done, you record it with a mark on the list.

Also included in the loose-leaf binder are sheets for small projects. They hold up to about 12 tasks per project or subproject. Although this is not much for medium projects, it is somewhat more than is available in other systems. Some sample Time/Design worksheets are shown in Figure 13-8. Note how the task list or project sheet can be put opposite the diary page for easy transposition. Also, there is a vinyl unit that can be snapped out and folded to pocket size.

To go further on projects, I have found that you can take a letter-size sheet that has a list of activities and a schedule on it, punch holes on one end, and fold it into your book. Then when it is opened up against the calendar, you can enter start and finish dates of tasks that you must work on.

The second most important part of the system is the software called Control Center™. It is sold by a separate organization, but it integrates with the loose-leaf binder. You can print out sheets in the right size for the binder. With a computer, you can do sortings and selections that are quite useful, and you can access other project data in your computer files. When you are away from your computer, you need a connection between your mind and the computer. The Time/Design loose-leaf binder is that connection. You can take it with you. In addition, Time/Design has a small snap-in section that can fit in your shirt pocket. Thus, you still have a connection with your system even when you don't have the binder with you. The whole system is well thought out. It is so good that I am sure other suppliers will develop similar systems in the near future. In the meantime, if you are busy on multiple projects, I recommend that you look into this

Figure 13-8. Time/Design™ project worksheet.

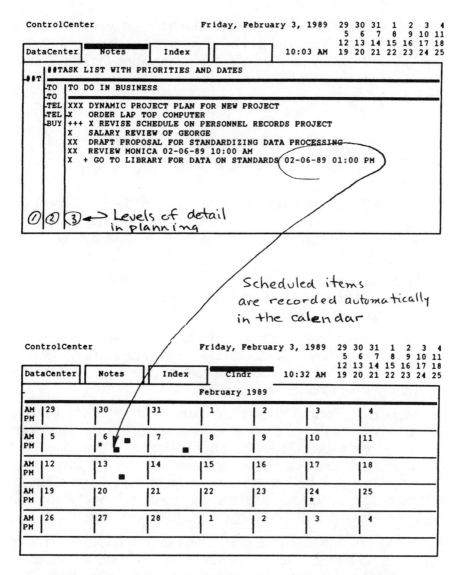

Figure 13-9. Control Center, for the project manager with a portable computer.

system. The project manager of the near future will undoubtedly have a laptop computer that will work well with this computer integrated software. Examples of Control Center features are shown in Figure 13-9.

Time/Design also has its own software that integrates with the loose-leaf binder. NameBank allows you to record and select names of people or tasks by projects. (Source information for Day-Timer, Time/Design, NameBank, and Control Center is given in Appendix B.)

QUESTIONS FOR ASSIGNMENT OR DISCUSSION

1. Discuss the essential differences in Harry's and Jack's time problems. Use one paragraph to outline Harry's time problems and a second paragraph for Jack's. The third paragraph should contrast the two.

2. In about 500 words, explain the essential differences in time management between a full-time operations manager and a full-time project manager.

3. Explain the essential difference between long-term payoff and urgency and how they should affect priority on your time. Explain why urgency tends to take over from long-term payoff. Confine your answer to about 500 words.

4. Make a list of about 10 tasks that you have ahead of you. Include such items as things to do, telephone calls to make, and things to buy and pick up. These tasks can be both in your work life and in your personal life. Mark the items on your list with X's for long-term payoff. Then go through them again and consider their urgency; add +'s for the degree of urgency. When you have finished, you should apply the following tests:

    a. Be sure that you have good variation in the total number of marks for the items. If you sum the X's and the +'s for each item, they should range from zero to six. This provides discrimination in your use of time. If all items on your list have three or four marks, there is not much discrimination, so the marks would not be of much use to you.

    b. The next test is to imagine that you start out your day by doing the items with the most marks, and you get the first one or two items done. Then you are called away for the rest of the day. Was that the best use of your time? If not, something else needs more marks.

QUESTIONS FOR ASSIGNMENT OR DISCUSSION

    c. Another test is to consider that you have had a very fruitful day and have done every item except those with one or zero marks. These would be put off until the next day. Is that okay? In the days to follow, the tasks that did not get done should either increase in urgency or be replaced by more important things.

    Take an item with a high number of marks and one with a low number of marks and explain to another person why you have marked them in that way.

5. What is the essential reason for minimizing the number of interruptions in your workday?
6. What is the main reason for doing a workload analysis? If you are doing project work, do a workload analysis of your own projects? If you have an overload, explain what you propose to do about it.

APPENDIX A

LOGIC DIAGRAMS

A COMPARISON OF THE TWO KINDS OF LOGIC DIAGRAMS

A logic diagram is a graphic aid to help you determine the best sequence of the activities (or tasks) of a project. The end result is a list of predecessors for each activity. If you can easily list the predecessors of a small project with certainty, you do not need a graphic aid. However, it is not possible to carry in your head the relationship of more than about seven items. The logic diagram is a useful tool for many small projects, and it is certainly needed for medium and large projects.

Originally, logic diagrams were made with arrows and small circles. They are called *arrow-node diagrams*. Then someone came up with the idea of labeling the circles, instead of the arrows, as the activities. These were called *activity-on-node diagrams*. Today they are better known as *precedence diagrams*. Sometimes, the word *network* is used in place of *diagram*.

To simplify your first lesson in logic diagrams, I chose to illustrate precedence diagrams in Chapter 4. However, in your dealings with other people, especially with organizations such as contractors, you will see both kinds of diagrams. So when and if your work involves communicating with people who use arrow-node diagrams, then it will be to your advantage to be able to understand them. Ultimately, you should be conversant with both kinds of diagrams. The following instruction is designed to show the relationships between the two kinds of diagrams, so that if you know one, you can easily understand the other.

The Projectics method includes the construction of a logic diagram composed of symbols that represent the activities and the events. An activity (or task) that needs to be done on the project is represented by an arrow or a box. The start of the activity is the tail

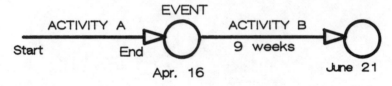

Figure A-1. An arrow-node diagram.

A COMPARISON OF THE TWO KINDS OF LOGIC DIAGRAMS 285

of the arrow or the left-hand side of the box. The finish is the arrow point or the right-hand side of the box.

An event is a point in time. An event is represented by a node (circle) in the arrow-node diagram or by the edge of a box in a precedence diagram. In the Figures A-1 and A-2, activity B depends on the completion of activity A before it can start.

Figure A-1 is an arrow-node diagram; Figure A-2 is the equivalent in a precedence diagram.

Actually, these are related logic diagrams. Imagine that you can rotate the boxes 90 degrees about the line that joins them. You would then be looking at the edge of the box, which would appear as a line that you can imagine to be an arrow. Imagine, also, that the line joining the boxes turned out to be the edge of a disk. Then the precedence diagram becomes an arrow-node diagram. Except for the arrow points, this is a good way to learn that one diagram is equivalent to the other. Try this now and learn it. Then, whichever diagram you use, you will be able to relate it to the other kind when and if you need to. Project managers who deal with outside contractors find it convenient to be able to understand both kinds of logic diagrams. Another way to see the relationship is depicted in Figure A-3.

Now let's add milestones for monitoring project progress at the management level (see Figure A-4). In arrow-node diagrams, an event can be identified as a milestone. In precedence diagrams, we have to create a milestone by adding an activity of zero time duration.

The advantage of precedence diagrams is that you don't have to be concerned about a "dummy activity," which is needed for some arrow-node diagrams. On the other hand, precedence diagrams require many interconnections. I have had considerable experience

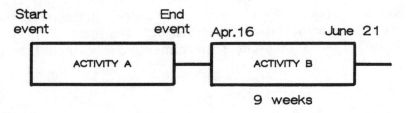

Figure A-2. A precedence diagram.

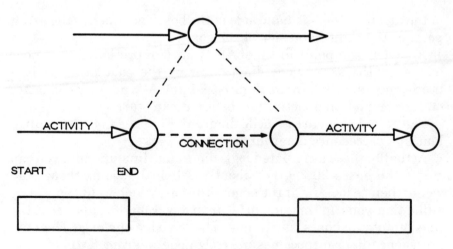

Figure A-3. Nodes become edges joined by a line.

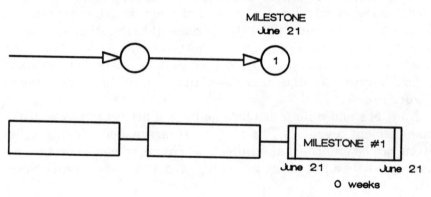

Figure A-4. Adding milestones.

with both kinds of diagrams. Currently, I favor precedence diagrams for small to medium projects. I see advantages in using arrow-node diagrams for large projects. However, the last word has not yet been spoken. We are being very much influenced by the project management software that is being used successfully. The software that sells the most may determine our choices in the future

ANSWERS TO EXERCISES IN CHAPTER 4

Figure A-5 is the answer to the exercise in Figure 4-6.

The following are the answers to the questions asked about that exercise:

1. The successor to W is Y.
2. The successors to X are Y and Z.
3. The immediate predecessors to the END milestone are Y and Z.

Figures A-6, A-7, and A-8 are the answers to the exercises in Figures 4-7, 4-8, and 4-12, respectively.

ACTIVITY OR MILESTONE	PREDECESSORS
Start	--
W	Start
X	Start
Y	W, X
Z	X
End	Y, Z

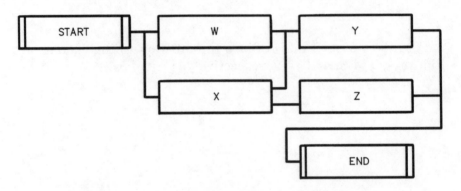

Figure A-5. Answers to exercise in Figure 4-6.

ACTIVITY OR MILESTONE (MS)	PREDECESSORS
Start	--
A. Analyze data	Start
B. Draft report	A
MS. Draft approved	B
C. Print report	MS
D. Get covers	Start
E. Distribute	C,D
End	E

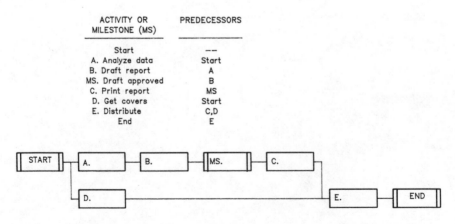

Figure A-6. Answers to exercise in Figure 4-7.

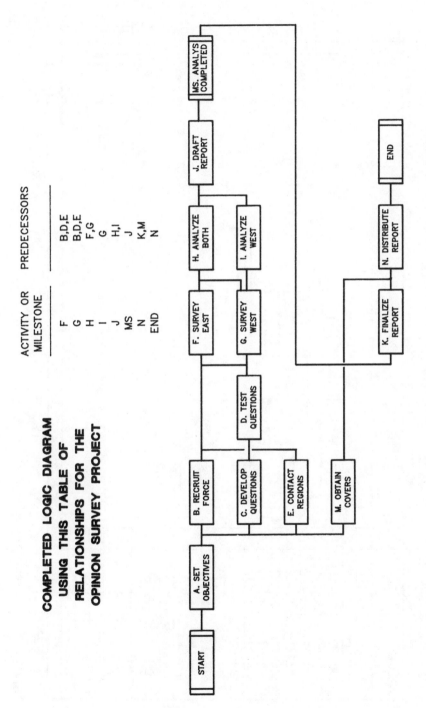

Figure A-7. Answers to exercise in Figure 4-8.

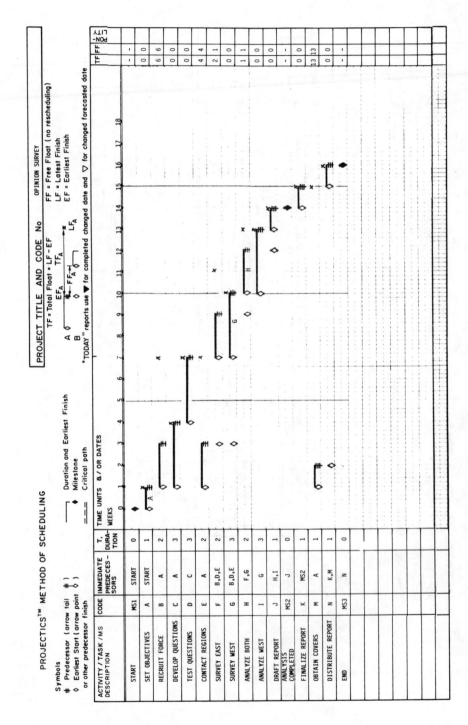

Figure A-8. Answers to exercise in Figure 4-12.

APPENDIX B

SOURCES FOR PROJECT MANAGEMENT MATERIALS

PROJECT MANAGEMENT SOFTWARE SUMMARIES

PM Solutions

1 Soft Decision Inc.
573 Wakerobin Lane, Suite B
P.O. Box 6123
San Rafael, CA 94903
(415)491–1616

This is a comprehensive and extensive hands-on evaluation report, not a compilation. More than 1200 items are looked at in each software program before the evaluation is done and the recommendations made. It covers most of the over 100 software programs available for project management on a PC. There are specific recommendations. The price in 1989 was $495.

Soft Decision News

1 Soft Decision Inc.
573 Wakerobin Lane, Suite B
P.O. Box 6123
San Rafael, CA 94903
(415)491–1616

This newsletter is published eight times a year. It contains information about new releases of project management software for a PC. The subscription price in 1988 was $50 per year.

Survey of Project Management Software Packages

Project Management Institute
P.O. Box 43
Drexel Hill, PA 19026
(215)622–1796

This is an annual compendium of information provided by vendors. It does not include evaluations. Some of the packages are software for PCs. The survey cost $60 in 1988.

Software Digest Ratings Reports

Software Digest
One Winding Drive
Philadelphia, PA 19131–2903
1–800–223–7093 (in Pennsylvania, 1–800–222–3315)

Software Digest currently publishes about one evaluation report per year on project management software for PCs. For example, a comparative test of 14 programs was published in February 1987. The issue was available for $45.

PROJECT MANAGEMENT SOFTWARE USED AS EXAMPLES IN THIS BOOK

Time Line

Symantec, Breakthrough Software Decision
10201 Torre Ave.
Cupertino, CA 95014–2132
(408)253–9600

Time Line offered a free demo disk in 1989.

Harvard Project Manager

Software Publishing Corporation
P.O. Box 7210
Mountain View, CA 94039–7210
1–800–255–5550

A free trial disk was offered in 1989.

PMS II

North America Mica, Inc.
11772 Sorrento Valley Rd., Suite 257
San Diego, CA 92121
(619)792–1012

TIME MANAGEMENT ORGANIZERS AND SOFTWARE MENTIONED IN CHAPTER 13

Time/Design and NameBank

Time/Design
11835 W. Olympic Blvd., Suite 450
Los Angeles, CA 90064
(213)312-0288

Day-Timers, Inc.

P.O. Box 2368
Allentown, PA 18001
(215)395-5884

Control Center

Viable Technology/Workplace
1914 Wilshire Blvd.
Santa Monica, CA 90403-5606
(213)453-6445

The Creative Organizer

Scan/Plan Inc.
P.O. Box 1662
Santa Monica, CA 90406
(213)829-2888

INDEX

A

Activities (*See* Tasks)
Arrow-node diagrams (*See* Logic diagrams)
Authority:
   granted by Dynamic Project Plan, 19–20, 120–129
   in a matrix organization, 24–25, 192–193
   of project managers, 187–190
   with the team approach, 24, 194
Available time (*See* Quiet time)

B

Bank's Goodwill Project (*See* Goodwill Project)
Bar (Gantt) Charts (*See* Schedule)
Baseline plan, 149
Budgets, 100–116
   controlling, 111–116
   estimating, 108–110, 138–139

C

Cases (*See* Goodwill Project; Personnel Records Project; Insurance company multiple projects; Computerization of a small company)
Cash flow, 112
Charter, for project, 194
Client, 17–18, 53
Commitment, 17–18, 139
Computer assistance, 202–227
   export and import of data, 213–215
   lap top, 216–217
   software selection, 217–225, 292–293
Computerization of a small company, a case, 4–5, 205–206, 209–213
Conflict in a matrix organization, 193
Contingency fund, 158
Control, 21–23, 39–42
Control Center software, 279–280, 294
Cost control, 115–116 (*See also* Budgets)
   code of accounts and WBS, 94
   committed cost, 112–113
   control by tradeoffs, 113

INDEX

Cost control (*cont.*)
  control with milestone budgets, 111–114
  cost per day of delay, 115
  estimating, budgeting, 110
  reports, 111–113
CPM, Critical Path Method (*See* Logic diagrams; Scheduling; Float)
Crisis management, 49, 241–247
Critical Path, 89–94 (*See also* Float)
C/SCSC, 159–160

D

Decision reviews: milestone decision reviews, 42, 156
Delegating tasks, 139, 194–198
Dependencies (*See* Logic diagrams)
Documentation, 23
Dummy activity, 287
Dynamic Project Plan, 120–129
  authorization, 16–19
  details of, 38–44
  examples, 34, 36, 45–48
  forms, 52–53
  need for, 33, 37

E

Earliest start and finish, 82–87
Earned value reporting, 160
Estimating (*See* Cost control)
Events (*See* Milestones)

F

Float, 84–87
  free, 84
  in software, 221
  total, 84
Forecasting, 84, 151–154
  estimate at completion, 154
  forecasted completion date, 151
Functional manager, 191–192

G

Gantt chart (*See* Schedule)
Goals (*See* Objectives)

Goodwill Project, 30–31, 33–34, 56, 59, 72–73, 87–89, 100–101, 103–104, 120–121, 124, 132, 134, 144–145, 146–147, 164–165, 167, 182–183, 185, 256–257, 260–262

H

Harry (*See* case: Goodwill Project)
Harvard Project Manager, 221, 225, 252, 293

I

Implementation (*See* Control)
Insurance company multiple projects, 12–16, 61–62, 106–107, 123–124, 202–203, 206–209, 230–233, 235, 240
Interdependencies (*See* Logic diagrams)

J

Jack (*See* case: Personnel Records Project)
Jobs (*See* Tasks)

K

Kotter, John P., 178

L

Large projects, 94, 128–129
Latest start and finish, 82–87
Levels (*See* WBS)
Logic diagrams:
  arrow-node style, 283–285
  precedence style, 75–82
  predecessors, 77
Love, Sydney F., 150, 267

M

Managing by Projects, MBP, 16–23, 26
Manpower, personpower (*See* Cost)
Mary-Helen (*See* case: Insurance company multiple projects)

INDEX 297

Matrix organization:
  conflict in, 192
  nature of, 24–25, 192–193
  separation of what and how, 187, 192
Meetings:
  agenda and instant minutes, 273
  milestone decision reviews, 156
  periodic, 147
  that waste time, 271
  time-shared, 272
Milestone:
  for budgets, 113
  for reporting, decision reviews, 43, 156
  symbols, 77
Monitoring and updating, 144–161
  balanced reporting, 154–155
  by periodic meetings, 146
  updating, 151–152
Motivation, 132–140, 164–179
  participation, 139, 175–176
  peer praise, 172–173
  power and influence, 178–179
  praise, 168–171
  project, 168–171
Multiple projects, 230–253
  priorities on resources, 238–244
  resource forecasting, 10, 15, 236–237
  resource leveling, 236, 244–246
  software selection, 247–251

N

Negotiations (*See* Task; Motivation)
Network diagrams (*See* Logic diagrams)

O

Objectives:
  joint setting, commitment, 139–140
  setting of, 63–68
  what and not how, 187, 192
Overhead (*See* Cost, estimating)
Overtime, 158

P

Participation:
  as a motivator, 139, 175–178
  when to do it, 176–177
Performance (*See* Results)
Periodic meetings, 147–149
Periodic updates, 151–152
Personnel Records Project, 31–33, 34–36, 57–58, 73–74, 89–94, 101–102, 104–106, 121–122, 126–127, 133, 145–146, 147–149, 165–166, 167, 183–184, 186–187, 233–234, 258–259, 262–263
PERT (*See* Logic diagrams; Scheduling)
Planning:
  advantages and disadvantages, 44, 49
  and control, 16–23
  (*See also* Project, planning; Dynamic Project Plan; Control)
PMS II, 212, 293
Power and influence, 178–1'79
Praise:
  as a motivator, 168–173
  peer praise, 172–173
Predecessors (*See* Logic diagrams)
Principles, 6, 33, 57, 74, 102, 124, 134–136, 146, 166, 185, 206, 235, 260
Priority:
  between projects, 239
  between tasks and personal life, 265–268
  changing, 241–244
Progress (*See* Monitoring and updating; Project, reporting)
Project:
  as a motivator, 173–175
  budget (*See* Cost control)
  definition, 60–61
  manager, leader, officer (*See* Project manager)
  planning, 44, 49
  reporting, 144–161
  results definition (*See* Objectives)

Project (cont.)
  reviews, 145, 149, 156
  schedule (See Schedule)
  small to medium, 94
  with multiple projects (See Multiple projects)
  (See also Dynamic Project Plan)
Project manager:
  competition between, 237–238
  rights of, 187–191
  role of, 23–25

Q

Quiet time, 270–271

R

Reinforcement (See Motivation)
Relationships among activities and tasks (See Logic diagrams)
Reporting (See Monitoring and updating)
Resources, 132–140, 235–237 (See also Budgets; Cost control)
Responsibility (See Authority)
Results:
  criteria to measure them, 64–69
  definition of project, 57–58
  definition of tasks, 194–198
  what and not how, 187–191
  (See also Objectives)
Reviews (See Monitoring and updating, Meetings)
Rights of project managers (See Authority)
Risk Chart, 179

S

Scan/Plan Creative Organizer, 274–277, 294
Schedule:
  computer assisted production, 202–227, 247–253
  forms, 85
  manual production, 74–87
  milestone (See Milestone)
  progress, 151–152
Slack (See Float)

Software (See Computer assistance)
Status (See Monitoring and updating)
Stress, 258–259
Subsystem (See Levels, WBS)

T

Task:
  commitment, 139–140
  examples, 195–196
  forms, 196–197
  objectives, 63–68
  reporting in an organization, 191–192
Team:
  full-time project team, 194
  motivation, 132–140, 164–179
  selection, 189
Time/Design organizer, 277–278, 293
Time Line, 225, 226, 250, 251, 293
Time management, 256–280
  book, *Mastery and Management of Time,* 267
  organizers, 274–280, 293–294
  software, 278–280, 294
  examples of task lists and schedules, 260, 261, 263
  interruptions, 263–268
  meetings that waste time, 271–273
  quiet time, 270–271
  task lists and schedules, 260–268
  urgency and payoff, 265–268
  (See also Priorities)
Time pressures (See Time management)
Tradeoff:
  control by, 114
  guidelines, 128–129
Trends (See Monitoring and updating)

U

Uncertainty, coping with, 157–158
User needs, 41

W

WBS (Work breakdown structure), 94